Teach Yourself VISUALLY™

iPhone®
2nd Edition

by Guy Hart-Davis

Visual
A Wiley Brand

Teach Yourself VISUALLY™ iPhone® 2nd Edition

Published by
John Wiley & Sons, Inc.
10475 Crosspoint Boulevard
Indianapolis, IN 46256

www.wiley.com

Published simultaneously in Canada

Wiley publishes in a variety of print and electronic formats and by print-on-demand. Some material included with standard print versions of this book may not be included in e-books or in print-on-demand. If this book refers to media such as a CD or DVD that is not included in the version you purchased, you may download this material at http://booksupport.wiley.com. For more information about Wiley products, visit www.wiley.com.

Library of Congress Control Number: 2014943274

ISBN: 978-1-118-93222-3

Manufactured in the United States of America

10 9 8 7 6 5 4 3 2 1

Trademark Acknowledgments

Contact Us

For general information on our other products and services please contact our Customer Care Department within the U.S. at 877-762-2974, outside the U.S. at 317-572-3993 or fax 317-572-4002.

For technical support please visit www.wiley.com/techsupport.

Credits

Acquisitions Editor
Aaron Black

Project Editor
Lynn Northrup

Technical Editor
Dwight Spivey

Copy Editor
Lauren Kennedy

Project Coordinator
Lauren Buroker

Manager, Content Development & Assembly
Mary Beth Wakefield

Publisher
Jim Minatel

About the Author

Guy Hart-Davis is the author of *Teach Yourself VISUALLY iPad; Teach Yourself VISUALLY iMac, 3rd Edition; Teach Yourself VISUALLY MacBook Pro, 2nd Edition; Teach Yourself VISUALLY MacBook Air; iMac Portable Genius, 4th Edition;* and *iWork Portable Genius, 2nd Edition.*

Author's Acknowledgments

My thanks go to the many people who turned my manuscript into the highly graphical book you are holding. In particular, I thank Aaron Black for asking me to write the book; Lynn Northrup for keeping me on track and guiding the editorial process; Lauren Kennedy for skillfully editing the text; Dwight Spivey for reviewing the book for technical accuracy and contributing helpful suggestions; and EPS for laying out the book.

How to Use This Book

Who This Book Is For

This book is for the reader who has never used this particular technology or software application. It is also for readers who want to expand their knowledge.

The Conventions in This Book

① Steps

This book uses a step-by-step format to guide you easily through each task. **Numbered steps** are actions you must do; **bulleted steps** clarify a point, step, or optional feature; and **indented steps** give you the result.

② Notes

Notes give additional information — special conditions that may occur during an operation, a situation that you want to avoid, or a cross reference to a related area of the book.

③ Icons and Buttons

Icons and buttons show you exactly what you need to click to perform a step.

④ Tips

Tips offer additional information, including warnings and shortcuts.

⑤ Bold

Bold type shows command names, options, and text or numbers you must type.

⑥ Italics

Italic type introduces and defines a new term.

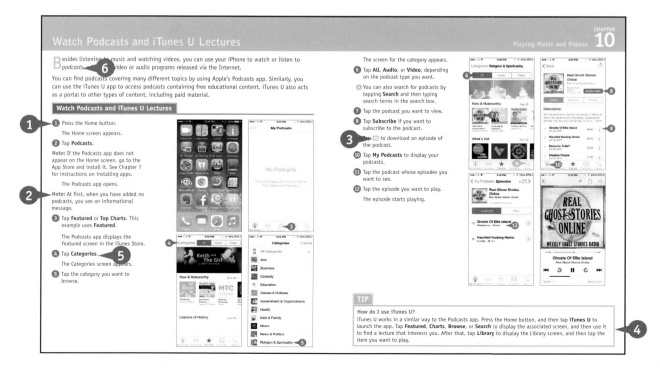

Watch Podcasts and iTunes U Lectures

Besides listening to music and watching videos, you can use your iPhone to watch or listen to podcasts, video or audio programs released via the Internet.

You can find podcasts covering many different topics by using Apple's Podcasts app. Similarly, you can use the iTunes U app to access podcasts containing free educational content. iTunes U also acts as a portal to other types of content, including paid material.

Watch Podcasts and iTunes U Lectures

① Press the Home button.

The Home screen appears.

② Tap **Podcasts**.

Note: If the Podcasts app does not appear on the Home screen, go to the App Store and install it. See Chapter 7 for instructions on installing apps.

The Podcasts app opens.

Note: At first, when you have added no podcasts, you see an informational message.

③ Tap **Featured** or **Top Charts**. This example uses **Featured**.

The Podcasts app displays the Featured screen in the iTunes Store.

④ Tap **Categories**.

The Categories screen appears.

⑤ Tap the category you want to browse.

The screen for the category appears.

⑥ Tap **All**, **Audio**, or **Video**, depending on the podcast type you want.

● You can also search for podcasts by tapping **Search** and then typing search terms in the search box.

⑦ Tap the podcast you want to view.

⑧ Tap **Subscribe** if you want to subscribe to the podcast.

⑨ Tap ⬇ to download an episode of the podcast.

⑩ Tap **My Podcasts** to display your podcasts.

⑪ Tap the podcast whose episodes you want to see.

⑫ Tap the episode you want to play.

The episode starts playing.

TIP

How do I use iTunes U?

iTunes U works in a similar way to the Podcasts app. Press the Home button, and then tap **iTunes U** to launch the app. Tap **Featured**, **Charts**, **Browse**, or **Search** to display the associated screen, and then use it to find a lecture that interests you. After that, tap **Library** to display the Library screen, and then tap the item you want to play.

Table of Contents

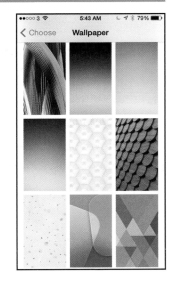

Chapter 3   Working with Voice and Accessibility

Chapter 4   Setting Up Communications

Table of Contents

Chapter 7	Working with Apps

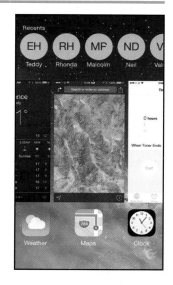

Table of Contents

Chapter 10 Playing Music and Videos

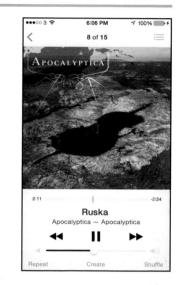

Chapter 11 Working with Photos and Books

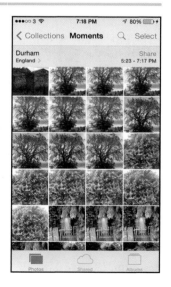

Table of Contents

Chapter 12   Using the Built-In Apps

Chapter 13   Taking Photos and Videos

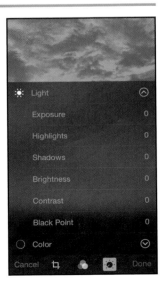

Chapter 14 Troubleshooting Your iPhone

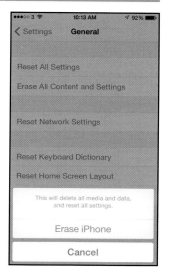

CHAPTER 1

Getting Started with Your iPhone

In this chapter, you set up your iPhone to work with your computer or iCloud. You choose items to sync and learn to use the iPhone interface.

Take a Look at the iPhone Models

The iPhone is a series of hugely popular smartphones designed by Apple. At this writing, the iPhone comes in four versions that differ in size, power, and price. This section explains the common features and differences between the iPhone models to enable you to distinguish them and choose among them.

Understand the Common Features of the iPhone Models

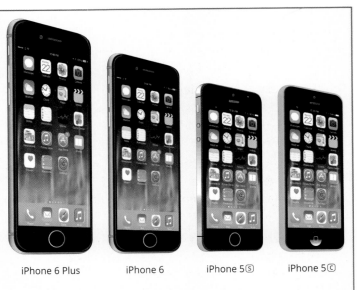

Each iPhone comes with the Apple EarPods headset, which incorporates a remote control and a microphone; a USB power adapter; and a Lightning-to-USB cable.

Each iPhone runs iOS 8, the latest operating system from Apple, which comes with a suite of built-in apps, such as the Safari web browser and the Mail e-mail app.

The iPhone 6 models and the iPhone 5s come in three colors: silver, gold, and space gray. The iPhone 5c comes in five colors: white, pink, yellow, blue, and green.

The iPhone 6 models and the iPhone 5s have the Touch ID fingerprint-recognition feature. The iPhone 5c does not have Touch ID.

Each iPhone has an 8-megapixel main camera on the back and a 1.2-megapixel camera on the screen size.

Compare the iPhone 6 Models with the iPhone 5 Models

The iPhone 6 models have larger screens than the iPhone 5 models, enabling you to see more on the screen at once. The iPhone 6 screens also have higher contrast than the iPhone 5 models do.

The iPhone 6 models have faster processors, both using an A8 chip with an M8 motion coprocessor. The iPhone 5s has an A7 chip with an M7 motion coprocessor. The iPhone 5c has an A6 chip with no motion coprocessor.

The iPhone 6 models have new camera features, including the Focus Pixels feature for faster focusing and slow-motion video recording at 240 frames per second.

iPhone 6 Plus   iPhone 6   iPhone 5ⓢ   iPhone 5ⓒ

The iPhone 6 models have a Near Field Communication (NFC) chip that enables you to use the Apple Pay service to make payments from your iPhone. The iPhone 5 models do not have NFC and cannot use Apple Pay.

Compare the iPhone 6 with the iPhone 6 Plus

The main difference between the iPhone 6 Plus and the iPhone 6 is that the iPhone 6 Plus is substantially bigger than the iPhone 6. The iPhone 6 Plus has a larger screen and higher resolution than the iPhone 6. You see the amount of Home screen or app screen on each phone, but the display may look better on the iPhone 6 Plus.

The iPhone 6 Plus also has optical image stabilization to help minimize camera shake. If you take many photos, you may find this feature helpful.

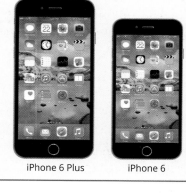

iPhone 6 Plus   iPhone 6

Compare the iPhone 5s with the iPhone 5c

The most visible difference between the iPhone 5s and the iPhone 5c is in their design. The iPhone 5s has a sleek aluminum case, whereas the iPhone 5c has a case made of colorful polycarbonate.

Under the skin, the iPhone 5s is more powerful than the iPhone 5c. It has a faster processor than the iPhone 5c; it has a motion coprocessor, which the iPhone 5c does not; and it has a better flash unit for the rear camera.

Evaluate iPhone Storage Capacity

The iPhone models are available with different amounts of storage capacity: 8GB, 16GB, 32GB, 64GB, and 128GB. The iPhone 6 and iPhone 6 Plus come in 16GB, 64GB, and 128GB versions; the iPhone 5s comes in 16GB and 32GB models; and the iPhone 5c has only an 8GB model.

Having more storage enables you to install more apps and carry more music, movies, and other files with you. Having plenty of storage is especially important for shooting videos with your iPhone. The diagram shows sample amounts of contents.

Higher capacities command substantially higher prices, so you must decide how much you are prepared to spend. Generally speaking, higher-capacity devices get more use in the long run and are worth the extra cost.

8GB	16GB	32GB	64GB	128GB
675 songs	1250 songs	2500 songs	5000 songs	10000 songs
500 photos	1000 photos	2000 photos	4000 photos	8000 photos
2.5 hours video	5 hours video	10 hours video	20 hours video	40 hours video

Meet Your iPhone's Hardware Controls

After unboxing your iPhone, connect it to its charger and charge the battery fully. Then turn your iPhone on and meet its hardware controls. For essential actions, such as turning on and controlling volume, the iPhone has a Power/Sleep button, a Ringer On/Off switch, a Volume Up button and a Volume Down button, together with the Home button below the screen. Most stores and carriers insert a SIM card in your iPhone for you. But in some cases, you may need to insert a suitable SIM card yourself.

Meet Your iPhone's Hardware Controls

1 Press and hold the Power/ Sleep button for a couple of seconds.

Note: The Power/Sleep button is on the right side of the iPhone 6 models and on the top of the iPhone 5 models.

As the iPhone starts, the Apple logo appears on the screen.

Above the iPhone's screen are:

Ⓐ The front-facing camera.

Ⓑ The receiver speaker, which plays phone calls into your ear when you hold the iPhone up to your face.

Ⓒ Below the iPhone's screen is the Home button, which you press to display the Home screen.

At the bottom of the iPhone are:

Ⓓ The headphone socket.

Ⓔ The microphone.

Ⓕ The Lightning connector.

Ⓖ The speakers.

6

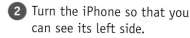 Turn the iPhone so that you can see its left side.

3 Move the Ringer On/Off switch to the rear, so that the orange background appears, when you want to turn off the ringer.

Note: Turn the ringer off when you do not want the iPhone to disturb you or the peace. Move the Ringer On/Off switch back to the front when you want to turn the ringer back on.

4 Press the Volume Up (+) button to increase the ringer volume.

Note: When the Camera app is displayed, you can press the Volume Up (+) button to take a picture with the camera.

5 Press the Volume Down (−) button to decrease the ringer volume.

6 When the lock screen appears, tap the **slide to unlock** prompt, and then drag your finger to the right.

The iPhone unlocks, and the Home screen appears.

TIP

How do I insert a SIM card in my iPhone?
If the store or carrier has not inserted a SIM card, insert the SIM removal tool in the SIM hole on the right side of the iPhone. If you do not have a SIM removal tool, straighten out the end of a small paperclip and use that instead. Push gently until the tray pops out, and then pull it with your fingernails. Insert the SIM in the tray, and then push the tray in fully.

Download, Install, and Set Up iTunes

To sync your iPhone with your computer, you use Apple's iTunes application. iTunes comes preinstalled on every Mac but not on PCs; to get iTunes for Windows, you download it from the Apple website and then install it on your PC.

If you do not have a computer, or you do not want to sync your iPhone with your computer, you can set up and sync your iPhone using Apple's iCloud service, as described later in this chapter.

Download, Install, and Set Up iTunes

1 On your PC, open the web browser (Internet Explorer in this example).

2 Click the Address box, type **www.apple.com/itunes/download**, and then press **Enter**.

The Download iTunes Now web page appears.

3 Click the check boxes (☑ changes to ☐) unless you want to receive e-mail from Apple.

4 Click **Download Now**.

The download bar appears.

5 Click the drop-down arrow.

The Save pop-up menu opens.

6 Click **Save and run**.

Internet Explorer downloads the file, and then starts running it.

The iTunes installation begins, and the Welcome to iTunes dialog opens.

7 Click **Next**, and then follow the steps of the installer.

Note: You must accept the license agreement to install iTunes.

⑧ On the Installation Options screen, click the **Add iTunes shortcut to my desktop** check box (☑ changes to ☐) unless you want this shortcut.

⑨ Select (☑) or deselect (☐) the **Use iTunes as the default player for audio files** check box, as needed.

⑩ Click **Install**.

When the installation finishes, the installer displays the Congratulations screen.

⑪ Click **Open iTunes after the installer exits** (☑ changes to ☐) if you do not want iTunes to launch automatically when you close the installer.

⑫ Click **Finish**.

The installer closes.

Unless you chose not to open iTunes automatically, iTunes opens.

iTunes

Installation Options

Select folder where iTunes files will be installed and choose installation options.

⑧ ☑ Add iTunes shortcut to my desktop

☑ Use iTunes as the default player for audio files

⑨

Default iTunes language: English (United States)

Destination Folder

C:\Program Files (x86)\iTunes\   Change...

< Back   Install ⑩ Cancel

iTunes

Congratulations.

iTunes has been successfully installed on your computer.

⑪ ☑ Open iTunes after the installer exits.

Click Finish to exit the installer.

< Back   Finish ⑫ Cancel

TIP

How do I set up iTunes on a Mac?

If you have not run iTunes already, click the **iTunes** icon (🅾) that appears on the Dock by default. If the Dock contains no iTunes icon, click **Launchpad** (🅾) on the Dock, and then click **iTunes** (🅾) on the Launchpad screen. The iTunes Setup Assistant launches. Follow the steps to set up iTunes.

Begin Setup and Activate Your iPhone

Before you can use your iPhone, you must begin setup and activate the device. The first stage of setup involves choosing the language to use, specifying your country or region, connecting to the Internet through either a Wi-Fi network or the cellular network, and choosing whether to use Location Services. You then activate the iPhone, registering it with Apple's servers. At the end of the first stage of setup, you choose whether to set up the iPhone as a new iPhone, restore it from an iCloud backup, or restore it from an iTunes backup.

Begin Setup and Activate Your iPhone

1 Turn on the iPhone by pressing and holding the Power/Sleep button for a couple of seconds until the Apple logo appears on-screen.

2 When the initial iPhone screen appears, tap the prompt and slide your finger to the right.

The iPhone unlocks and begins the setup routine.

The Language screen appears.

3 Tap the language you want to use.

The Select Your Country or Region screen appears.

4 Tap your country or region.

The Choose a Wi-Fi Network screen appears.

5 Tap the wireless network you want to use.

Ⓐ If your Wi-Fi network does not appear because it does not broadcast its network name, tap **Choose another network**. You can then type the network's name.

Ⓑ If your Wi-Fi network does not appear because it is out of range, tap **Use Cellular Connection**.

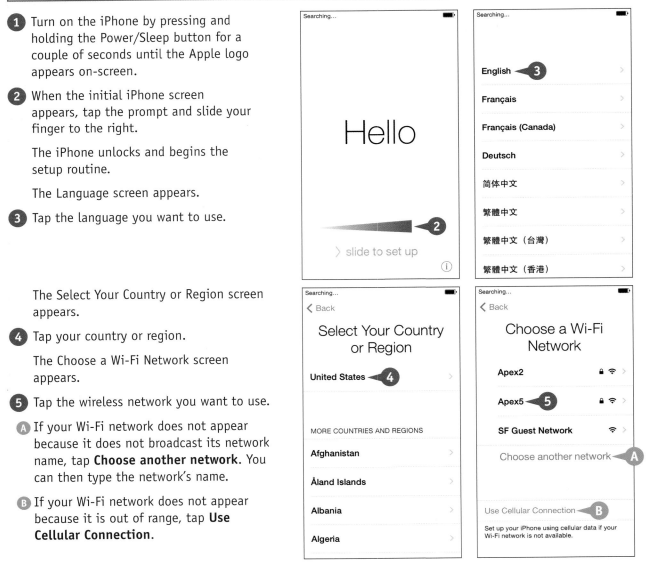

6 On the Enter Password screen, type the password.

7 Tap **Join**.

Your iPhone joins the wireless network and connects to the Internet.

C The Activating Your iPhone screen appears while iOS activates your iPhone.

8 On the Location Services screen, tap **Enable Location Services** or **Disable Location Services**, as needed. See the tip for advice.

9 On the Set Up iPhone screen, tap the appropriate button:

D Tap **Set Up as New iPhone** to set up your iPhone from scratch using iCloud. See the next section, "Set Up Your iPhone as New Using iCloud" for details.

E Tap **Restore from iCloud Backup** to set up your iPhone using a backup stored in iCloud. See the section "Set Up Your iPhone from an iCloud Backup," later in this chapter, for details.

F Tap **Restore from iTunes Backup** to set up your iPhone using a backup stored on your computer. See the section "Set Up Your iPhone from iTunes," later in this chapter, for details.

TIP

Should I enable Location Services?
Normally, enabling Location Services is helpful because it lets apps such as Maps determine your exact location, which makes them more useful. Using Location Services does mean that your iPhone continually tracks your location, but this is something the cellular network does anyway for cell phones. That said, it is a good idea to open the Location Settings screen in the Settings app and turn off the switch for any app you do not want to track you.

Set Up Your iPhone as New Using iCloud

If you want to set up and use your iPhone without syncing it to your computer, you can set it up using Apple's iCloud online service. With this approach, you sync your data to your account on iCloud, from which you can access it using other iOS devices, a Mac, or a web browser on any computer.

To set up a new iPhone to use iCloud, follow the instructions in the previous section to begin setup, and then continue with the instructions in this section. If you have backed up your iPhone to iCloud, and want to restore it from that backup, turn to the next section instead.

Set Up Your iPhone as New Using iCloud

1 Begin setup as explained in the previous section, "Begin Setup and Activate Your iPhone."

2 On the Set Up Your iPhone screen, tap **Set Up as New iPhone**.

The Set Up Your Apple ID screen appears.

3 Tap **Sign In with Your Apple ID**.

Note: If you do not yet have an Apple ID, tap **Create a Free Apple ID** and follow the prompts on the screens that appear.

The Apple ID screen appears.

4 Type your Apple ID.

5 Type your password.

6 Tap **Next**.

The Terms and Conditions screen appears.

7 Tap **Agree**.

The Terms and Conditions dialog opens.

8 Tap **Agree**.

The Set Up iCloud screen appears.

9 Tap **Use iCloud** if you want to use iCloud.

Note: Normally, you will be able to get more out of your iPhone by using iCloud. Using iCloud enables you to use the Find My iPhone feature to track your iPhone if it goes missing.

The Find My iPhone screen appears.

10 Tap **Next**.

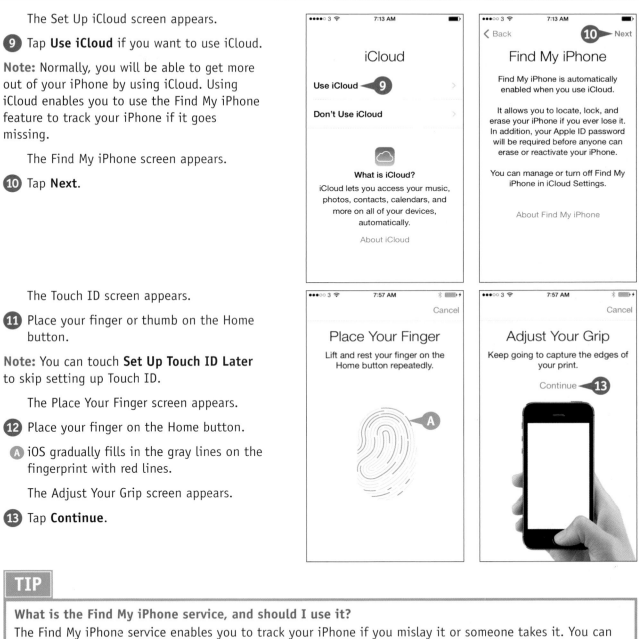

The Touch ID screen appears.

11 Place your finger or thumb on the Home button.

Note: You can touch **Set Up Touch ID Later** to skip setting up Touch ID.

The Place Your Finger screen appears.

12 Place your finger on the Home button.

A iOS gradually fills in the gray lines on the fingerprint with red lines.

The Adjust Your Grip screen appears.

13 Tap **Continue**.

TIP

What is the Find My iPhone service, and should I use it?

The Find My iPhone service enables you to track your iPhone if you mislay it or someone takes it. You can play a tone on your iPhone to help you locate it, lock your iPhone with a passcode, or erase its contents remotely. See Chapter 14 for instructions on using Find My iPhone.

continued ▶

When you set up your iPhone using iCloud, use an e-mail address that you intend to keep for the long term. This is especially true if you use the same e-mail address for the Apple ID you use for the App Store; each app you buy is tied to that e-mail address, so if you change the address, you will need to authenticate again for each app update. When setting up your iPhone using iCloud, you can apply a passcode lock to protect your iPhone, use iCloud Keychain to protect your passwords and credit card data, and enable the Siri voice-controlled assistant.

Set Up Your iPhone as New Using iCloud (continued)

The second Place Your Finger screen appears.

14 Place the edges of your finger on the Home button repeatedly.

The Complete screen appears.

15 Tap **Continue**.

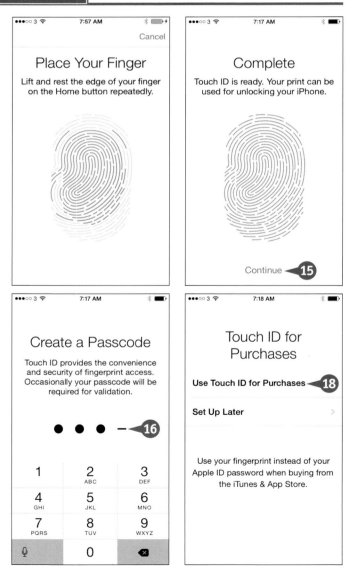

The Create a Passcode screen appears.

16 Tap the keys to create a four-digit passcode.

Note: If you use a weak passcode, such as 1111, your iPhone displays a warning dialog prompting you to try again.

The Create a Passcode screen prompts you to reenter your passcode.

17 Type your passcode again to confirm the number.

The Touch ID for Purchases screen appears.

18 Tap **Use Touch ID for Purchases** screen or **Set Up Later**, as needed.

The Siri screen appears.

19 Tap **Use Siri** or **Don't use Siri**, as appropriate.

Note: You can turn Siri on or off at any point after setup.

The Diagnostics screen appears.

20 Tap **Automatically Send** or **Don't Send**, as needed.

Note: To learn which details the diagnostics and usage reports contain, tap **About Diagnostics and Privacy**.

The App Analytics screen appears.

21 Tap **Share with App Developers** if you want to share usage statistics and crash data with the developers of the apps you use. Otherwise, tap **Don't Share**.

The Welcome to iPhone screen appears.

22 Tap **Get Started**.

The Home screen appears, and you can begin using your iPhone.

TIP

Why should I use iCloud Keychain?

iCloud Keychain gives you an easy way to store your passwords and credit card information securely on your iPhone, other iOS devices, and Mac. Instead of having to remember the password for each website, or look at a credit card when you need to enter its details, you can have iCloud Keychain automatically provide the details.

iCloud Keychain encrypts your data, but you must use a complex passcode to keep it secure. A standard four-digit numeric passcode is not strong enough to keep your iCloud Keychain secure against serious attacks.

Set Up Your iPhone from an iCloud Backup

Instead of setting up your iPhone as new using iCloud, you can set it up by restoring it from an iCloud backup. This backup can be from either another iPhone or iOS device or from the same iPhone. For example, if you are upgrading to the iPhone 6, you can restore the backup of your previous iPhone.

When you restore your iPhone from an iCloud backup, you choose which backup to use — normally, the most recent one. iOS automatically restores your settings, downloads your apps from the App Store, and then installs them on the iPhone.

Set Up Your iPhone from an iCloud Backup

1 Begin setup as explained in the section "Begin Setup and Activate Your iPhone," earlier in this chapter.

2 On the Set Up Your iPhone screen, tap **Restore from iCloud Backup**.

The iCloud Sign In screen appears.

3 Type your Apple ID.

4 Type your password.

5 Tap **Next**.

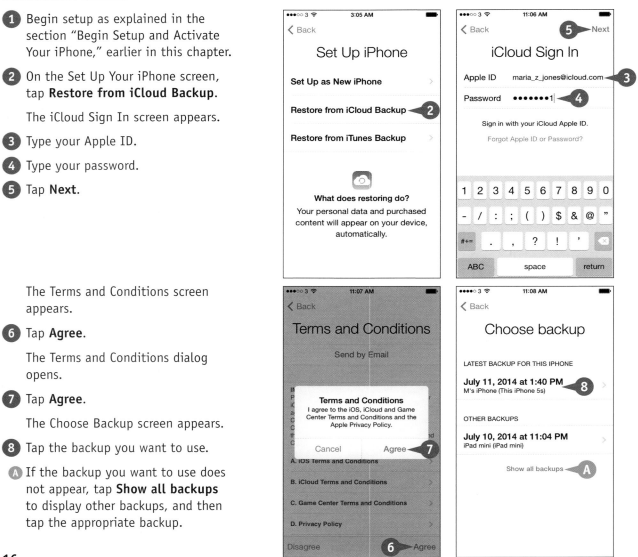

The Terms and Conditions screen appears.

6 Tap **Agree**.

The Terms and Conditions dialog opens.

7 Tap **Agree**.

The Choose Backup screen appears.

8 Tap the backup you want to use.

A If the backup you want to use does not appear, tap **Show all backups** to display other backups, and then tap the appropriate backup.

iOS restores the backup to your iPhone.

Your iPhone restarts.

A screen for signing into iCloud appears.

9 Type your password.

10 Tap **Next**.

The Find My iPhone screen appears.

11 Tap **Use Find My iPhone** or **Don't Use Find My iPhone**, as appropriate.

The Touch ID screen appears.

12 Follow Steps **11** to **15** in the previous section to set up Touch ID with your fingerprint.

The Create a Passcode screen appears.

13 Tap the keys to create a four-digit passcode.

The Create a Passcode screen prompts you to reenter your passcode.

14 Type your passcode again to confirm the number.

The Welcome to iPhone screen appears.

15 Tap **Get Started**.

The Home screen appears, and you can start using your iPhone.

Which iPhone backup should I use?

Normally, it is best to use the most recent backup available for this iPhone or for the iPhone whose backups you are using. But sometimes you may find a problem exists with the latest backup. In this case, try the previous backup.

Set Up Your iPhone from iTunes

Instead of setting up your iPhone using iCloud, as described in the previous two section, you can set it up using iTunes. You can either restore an iTunes backup to the device or set up the iPhone from scratch using iTunes.

When setting up your iPhone for the first time, you can restore it from an iTunes backup of another iPhone — for example, your previous iPhone. If you have already set up this iPhone, you can restore it from its own backup.

Set Up Your iPhone from iTunes

1. Begin setup as explained in the section "Begin Setup and Activate Your iPhone," earlier in this chapter.

2. On the Set Up Your iPhone screen, tap **Restore from iTunes Backup**.

   The Connect to iTunes screen appears.

3. Connect your iPhone to your computer via the USB cable.

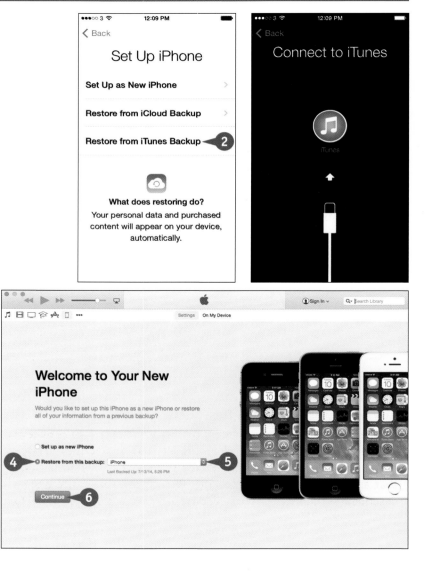

   On your computer, iTunes opens or becomes active.

   The Welcome to Your New iPhone screen appears.

4. Make sure the **Restore from this backup** radio button is selected (○).

5. Click ⬦ and select the appropriate iPhone from the menu.

6. Click **Continue**.

iTunes restores your iPhone from the backup.

When the restore is complete, your iPhone restarts.

Your iPhone's control screens appear in the iTunes window.

You can now choose sync settings for the iPhone as explained in the next section, "Choose Which Items to Sync from Your Computer."

How do I set up my iPhone from scratch using iTunes?

On the Set Up Your iPhone screen, tap **Restore from iTunes Backup**, and then connect your iPhone to your computer via the USB cable. When the Welcome to Your New iPhone screen appears in iTunes on your computer, click **Set up as new iPhone** (☐ changes to ◉). Click **Continue**. On the Sync with iTunes screen that appears, click **Get Started**. The iPhone's control screens appear, and you can set up synchronization as described in the next section, "Choose Which Items to Sync from Your Computer."

Choose Which Items to Sync from Your Computer

After specifying that you will use iTunes to sync your iPhone, as explained in the previous section, "Set Up Your iPhone from iTunes," you use the iPhone's control screens in iTunes to choose which items to sync between your computer and your iPhone. When setting your sync preferences, the best place to start is the Summary tab. Here, you can change your iPhone's name, choose whether to back up the iPhone to iCloud or to your computer, decide whether to encrypt the backup, and set general options for controlling syncing.

Choose Which Items to Sync from Your Computer

Connect Your iPhone and Choose Options on the Summary Tab

1 Connect your iPhone to your computer via the USB cable.

The iTunes window appears.

2 If your iPhone's control screens do not automatically appear, click iPhone (⬚) on the navigation bar at the top of the screen.

Note: Your iPhone appears in iTunes with either a default name or the name you have given it.

The iPhone's control screens appear.

3 Click **Summary** if the Summary screen is not already displayed.

The Summary screen appears.

4 To change the iPhone's name, click the existing name, type the new name, and press Enter or Return.

5 In the Automatically Back Up area, click **iCloud** (⬚ changes to ⦿) or **This computer** (⬚ changes to ⦿) to specify where to back up your iPhone.

6 If you choose to back up to this computer, click **Encrypt iPhone backup** (⬚ changes to ☑).

7 In the Set Password dialog, type a password twice.

8 On a Mac, click **Remember this password in my keychain** (☐ changes to ☑) if you want to save the password in your keychain.

9 Click **Set Password**, and the dialog closes.

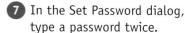

10 Scroll down the iTunes window.

11 Click the **Automatically sync when this iPhone is connected** check box (☐ changes to ☑) if you want to sync your iPhone automatically when you connect it.

12 Click the **Sync only checked songs and videos** check box (☐ changes to ☑) if you want syncing to omit any song or video whose check box you have deselected (☐).

13 Click the **Convert higher bit rate songs to AAC** check box (☐ changes to ☑) if you want to compress larger songs to fit more on your iPhone. In the pop-up menu, choose the bit rate.

TIP

Should I back up my iPhone to my computer or to iCloud?

If you plan to use your iPhone mostly with your computer, back up the iPhone to the computer. Doing so makes iTunes store a full backup of the iPhone on the computer, so you can restore all the data to your iPhone, or to a replacement iPhone, if necessary. You can also encrypt the backup. To keep your data safe, you must back up your computer as well. For example, you can use Time Machine to back up a Mac.

Backing up your iPhone to iCloud enables you to access the backups from anywhere via the Internet, but make sure your iCloud account has enough storage to contain the backups.

continued ▶

When syncing your iPhone with your computer using iTunes, you can quickly set up the communications accounts you want the iPhone to use. On the Info tab of the iPhone's control screens in iTunes, you can set your contacts, calendars, e-mail accounts, bookmarks, and notes to sync to your iPhone. When you need to resolve problems such as data corruption on the iPhone, you can also set iTunes to overwrite particular items on the iPhone during the next sync.

Choose Which Items to Sync from Your Computer (continued)

Sync Your Communications Information to Your iPhone

1 Click **Info**.

2 Click **Sync Contacts** (☐ changes to ☑).

iTunes selects the All Contacts radio button by default.

Note: In Windows, select the program that contains the contacts — for example, Outlook.

3 To sync only some contacts, click **Selected groups** (☐ changes to ◉).

4 Click each contacts group to sync (☐ changes to ☑).

5 Click **Add contacts created outside of groups on this iPhone to** (☐ changes to ☑).

6 Click ⬍ and then click the contacts group to which you want to add contacts created outside the iPhone.

7 Click **Sync Calendars**
(☐ changes to ☑).

8 To sync only some calendars,
click **Selected calendars**
(☐ changes to ◉).

9 Click each calendar to sync
(☐ changes to ☑).

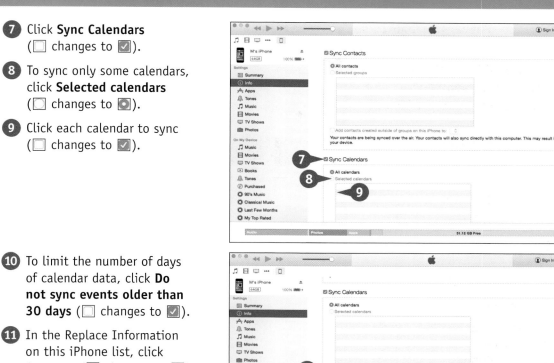

10 To limit the number of days
of calendar data, click **Do
not sync events older than
30 days** (☐ changes to ☑).

11 In the Replace Information
on this iPhone list, click
Contacts (☐ changes to ☑)
if you need to replace your
iPhone's contact data at the
next sync.

12 Click **Calendars** (☐ changes
to ☑) if you need to replace
your iPhone's calendar data
at the next sync.

TIPS

**When should I select the Contacts check box
and Calendars check box in the Advanced box?**
Select these check boxes (☑) only when you
need to overwrite the data on the iPhone.
Normally, you would need to do this only if the
data on the iPhone becomes corrupted.

**Why does Info not appear on the iPhone's control
screens?**
If your Mac is running OS X Mavericks, version 10.9, Info
does not appear on the iPhone's control screens. To sync
your contacts and calendars, set up your Internet
accounts on your iPhone as explained in Chapter 4.

continued ▶

When syncing your iPhone with your computer using iTunes, you can choose which apps to install on your iPhone from those you have purchased from the App Store.

Similarly, you can choose which music to sync by choosing playlists, artists, genres, and albums on the Music screen. And if you have ringtones on your computer, you can sync them to your iPhone by using the Tones screen.

Choose Which Items to Sync from Your Computer (continued)

Choose Which Apps to Sync

1 Click **Apps**.

Ⓐ You can click ⬢ and choose how to sort the apps: Click **Sort by Name**, **Sort by Kind**, **Sort by Category**, **Sort by Date**, or **Sort by Size**, as needed.

2 Click **Install** for each app you want to sync to the iPhone (Install changes to Will Install).

3 Scroll down the screen and click **Automatically install new apps** (☐ changes to ☑) if you want to sync new apps automatically. This is usually helpful.

Choose Which Music and Tones to Sync

1 Click **Music**.

2 Click **Sync Music** (☐ changes to ☑).

3 To load a selection of music, click **Selected playlists, artists, albums, and genres** (☐ changes to ◉) instead of **Entire music library**.

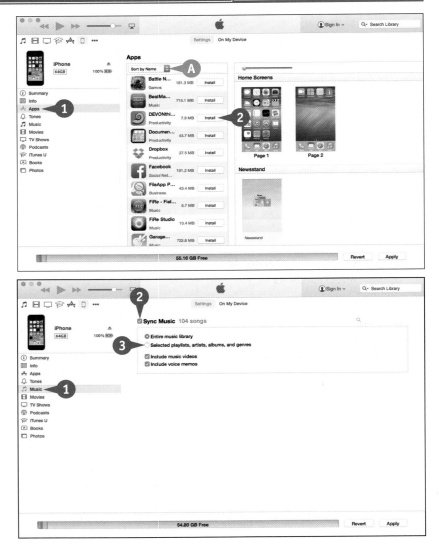

B Click **Automatically fill free space with songs** (☐ changes to ☑) if you want to put as much music as possible on your iPhone.

4 In the Playlists area, click the check box (☐ changes to ☑) for each playlist to include.

5 In the Artists area, click the check box (☐ changes to ☑) for each artist to include.

6 In the Genres area, click the check box (☐ changes to ☑) for each genre to load.

7 In the Albums area, click the check box (☐ changes to ☑) for each album to load.

8 Click **Tones**.

The Tones tab appears.

9 Click **Sync Tones** (☐ changes to ☑).

10 Click **All tones** (☐ changes to ◉) or **Selected tones** (☐ changes to ◉), as needed.

11 If you choose Selected Tones, click the check box (☐ changes to ☑) for each tone to load.

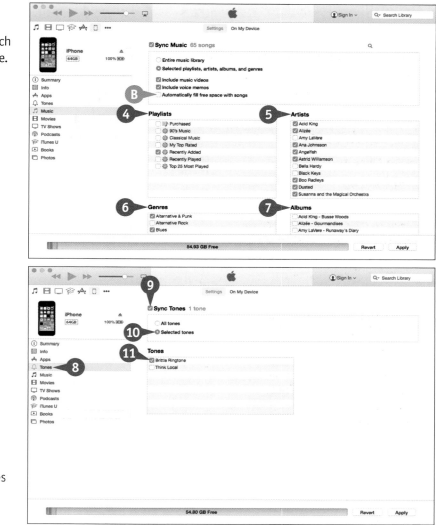

TIP

Should I sync my entire music library to my iPhone?

This depends on how big your music library is, how high your iPhone's capacity is, and how much other data you need to put on the iPhone. Normally, it is best to put a selection of your favorite music, and perhaps your newest music, on your iPhone and leave plenty of space for other content. Leave the **Automatically fill free space with songs** check box deselected (☐) to prevent iTunes from filling all the free space, because this may prevent you from shooting video, taking photos, or recording audio.

You can also click **Manually manage music and videos** (☐ changes to ☑) on the Summary screen and drag songs and videos to the iPhone instead of loading them automatically.

continued ▶

The wide range of content you can sync to your iPhone using iTunes includes movies, TV shows, podcasts, iTunes U lessons, books, and photos. To choose which items to sync, you click the appropriate tab, and then make your selection using the controls that appear on it. For each category of content, you can choose between syncing all the items and only selected ones.

Choose Which Items to Sync from Your Computer (continued)

Sync Movies, TV Shows, Podcasts, and iTunes U Lessons

1 Click an item, **Movies**, for example.

2 Click **Sync Movies** (☐ changes to ☑).

3 Click **Automatically include** (☐ changes to ☑) to have iTunes load some movies automatically.

4 Click ☐ and choose what to include — for example, click **all unwatched** or **10 most recent**.

5 Specify other items to sync (☐ changes to ☑).

Sync Books

1 Click **Books**.

2 Click **Sync Books** (☐ changes to ☑).

3 To sync only some books, click **Selected books** (☐ changes to ◉).

4 Click each book or PDF file to sync (☐ changes to ☑).

5 Click **Sync Audiobooks** (☐ changes to ☑).

6 Choose which audiobooks to sync.

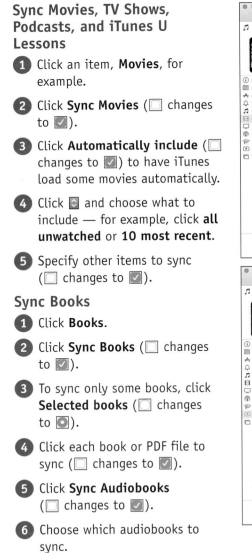

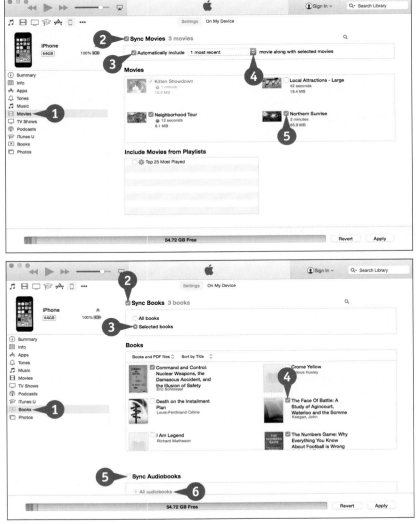

Sync Photos

1 Click **Photos**.

2 Click **Sync Photos from**
(☐ changes to ☑).

Note: In Windows, click **Sync Photos with** (☐ changes to ☑), and then choose the folder in the drop-down list.

3 Click ☐ and choose the source of the photos — for example, iPhoto.

4 Choose which photos to sync. For example, click **Selected albums, Events, and Faces, and automatically include** (☐ changes to ◉), and then choose which albums, events, and faces to include.

Apply Your Changes and Sync

1 Click **Apply** or **Sync**.

iTunes syncs the items to your iPhone.

D The readout shows you the sync progress.

E If you need to stop the sync, click ☒.

2 When the sync finishes, disconnect your iPhone.

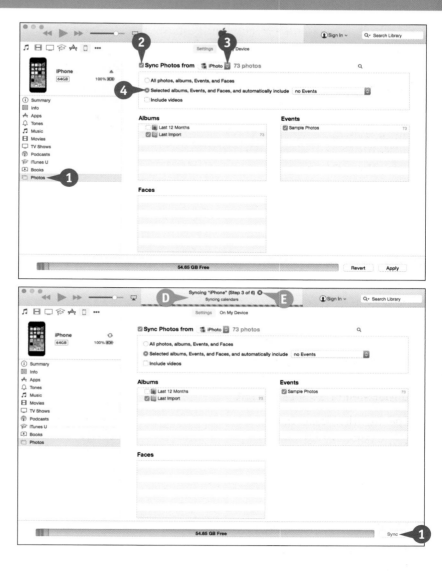

How can I fit more content on my iPhone?

You cannot increase your iPhone's storage capacity — with some other phones, you can install a memory card — so the way to fit more content on is to prune and compress the existing content.

Video and music files tend to take the most space. For video, your only option is to remove files you do not need on your iPhone. For music, click the **Convert higher bit rate songs** check box (☐ changes to ☑) on the Summary tab and choose a low bit rate, such as 128 Kbps, to reduce the size of music files while retaining acceptable audio quality.

Sync Your iPhone with iTunes via Wi-Fi

Instead of syncing your iPhone with iTunes via USB, you can sync it wirelessly. This is called syncing "over the air." You must connect your iPhone and your computer to the same network.

To use wireless sync, you must first enable it in iTunes. You can then have the iPhone sync automatically when connected to a power source and to the same wireless network as the computer. You can also start a sync manually from the iPhone, even if it is not connected to a power source.

Sync Your iPhone with iTunes via Wi-Fi

Set Your iPhone to Sync with iTunes via Wi-Fi

1. Connect your iPhone to your computer with the USB cable.

   The iTunes window appears.

2. Click ⬚.

Note: Your iPhone appears in iTunes with the name you gave it.

   The iPhone's control screens appear.

3. Click **Summary**.

   The Summary screen appears.

4. Click **Sync with this iPhone over Wi-Fi** (⬚ changes to ☑).

5. Click **Apply**.

   iTunes applies the change.

6. Disconnect your iPhone from your computer.

Perform a Manual Sync via Wi-Fi

1. Press the Home button.

   The Home screen appears.

2. Tap **Settings**.

   The Settings screen appears.

3. Tap **General**.

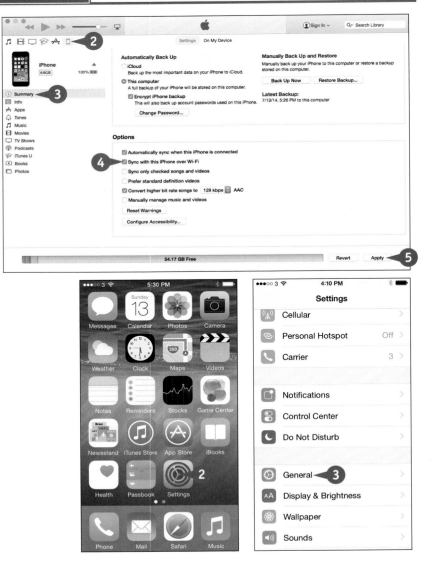

The General screen appears.

4 Tap **iTunes Wi-Fi Sync**.

The iTunes Wi-Fi Sync screen appears.

5 Tap **Sync Now**.

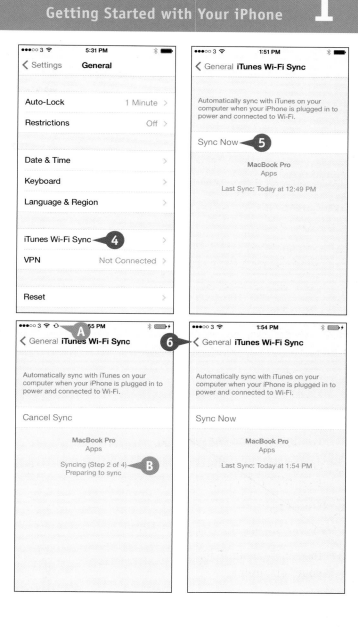

The sync runs.

A The Sync symbol (⟳) appears in the status bar.

B The readout shows which part of the sync is currently running.

6 When the sync completes, tap **General**.

The General screen appears.

TIP

Can I sync my iPhone automatically via Wi-Fi?

To sync your iPhone automatically via Wi-Fi, connect your iPhone to a power source — for example, the iPhone power adapter. Make sure your computer is on and connected to your network, and that iTunes is running. Your iPhone automatically connects to your computer across the wireless network. iTunes syncs the latest songs, videos, and data.

Explore the User Interface and Launch Apps

After you set up your iPhone with iCloud or iTunes, you are ready to start using the device. When you press the Home button to wake the iPhone from sleep, it displays the lock screen. You then unlock the iPhone to reach the Home screen, which contains icons for running the apps installed on the iPhone.

You can quickly launch an app by tapping its icon on the Home screen. From the app, you can return to the Home screen by pressing the Home button. You can then launch another app as needed.

Explore the User Interface and Launch Apps

1 Press the Home button.

The iPhone's screen lights up and shows the lock screen.

2 Tap the slider and drag it to the right.

The iPhone unlocks, and the Home screen appears.

Ⓐ The iPhone has two or more Home screens, depending on how many apps are installed. The gray dots at the bottom of the Home screen show how many Home screens you have. The white dot shows the current Home screen.

3 Tap **Notes**.

The Notes app opens.

Note: If you chose to sync notes with your iPhone, the synced notes appear in the Notes app. Otherwise, the list is empty until you create a note.

4 Tap **New**.

A new note opens, and the on-screen keyboard appears.

5 Type a short note by tapping the keys.

B If the middle button in the suggestion bar shows the word you want, tap Spacebar to accept it. If one of the other buttons shows the right word, tap that button.

6 Tap **Done**.

The on-screen keyboard closes.

7 Tap **Back**.

C The Notes list appears, with your note in it.

8 Press the Home button.

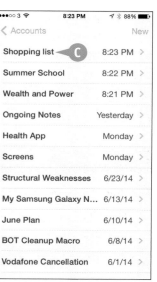

The Home screen appears.

9 Tap and drag to the left to display the second Home screen.

Note: You can also tap at the right end of the row of dots on the Home screen to move one screen to the right. Tap at the left end to move one screen to the left.

You can now launch another app by tapping its icon.

10 Press the Power/Sleep button.

Your iPhone goes to sleep.

TIP

Where do I get more apps to perform other tasks?
You can find an amazingly wide selection of apps — both free and ones you pay for — on Apple's App Store. See Chapter 7 for instructions on finding and downloading the apps you need.

Using Notification Center

As your communications hub, your iPhone handles many different types of alerts for you: missed phone calls, text messages, reminders, meetings, and so on. To help you keep on top of all these alerts, your iPhone integrates them into Notification Center, together with information about the current weather and stock prices. You can quickly access Notification Center from the Home screen or any other screen. After you display Notification Center, you can respond to an alert, view your upcoming appointments, check on the weather, or look at your current stock prices.

Using Notification Center

Open Notification Center

1 Tap at the top of the screen and swipe your finger down.

Notification Center appears.

A The Today tab shows you a list of today's commitments.

B A summary of the weather and your appointments appears at the top of the screen.

C Your calendar appears below that.

2 Scroll down the screen.

D Your Stocks list appears, showing current data.

E A summary of your commitments for tomorrow appears at the bottom of the screen.

3 Tap **Notifications**.

The full list of notifications appears.

F Tap a notification to access the app to which it belongs.

4 Tap and drag up from the bottom of the screen.

Notification Center closes.

Open the Weather App from Notification Center

1 In Notification Center, tap the weather item at the top of the screen.

The Weather app opens, displaying the current weather.

You can then swipe your finger to the left or right across the timeline to display other hourly details.

Swipe your finger left or right below the timeline to view the weather for another location.

Open the Stocks App from Notification Center

1 In Notification Center, tap anywhere in the Stocks section.

The Stocks app opens, displaying the current stock prices, market capitalizations, and charts.

Note: You can customize Notification Center to show the notifications you want to see. See Chapter 2 for details.

TIP

What happens if I receive a notification when my iPhone is locked?

What happens when you receive a notification while the screen is locked depends on the type of notification. For most types of notifications, your iPhone displays an alert on the lock screen to alert you to the notification. Unlocking your iPhone while the alert is showing takes you directly to the notification in whatever app it belongs to — for example, to an instant message in the Messages app.

Using Control Center

Control Center puts your iPhone's most essential controls right where you need them. From Control Center, you can turn Airplane mode, Wi-Fi, Bluetooth, Do Not Disturb mode, and Orientation Lock on or off; control music playback and volume, and direct your iPhone's audio output to AirPlay devices; change the setting for the AirDrop sharing feature; and quickly access the Flashlight, Clock, Calculator, and Camera apps. Control Center appears as a pane that you open by swiping upward from the bottom of the screen. After using Control Center, you can drag the pane closed or simply tap the screen above it.

Using Control Center

Open Control Center

1 Tap and swipe up from the very bottom of the screen.

Control Center opens.

Note: You can open Control Center from most apps and screens. You may find some exceptions — for example, where iOS interprets an upward swipe as an action within the app.

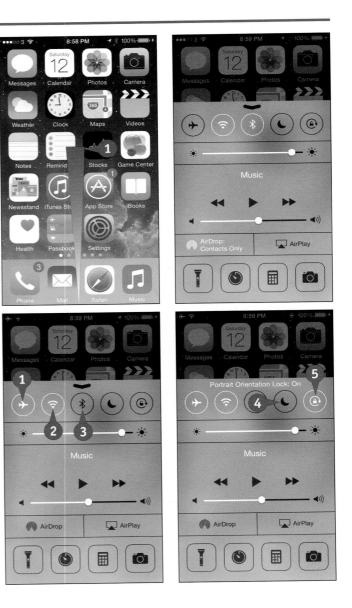

Control Essential Settings

1 Tap **Airplane Mode** (□) to turn Airplane mode on or off.

2 Tap **Wi-Fi** (□) to turn Wi-Fi on or off.

3 Tap **Bluetooth** (□) to turn Bluetooth on or off.

4 Tap **Do Not Disturb** (□) to turn Do Not Disturb mode on or off.

5 Tap **Orientation Lock** (□) to turn Orientation Lock on or off.

Choose an AirPlay Device

1 In Control Center, tap **AirPlay**.

The AirPlay dialog opens.

2 Tap the AirPlay speaker or Apple TV you want to use.

3 If you choose an AirPlay TV, set the **Mirroring** switch to On (⬛) or Off (⬜), as needed.

4 Tap **Done**.

The AirPlay dialog closes.

Open Flashlight, Clock, Calculator, or Camera

1 In Control Center, tap the appropriate icon:

A Tap **Flashlight** (🔦) to turn on the Flashlight.

B Tap **Clock** (🕐) to display the Clock app.

C Tap **Calculator** (🔢) to display the Calculator app.

D Tap **Camera** (📷) to display the Camera app.

The Flashlight turns on, or the app opens.

TIP

Can I use Control Center in landscape mode as well?
Yes, Control Center works in landscape orientation. Simply swipe up from the bottom of the screen in an app that supports the rotated orientation. Control Center has a different landscape layout, but the controls work the same way.

Using the Reachability Feature

On the iPhone 6, iOS provides a feature called Reachability to help you reach the top of the screen when you are using the iPhone one-handed. Reachability is especially useful if you have small hands or if your iPhone is the iPhone 6 Plus model with its large screen.

You can turn Reachability on or off in the Settings app. Once it is turned on, you can use it whenever you need it.

Using the Reachability Feature

Turn the Reachability Feature On

 Press the Home button.

The Home screen appears.

2 Tap **Settings**.

The Settings screen appears.

3 Tap **General**.

The General screen appears.

4 Tap **Accessibility**.

The Accessibility screen appears.

5 At the bottom of the screen, set the **Reachability** switch to On (⬜).

Use the Reachability Feature

 Press the Home button.

The Home screen appears.

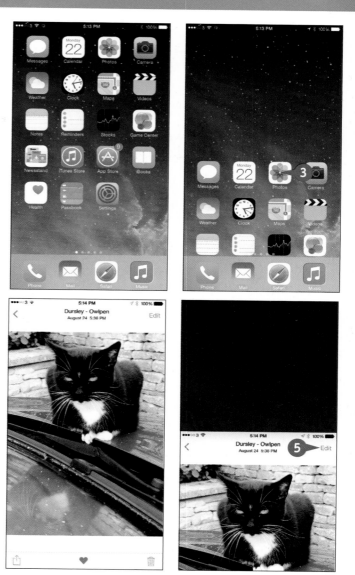

2 Double-tap the **Home** button.

Note: Double-tap the Home button lightly with your finger. Do not double-press the Home button, because that displays the App Switcher instead.

The screen slides down so that its top half is within easy reach.

3 Tap the appropriate button. For example, tap **Photos** to launch the Photos app.

The app opens, and you can use it as normal.

4 When you need to reach the top of the screen easily, double-tap the **Home** button.

The screen slides down.

5 Tap the appropriate button.

The screen resumes its normal appearance.

Note: If you do not tap the screen for a few seconds after activating Reachability, the feature automatically returns the screen to normal.

TIP

How can I make the Home screen icons larger on an iPhone 6?

You can turn on Zoomed view, which makes the Home screen icons and other interface elements appear larger.

Press the Home button and then tap **Settings** to display the Settings screen. Tap **Display & Brightness** to display the Display & Brightness screen, and then tap **View** in the Display Zoom section. On the Display Zoom screen, tap **Zoomed** and then tap **Set**.

CHAPTER 2

Personalizing Your iPhone

To make your iPhone work the way you prefer, you can configure its many settings. In this chapter, you learn how to control iCloud sync, notifications, audio preferences, screen brightness, and other key aspects of the iPhone's behavior.

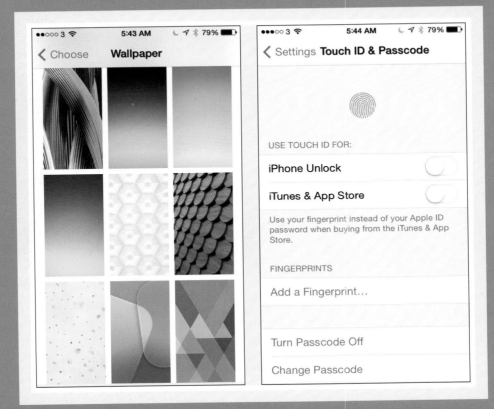

Find the Settings You Need

The iOS operating system includes many settings that enable you to configure your iPhone to work the way you prefer. The central place for manipulating settings is the Settings app, which contains settings for the iPhone's system software, the apps the iPhone includes, and third-party apps you have added. To reach the settings, you first display the Settings screen and then the category of settings you want to configure.

Find the Settings You Need

Display the Settings Screen

1. Press the Home button.

   The Home screen appears.

2. Tap **Settings**.

   The Settings screen appears.

Ⓐ The top part of the Settings screen contains settings you are likely to use frequently, such as Airplane Mode, Wi-Fi, and Bluetooth.

3. Tap and drag up to scroll down the screen.

Ⓑ This section contains settings for built-in apps developed by Apple.

4. Tap and drag up to scroll further down the screen.

Ⓒ This section contains settings for built-in apps developed by third-party developers.

Note: Settings for apps you install appear even further down the Settings screen.

Display a Settings Screen

1 On the Settings screen, tap the button for the settings you want to display. For example, tap **Sounds** to display the Sounds screen.

2 Tap **Settings** when you are ready to return to the Settings screen.

Display the Settings for an App

1 On the Settings screen, scroll down toward the bottom.

2 Tap the button for the app whose settings you want to display. For example, tap **DEVONthink** to display the DEVONthink settings.

3 Tap **Settings** when you are ready to return to the Settings screen.

4 Press the Home button.

The Home screen appears again.

TIP

Why do only some apps have an entry in the Settings app?

The Settings app contains entries for only those apps that have settings you can configure directly through iOS, the iPhone's operating system. Other apps include settings that you configure directly from within the app. This approach is more convenient for apps that have settings you are likely to change frequently while you use the app.

Choose Which iCloud Items to Sync

pple's iCloud service enables you to sync your e-mail account, contacts, calendars, reminders, Safari bookmarks, shared photos, and files online so you can access them from any of your devices. You can also use the Find My iPhone feature to locate your iPhone when it goes missing. To use iCloud, you set your iPhone to use your Apple ID, and then choose which features to use. If you set up your iPhone using iCloud, your account is already active, but you may want to choose different settings for iCloud.

Choose Which iCloud Items to Sync

1 Press the Home button.

The Home screen appears.

2 Tap **Settings**.

The Settings screen appears.

3 Tap **iCloud**.

Note: If you have not yet set up iCloud on your iPhone, type your Apple ID and password on the iCloud screen, and then tap **Sign In**. If you do not yet have an Apple ID, tap **Get a Free Apple ID** and follow the prompts.

4 Tap **Photos**.

5 Set the **iCloud Photo Library** switch to On (⬜) to store all your photos in iCloud.

6 Set the **My Photo Stream** switch to On (⬜) to use My Photo Stream.

7 Set the **Upload Burst Photos** switch to On (⬜) to upload burst shots.

8 Set the **iCloud Photo Sharing** switch to On (⬜) to use Photo Sharing.

9 Tap **iCloud**.

10 Tap **iCloud Drive**.

11 Set the **iCloud Drive** switch to On () to enable iCloud Drive.

12 Set each app's switch to On () or Off (), as needed.

13 Set the **Use Cellular Data** switch to On () if you want to transfer data across the cellular connection.

Note: If you set the **Use Cellular Data** switch to On (), monitor your data usage as explained in Chapter 6 to ensure that you do not exceed your data plan.

14 Tap **iCloud**.

15 On the iCloud screen, set the switches for **Mail**, **Contacts**, **Calendars**, **Reminders**, **Safari**, **Notes**, and **Passbook** to On () or Off (), as needed.

16 Tap **Backup**.

17 On the Backup screen, set the **iCloud Backup** switch to On ().

18 Tap **iCloud**.

19 Tap **Keychain** to display the Keychain screen, set the **iCloud Keychain** switch to On (), and follow the prompts to create a security code.

TIPS

How much space does iCloud provide?

iCloud provides 5GB of space for a free account; content and apps you acquire from Apple do not count against this space, nor do your Photo Stream photos or songs included in iTunes Match. You can buy more space by tapping **Storage**, tapping **Manage Storage** on the Storage screen, and then tapping **Change Storage Plan** on the Manage Storage screen.

Should I turn on Find My iPhone?

Yes. Find My iPhone enables you to locate your iPhone when you misplace it or learn where it is when someone misappropriates it.

Choose Which Apps Can Give Notifications

Some iPhone apps can notify you when you have received messages or when updates are available. You can choose which apps give which notifications, or prevent apps from showing notifications altogether. You can also choose the order in which the notifications appear in Notification Center and control which notifications appear on the lock screen.

iPhone apps use three types of notifications: badges on app icons, banners at the top of the screen, and alert dialogs. See the tip in this section for details.

Choose Which Apps Can Give Notifications

1 Press the Home button.

The Home screen appears.

2 Tap **Settings**.

The Settings screen appears.

3 Tap **Notifications** to display the Notifications screen.

4 In the Notifications View box, tap **Sort Manually** to sort the notifications in the order you set in the Include box. Tap **Sort By Time** to sort the apps by the times of their notifications.

5 Tap **Edit**.

6 Drag a handle (▭) to move an app up or down the list.

7 Tap **Done**.

8 Tap the app you want to configure.

9 Set the **Allow Notifications** switch to On (▣) to enable notifications.

10 Tap **Show in Notification Center**.

11 Tap the number of recent items to show.

12 Tap **Back**.

13 Tap **Notification Sound** and select a sound.

14 Set the **Badge App Icon** switch to On (▣) to show badges.

15 Set the **Show on Lock Screen** switch to On (▣) or Off (▢), as needed.

16 Tap **Alerts**, **Banners**, or **None** to choose what alerts to show.

17 Set the **Show Previews** switch to On (▣) if you want to see previews.

18 Tap **Show Alerts from Everyone** or **Show Alerts from My Contacts**, as needed.

19 Tap **Repeat Alerts**.

20 On the Repeat Alerts screen, tap the number of repeats you want, such as **Once** or **Twice**.

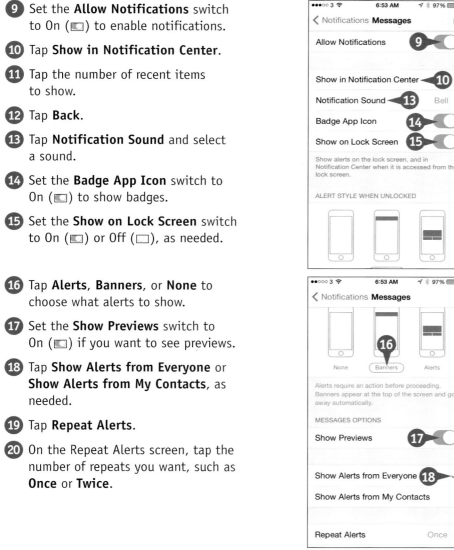

What are the three kinds of notifications?

A *badge* is a red circle or rounded rectangle that appears on the app's icon on the Home screen and shows a white number indicating how many notifications there are. A *banner* is a pop-up notification that appears briefly at the top of the screen and then disappears automatically. An *alert* is a dialog that appears in front of the running app; you need to dismiss the alert before you can take other actions on your iPhone. Whichever notification type you choose, you can also have your iPhone play a sound to get your attention.

Choose Sounds Settings

The Sounds screen in Settings enables you to control what audio feedback your iPhone gives you. You can have the iPhone vibrate always to signal incoming calls, or vibrate only when the ringer is silent. You can set the ringer and alerts volumes, choose your default ringtone and text tone, and choose which items can give you alerts. Your iPhone can play lock sounds to confirm you have locked or unlocked your iPhone. It can also play keyboard clicks to confirm each key press.

Choose Sounds Settings

1 Press the Home button.

The Home screen appears.

2 Tap **Settings**.

The Settings screen appears.

3 Tap **Sounds**.

The Sounds screen appears.

4 Set the **Vibrate on Ring** switch to On (⬜) or Off (☐), as needed.

5 Set the **Vibrate on Silent** switch to On (⬜) or Off (☐), as needed.

6 Tap and drag the **Ringer and Alerts** slider to set the volume.

A When the **Change with Buttons** switch is On (⬜), you can change the Ringer and Alerts volume by pressing the volume buttons on the side of the iPhone.

7 Tap **Ringtone**.

The Ringtone screen appears.

8 Tap the ringtone you want to hear.

9 Tap **Vibration**.

The Vibration screen appears.

 Tap the vibration pattern you want.

⑪ If you prefer a custom vibration, tap **Create New Vibration** in the Custom area.

The New Vibration screen appears.

⑫ Tap a rhythm.

⑬ Tap **Stop**.

⑭ Tap **Play** to play back the vibration.

⑮ Tap **Save**.

⑯ In the New Vibration dialog, type a name.

⑰ Tap **Save**.

⑱ On the Ringtone screen, tap **Sounds**.

The Sounds screen appears.

⑲ Repeat Steps **7** to **18** to set other tones, such as text tones.

⑳ Set the **Lock Sounds** switch to On (🔘) or Off (⬜), as needed.

㉑ Set the **Keyboard Clicks** switch to On (🔘) or Off (⬜), as needed.

TIP

How do I use different ringtones for different callers?

The ringtone and text tone you set in the Ringtone area of the Sounds screen are your standard tone for phone calls, FaceTime calls, and messaging calls. To set different tones for a contact, press the Home button, tap **Phone**, and then tap **Contacts**. In the Contacts list, tap the contact, tap **Edit**, and then tap **Ringtone**. On the Ringtone screen, tap the ringtone and then tap **Done**. You can also change other settings, such as the ringtone's vibration for the contact. Tap **Done** when you finish.

Set Display Brightness and Wallpapers

To make the screen easier to see, you can change its brightness. You can also have the iPhone's Auto-Brightness feature automatically set the screen's brightness to a level suitable for the ambient brightness.

To make the screen attractive to your eye, you can choose which picture to use as the wallpaper that appears in the background. You can use either a static wallpaper or a dynamic, changing wallpaper. You can set different wallpaper for the lock screen and for the Home screen.

Set Display Brightness and Wallpapers

1 Press the Home button.

The Home screen appears.

2 Tap **Settings**.

The Settings screen appears.

3 Tap **Display & Brightness**.

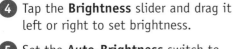

4 Tap the **Brightness** slider and drag it left or right to set brightness.

5 Set the **Auto-Brightness** switch to On (▢) or Off (▢), as needed.

A You can tap **Text Size** to set your preferred text size.

B You can set the **Bold Text** switch to On (▢) to turn the system text bold.

6 Tap **Settings**.

7 Tap **Wallpaper**.

The Wallpaper screen appears.

8 Tap **Choose a New Wallpaper**.

9 Tap **Dynamic** or **Stills** in the Apple Wallpaper area. This example uses **Stills**.

C To choose a picture from a different picture category, tap that category. For example, tap **Recently Added** to display pictures you have taken with the iPhone's camera, saved from e-mail or multimedia messages, or saved from web pages.

10 Tap the wallpaper you want to use.

The Wallpaper Preview screen appears.

11 Tap **Perspective Zoom: On** if you want to turn Perspective Zoom off to minimize 3D effects.

12 Tap **Set**.

13 Tap **Set Lock Screen**, **Set Home Screen**, or **Set Both**. Tap **Cancel** if you do not want to proceed.

14 Press the Home button.

The Home screen appears.

If you changed the Home screen wallpaper, the new wallpaper appears.

TIP

How do I use only part of a picture as the wallpaper?
The Apple wallpapers are the right size for the screen, so you do not need to resize them. But when you use a photo for the wallpaper, you usually need to choose which part of it to display. When you choose a photo as wallpaper, the iPhone displays the screen for moving and scaling the photo. Pinch in or out to zoom the photo out or in, and tap and drag to move the picture around. When you have chosen the part you want, tap **Set**.

Choose Privacy and Location Settings

Your iPhone contains a huge amount of information about you, the people you communicate with, what you do, and where you go. To keep this information safe, you need to choose suitable privacy and location settings.

Privacy settings enable you to control which apps may access your contacts, calendars, reminders, and photos. You can also choose which apps can use your iPhone's location services, and which track the iPhone's location via the Global Positioning System, or GPS.

Choose Privacy and Location Settings

 Press the Home button.

The Home screen appears.

 Tap **Settings**.

The Settings screen appears.

 Tap **Privacy**.

Note: To limit how ads can track your iPhone usage, tap **Advertising** at the bottom of the Privacy screen. On the Advertising screen, set the **Limit Ad Tracking** switch to On ( ). Tap **Reset Advertising Identifier** and then tap **Reset Identifier** in the confirmation dialog.

The Privacy screen appears.

 Tap the app or service you want to configure. This example uses **Photos**.

The screen for the app or service appears.

 Set the switches (changes to) to choose which apps can access the item — in this case, your photos.

 Tap **Privacy**.

The Privacy screen appears.

 Configure other apps and services as needed.

 Tap **Location Services**.

The Location Services screen appears.

9 If you need to turn location services off completely, set the **Location Services** switch to Off (☐).

10 Tap the app or feature you want to configure.

11 In the Location Access box, tap the appropriate button, such as **While Using the App** or **Always**.

Note: The buttons in the Location Access box vary depending on the app or feature.

12 Tap **Back**.

13 Set location access for other apps and features.

14 Tap **System Services**.

15 Set the switch for each system service to On (☐) or Off (☐), as needed.

Note: You may want to set the **Location-Based iAds** switch to Off (☐).

16 Set the **Status Bar Icon** switch to On (☐) to see the Location Services icon in the status bar when an app requests your location.

Why do some apps need to use location services?

Some apps and system services need to use location services to determine where you are. For example, the Maps app requires location services to display your location, and the Compass service needs your location to display accurate compass information.

If you allow the Camera app to use location services, it stores GPS data in your photos. You can then sort the photos by location in applications such as iPhoto on OS X. Other apps use location services to provide context-specific information, such as information about nearby restaurants. For privacy, review the apps using location services and turn off any you prefer not to have this information.

Configure and Use Spotlight Search

Your iPhone can put a huge amount of data in the palm of your hand, and you may often need to search to find what you need.

To make your search results more accurate and helpful, you can configure your iPhone's Spotlight Search feature. You can turn off searching for items you do not want to see in your search results, and you can change the order in which Spotlight displays the items it finds.

Configure and Use Spotlight Search

Configure Spotlight Search

1. Press the Home button.

   The Home screen appears.

2. Tap **Settings**.

   The Settings screen appears.

3. Tap **General**.

   The General screen appears.

4. Tap **Spotlight Search**.

   The Spotlight Search screen appears.

5 Tap to remove the check mark from each item you do not want to search.

6 Tap a movement handle and drag an item up or down the search order.

Note: Spotlight displays the search results in descending order, starting with the first item on the list.

7 Tap **General** to go back to the General screen.

8 Tap **Settings** to go back to the Settings screen.

Search for Items Using Spotlight

1 Press the Home button.

The Home screen appears.

2 Tap near the top of the screen and pull down.

The Search iPhone panel appears.

The keyboard appears.

3 Type your search term.

A list of results appears.

4 Tap the result you want to view.

Which items should I make Spotlight search?

This depends on what you need to be able to search for. For example, if you do not need to search for music, videos, or podcasts, remove the check marks for the Music, Podcasts, and Videos items on the Spotlight Search screen to exclude them from Spotlight searches. For normal use, you may want to leave all the check marks in place but move the items most important to you to the top of the Spotlight Search list.

Choose Locking and Control Center Settings

After a period of inactivity, your iPhone automatically locks itself. It then turns off its screen and goes to sleep to save battery power. You can choose how long your iPhone waits before locking itself. Setting your iPhone to lock quickly helps preserve battery power, but you may prefer to leave your iPhone on longer so that you can continue work, and then lock your iPhone manually. You can also choose whether to make Control Center accessible from the lock screen and from within apps.

Choose Locking and Control Center Settings

1 Press the Home button.

The Home screen appears.

2 Tap **Settings**.

The Settings screen appears.

3 Tap **General**.

The General screen appears.

4 Tap **Auto-Lock**.

The Auto-Lock screen appears.

5 Tap the interval — for example, **2 Minutes**.

Note: Choose **Never** for Auto-Lock if you need to make sure your iPhone never goes to sleep. For example, if you are playing music with the lyrics displayed, turning off auto-locking may be helpful.

6 Tap **General**.

The General screen appears.

7 Tap **Settings**.

The Settings screen appears.

8 Tap **Control Center**.

Note: Giving yourself access to Control Center from the lock screen is useful, especially if you play music a lot. But it also gives an unauthorized person access to important settings, such as Wi-Fi, without unlocking the iPhone.

The Control Center screen appears.

9 Set the **Access on Lock Screen** switch to On (◼) or Off (☐), as needed.

10 Set the **Access Within Apps** switch to On (◼) or Off (☐), as needed.

11 Tap **Settings**.

The Settings screen appears.

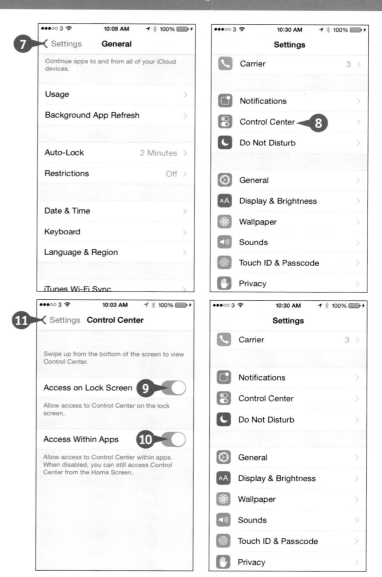

TIP

How do I put the iPhone to sleep manually?

You can put the iPhone to sleep at any point by pressing the Power/Sleep button for a moment.

Putting the iPhone to sleep as soon as you stop using it helps to prolong battery life. If you apply a passcode, as discussed later in this chapter, putting the iPhone to sleep also starts protecting your data sooner.

Set Up and Use Do Not Disturb Mode

When you do not want your iPhone to disturb you, turn on its Do Not Disturb mode. You can configure Do Not Disturb mode to turn on and off automatically at set times each day — for example, on at 10 p.m. and off at 7 a.m. You can turn Do Not Disturb mode on and off manually from Control Center.

You can allow particular groups of contacts to bypass Do Not Disturb mode so they can contact you even when Do Not Disturb is on. You can also allow repeated calls to ring when Do Not Disturb is on.

Set Up and Use Do Not Disturb Mode

Configure Do Not Disturb Mode

1. Press the Home button.

   The Home screen appears.

2. Tap **Settings**.

   The Settings screen appears.

3. Tap **Do Not Disturb**.

4. To turn on Do Not Disturb, set the **Manual** switch to On (⬜).

Note: You can turn Do Not Disturb on and off more easily from Control Center.

5. Set the **Scheduled** switch to On (⬜).

6. Tap **From, To**.

7. Tap **From**.

8. Use the spin wheels to set the From time.

9. Tap **To**.

10. Set the To time.

11. Tap **Back**.

12. Tap **Allow Calls From**.

The Allow Calls From screen appears.

13 Tap the group you will allow to call you during your quiet hours.

14 Tap **Back**.

15 Set the **Repeated Calls** switch to On () or Off (☐), as needed.

16 In the Silence area, tap **Always** or **Only while iPhone is locked**, as needed.

Turn Do Not Disturb Mode On or Off Manually

1 Press the Home button.

The Home screen appears.

2 Tap and drag up to scroll down the screen.

Control Center opens.

3 Tap **Do Not Disturb** to turn Do Not Disturb on (🌙 changes to 🌙) or off (🌙 changes to 🌙).

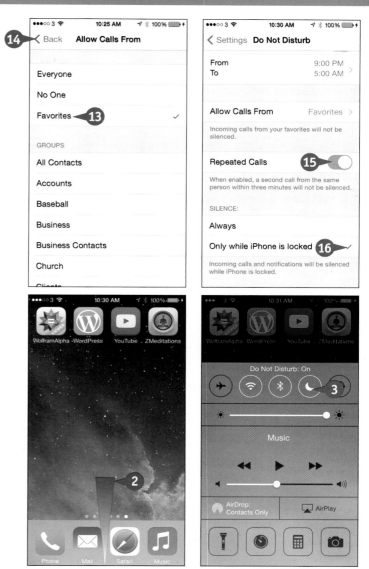

TIPS

How can I tell whether Do Not Disturb is on?

When Do Not Disturb is on, a crescent moon symbol appears in the status bar to the left of the battery readout.

How can I allow multiple groups of people to call me when Do Not Disturb is on?

The Allow Calls From screen lets you select only one group. Unless you can put all the relevant contacts into a single group, the best solution is to create a new group and add the existing groups to it. This is easiest to do in your iCloud account by working in a web browser on a computer.

Secure Your iPhone with Touch ID or a Passcode

To prevent anyone who picks up your iPhone from accessing your data, you can lock the iPhone with either Touch ID or a passcode. Touch ID uses your fingerprint to unlock the iPhone, which is usually faster and easier than typing a passcode; if Touch ID fails, you use the passcode as a backup means of unlocking your iPhone. You can also set the iPhone to automatically erase its data after ten failed passcode attempts. You can also choose between a standard, four-digit password and a longer password consisting of numbers, letters, and other characters.

Secure Your iPhone with Touch ID or a Passcode

1 Press the Home button.

The Home screen appears.

2 Tap **Settings**.

The Settings screen appears.

3 Tap **Touch ID & Passcode**.

The Touch ID & Passcode screen appears.

Ⓐ To set up Touch ID, tap **Add a Fingerprint** and follow the prompts. You can then set the **iPhone Unlock** switch and the **iTunes & App Store** switch to On (⬜).

4 To follow this example, set the **Simple Passcode** switch to On (⬜).

5 Tap **Turn Passcode On**.

6 Type your passcode.

The iPhone displays the message "Re-enter your passcode."

7 Type the passcode again.

The Touch ID & Passcode screen appears.

8 Tap **Require Passcode**.

The Require Passcode screen appears.

9 Tap the button for the length of time you want — for example, **After 1 minute** or **Immediately**.

10 Tap **Back**.

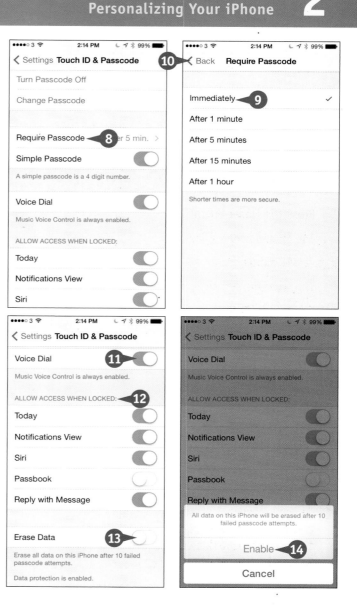

The Passcode Lock screen appears.

11 Set the **Voice Dial** switch to On (☑) or Off (☐), as needed.

12 In the Allow Access When Locked area, set the **Passbook** switch and the **Reply with Message** switch to Off (☐) or On (☑), as needed.

Note: Allowing access to Passbook when your iPhone is locked enables you to reach boarding passes and similar documents more quickly when you need them.

13 If you want the iPhone to erase all its data after ten failed passcode attempts, set the **Erase Data** switch to On (☑).

The iPhone displays a confirmation dialog.

14 Tap **Enable**.

How can I make my passcode even more secure?
If you feel a four-digit passcode is not secure enough, set the **Simple Passcode** switch on the Touch ID & Passcode screen to Off (☐). When you tap **Turn Passcode On**, the Set Passcode screen lets you set a passcode of any length.

What Require Passcode setting should I choose?
Choose **Immediately** for greatest security. Choose **After 1 minute** for good security but more convenience.

Configure Restrictions and Parental Controls

Like any other computer that can access the Internet, the iPhone can reach vast amounts of content not suitable for children or business contexts. You can restrict the iPhone from accessing particular kinds of content. You can use the restrictions to implement parental controls — for example, preventing the iPhone's user from buying content in apps or watching adult-rated movies.

Configure Restrictions and Parental Controls

1 Press the Home button.

The Home screen appears.

2 Tap **Settings**.

The Settings screen appears.

3 Tap **General**.

The General screen appears.

4 Scroll down, and then tap **Restrictions**.

The Restrictions screen appears.

5 Tap **Enable Restrictions**.

The Set Passcode screen appears.

Note: The passcode you set to protect restrictions is different from the passcode you use to lock the iPhone. Do not use the same code.

6 Type the passcode.

Note: The iPhone shows dots instead of your passcode digits in case someone is watching.

The iPhone displays the Set Passcode screen again, this time with the message "Re-enter your Restrictions Passcode."

7 Type the passcode again.

8 In the Allow area, set each switch to On (⬤) or Off (⬜), as needed.

9 Scroll down to the Allowed Content area.

10 If you need to change the country used for rating content, tap **Ratings For**. On the Ratings For screen, tap the country, and then tap **Restrictions**.

11 Choose settings for Music, Podcasts & iTunes U, Movies, TV Shows, Books, Apps, Siri, and Websites. For example, tap **Movies**.

The Movies screen appears.

12 Tap the highest rating you will permit.

13 Tap **Restrictions**.

14 Move the **In-App Purchases** switch to Off (⬜) to prevent the user buying items from within apps.

15 Choose other settings in the Privacy area.

16 Choose settings for Accounts, Cellular Data Use, Background App Refresh, and Volume Limit.

17 Set the **Multiplayer Games** switch and the **Adding Friends** switch to On (⬤) or Off (⬜), as needed.

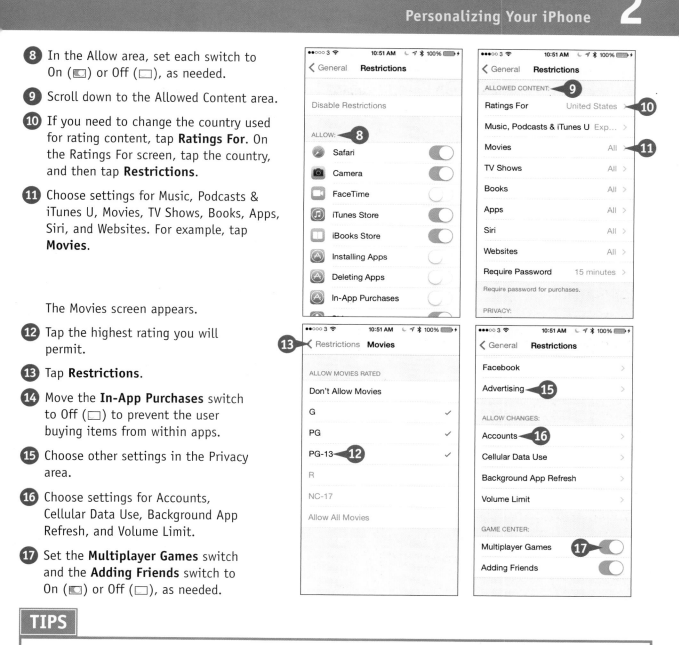

TIPS

What are in-app purchases?
In-app purchases are items that you can buy directly from within apps. These are a popular and easy way for developers to sell extra features for apps, especially low-cost apps or free apps. They are also an easy way for the iPhone's user to spend money.

What do the Privacy settings in Restrictions do?
The Privacy settings in Restrictions enable you to control which apps can access the iPhone's location information, contacts, and other apps, and whether the user can change the settings.

Set Up Family Sharing

Apple's Family Sharing feature enables you to share purchases from Apple's online services with other family members. You can also share photos and calendars, and you can use the Find My iPhone feature to find your iOS devices and Macs when they go missing.

This section assumes that you are the Family organizer, the person who gets to set up Family Sharing; to invite others to participate; and to pay for the content they buy on the iTunes Store, the iBooks Store, and the App Store.

Set Up Family Sharing

1. Press the Home button.

   The Home screen appears.

2. Tap **Settings**.

   The Settings screen appears.

3. Tap **iCloud**.

   The iCloud screen appears.

4. Tap **Set Up Family Sharing**.

   The Family Sharing screen appears.

5. Tap **Get Started**.

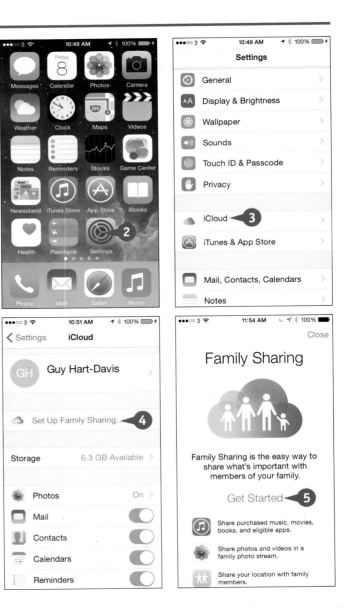

The Family Setup screen appears.

Ⓐ You can tap **add photo** and then either tap **Take Photo** to take a photo with your iPhone's camera or tap **Choose Photo** and select an existing photo for your profile.

6 Tap **Continue**.

The Share Purchases screen appears.

Ⓑ You can tap **Share purchases from a different account?** to change the account.

7 Tap **Continue**.

The Payment Method screen appears.

8 Verify that iOS has identified the means of payment that you want your family to belabor.

9 Tap **Continue**.

The Family screen appears.

10 Tap **iCloud**.

The iCloud screen appears.

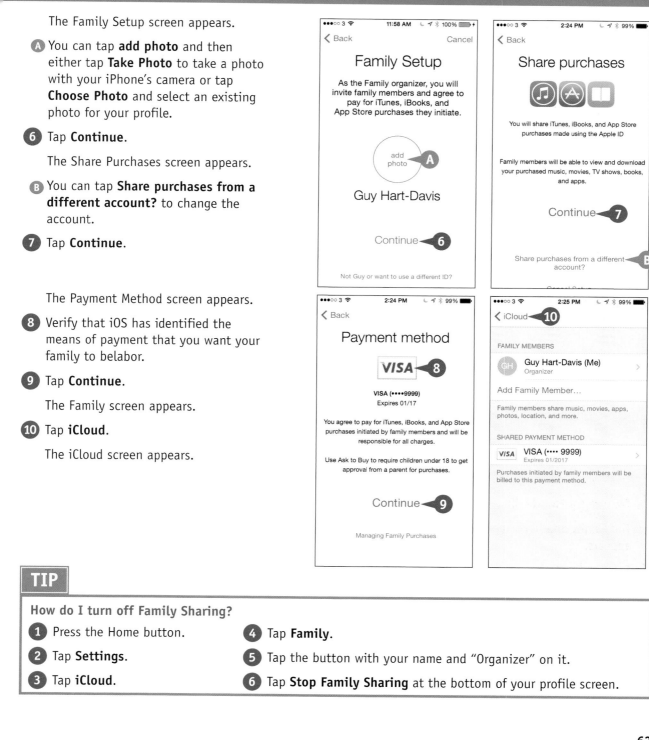

TIP

How do I turn off Family Sharing?

1 Press the Home button.

2 Tap **Settings**.

3 Tap **iCloud**.

4 Tap **Family**.

5 Tap the button with your name and "Organizer" on it.

6 Tap **Stop Family Sharing** at the bottom of your profile screen.

Add Family Members to Family Sharing

After setting up the basics of Family Sharing, you can add your family members to the group. You can either send an invitation to a family member to join the group or ask her to enter her Apple ID and password on your iPhone to join immediately.

If you send an invitation, the family member can join at a time of her choosing by using her own iPhone, iPad, iPod touch, or computer.

Add Family Members to Family Sharing

Add a Family Member to Family Sharing

1 Press the Home button.

The Home screen appears.

2 Tap **Settings**.

The Settings screen appears.

3 Tap **iCloud**.

The iCloud screen appears.

4 Tap **Family**.

The Family screen appears.

5 Tap **Add Family Member**.

The first Add Family Member screen appears.

6 Start typing the name.

A list of matches appears.

7 Tap the appropriate match.

The second Add Family Member screen appears.

A If the family member is not present, tap **Send an Invitation**. iOS sends the invitation.

8 If the family member is present, tap **Ask** *Name* **to Enter Password**.

The Enter password screen appears.

9 Ask the family member to enter her Apple ID and password.

10 Tap **Done**.

iOS adds the family member to Family Sharing.

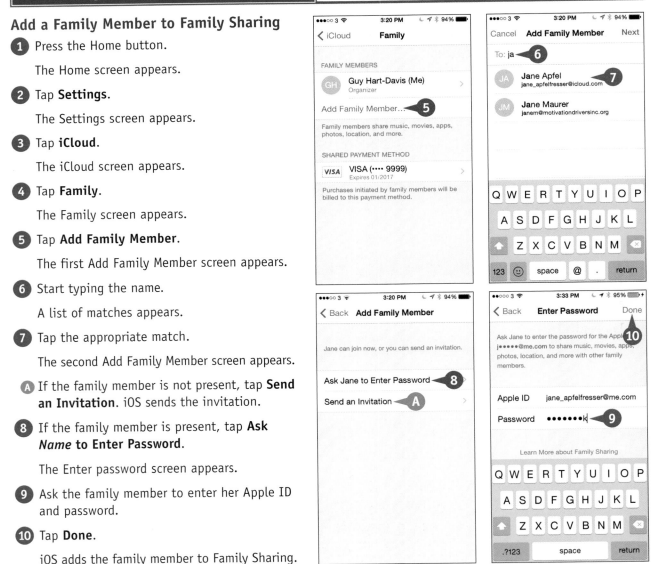

Accept an Invitation

Note: This example shows how a family member accepts your Family Sharing invitation on an iPad.

1 Tap the notification for the Family Sharing invitation.

The iCloud screen in the Settings app appears.

Note: You can also display the iCloud screen by pressing the Home button, tapping **Settings**, and then tapping **iCloud**.

2 Tap **Invitations**.

The Invitations screen appears, showing the Family Sharing Invitation.

3 Tap **Accept** to accept the invitation.

B You can tap **Decline** to decline the invitation.

The Confirm Account screen appears.

4 Tap **Confirm**.

TIPS

How many people can I add to Family Sharing?

Family Sharing works for up to six people, so you can add five other people to your account.

How do I control who can approve purchase requests from Family Sharing members?

On the Family screen in the Settings app, tap the name of the adult involved. The profile screen for the adult appears. Set the **Parent/Guardian** switch to On (⬜) to enable the adult to approve Ask to Buy requests.

Choose Date, Time, and International Settings

To keep yourself on time and your data accurate, you need to make sure the iPhone is using the correct date and time.

To make dates, times, and other data appear in the formats you prefer, you may need to change the iPhone's International settings.

Choose Date, Time, and International Settings

Choose Date and Time Settings

1. Press the Home button.

   The Home screen appears.

2. Tap **Settings**.

   The Settings screen appears.

3. Tap **General**.

   The General screen appears.

4. Scroll down, and then tap **Date & Time**.

   The Date & Time screen appears.

5. Set the **24-Hour Time** switch to On ( ) if you want to use 24-hour times.

6. To set the date and time manually, set the **Set Automatically** switch to Off ( ).

7. Use the controls to set the date and time.

8. Tap **General**.

   The General screen appears.

Choose International Settings

1 From the General screen, tap **Language & Region**.

The Language & Region screen appears.

A The Region Format Example area shows examples of the time, date, currency, and number formats for the current region.

2 Tap **iPhone Language**.

The iPhone Language screen appears.

3 Touch the language you want to use.

The Language & Region screen appears.

4 Tap **Region**.

The Region screen appears.

5 Tap the region you want, placing a check mark next to it.

6 Tap **Back**.

The Language & Region screen appears.

How does my iPhone set the date and time automatically?
Your iPhone sets the date and time automatically by using time servers, computers on the Internet that provide date and time information to computers that request them. The iPhone automatically determines its geographical location so that it can request the right time zone from the time server.

Why do my contacts' phone numbers appear in a different format from the region format example?
Your cellular carrier can override the setting that controls the format for phone numbers. You cannot change this, but you can change your carrier.

CHAPTER 3

Working with Voice and Accessibility

Your iPhone includes the Siri personal assistant, helpful accessibility features, and integration with your Mac and car.

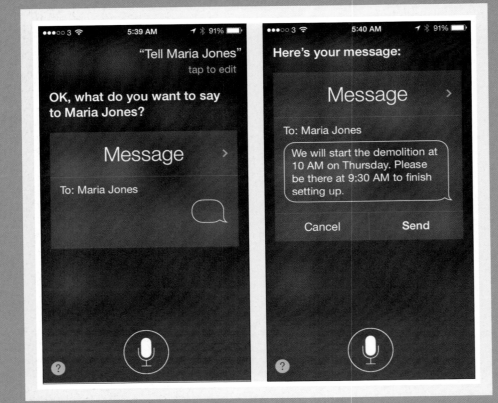

Give Commands with Siri

Often, speaking is even easier than using your iPhone's touch screen — especially when you are out and about or on the move. The iPhone's powerful Siri feature enables you to take essential actions by using your voice to tell your iPhone what you want. Siri requires a fast Internet connection because the speech recognition runs on servers in Apple's data center.

You can use Siri either with the iPhone's built-in microphone or with the microphone on a headset. Unless you are in a quiet environment, or you hold your iPhone close to your face, a headset microphone gives you much better results than the built-in microphone.

Open Siri

From the Home screen or any app, press the Home button or the headset clicker button for several seconds. If you have chosen to allow Siri access when your iPhone is locked, you can also activate Siri from the lock screen.

The Siri screen appears. A tone indicates that Siri is ready to take your commands. When your iPhone is connected to a power source, you can also activate Siri by saying "Hey Siri."

Send an E-Mail Message

Say "E-mail" and the contact's name, followed by the message. Siri creates an e-mail message to the contact and enters the text. Review the message, and then tap **Send** to send it.

If you prefer, you can start the message by saying "E-mail" and the contact's name, and then pausing. Siri then prompts you for the subject and text of the message in turn.

Set an Alarm

Say "Set an alarm for 5 a.m." and check the alarm that Siri displays.

You can turn the alarm off by tapping its switch (🔘 changes to 🔘).

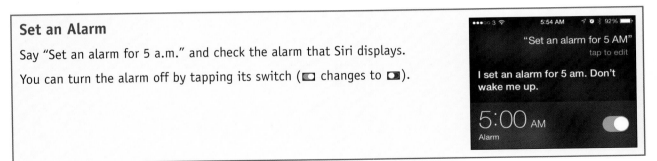

Set a Reminder for Yourself

Say "Remind me" and the details of what you want Siri to remind you of. For example, say "Remind me to take my iPad to Acme Industries tomorrow morning." Siri listens to what you say and creates a reminder. Check what Siri has written, and then tap **Confirm** if it is correct.

Send a Text Message

Say "Tell" and the contact's name. When Siri responds, say the message you want to send. For example, say "Tell Valerie Haller" and then "I am stuck in traffic but I'll be there in an hour." Siri creates a text message to the contact, enters the text, and sends the message when you say "Send" or tap **Send**.

You can also say "tell" and the contact's name followed immediately by the message. For example, "Tell Bill Sykes the package will arrive at 10 a.m."

Set Up a Meeting

Say "Meet with" and the contact's name, followed by brief details of the appointment. For example, say "Meet with Don Williamson for lunch at noon on Friday." Siri listens and warns you of any scheduling conflict. Siri then sends a meeting invitation to the contact if it finds an e-mail address, and adds the meeting to your calendar after you say "Yes" or tap **Yes**.

Dictate Text Using Siri

O ne of Siri's strongest features is the capability to transcribe your speech quickly and accurately into correctly spelled and punctuated text. Using your iPhone, you can dictate into any app that supports the keyboard, so you can dictate e-mail messages, notes, documents, and more. To dictate, simply tap the microphone icon (🎤), speak after Siri beeps, and then tap **Done**.

To get the most out of dictation, it is helpful to know the standard terms for dictating punctuation, capitalization, symbols, layout, and formatting.

Insert Punctuation

To insert punctuation, use standard terms: "comma," "period" (or "full stop"), "semicolon," "colon," "exclamation point" (or "exclamation mark"), "question mark," "hyphen," "dash" (for a short dash, –), or "em dash" (for a long dash, —). You can also say "asterisk" (*), "ampersand" (&), "open parenthesis" and "close parenthesis," "open bracket" and "close bracket," and "underscore" (_).

For example, say "buy eggs comma bread comma and cheese semicolon and maybe some milk period nothing else exclamation point" to enter the text shown here.

Insert Standard Symbols

To insert symbols, use these terms: "at sign" (@), "percent" (%), "greater than" (>) and "less than" (<), "forward slash" (/) and "backslash" (\), "registered sign" (®), and "copyright sign" (©).

For example, say "fifty-eight percent forward slash two greater than ninety-seven percent forward slash three" to enter the computation shown here.

Insert Currency Symbols

To insert currency symbols, say the currency name and "sign." For example, say "dollar sign" to insert $, "cent sign" to insert ¢, "euro sign" to insert €, "pound sterling sign" to insert £, and "yen sign" to insert ¥.

For example, say "dollar sign nine equals pound sterling sign six" to enter the equation shown here.

Control Layout

You can control text layout by creating new lines and new paragraphs as needed. A new paragraph enters two line breaks, creating a blank line between paragraphs. To create a new line, say "new line." To create a new paragraph, say "new paragraph."

For example, say "dear Anna comma new paragraph thank you for the parrot period new paragraph it's the most amazing gift I've ever had period" to enter the text shown here.

Control Capitalization

You can apply capitalization to the first letter of a word or to a whole word. You can also switch capitalization off temporarily to force lowercase:

- Say "cap" to capitalize the first letter of the next word.

- Say "caps on" to capitalize all the words until you say "caps off."

- Say "no caps" to prevent automatic capitalization of the next word — for example, "no caps Monday" produces "monday" instead of "Monday."

- Say "no caps on" to force lowercase of all words until you say "no caps off."

For example, say "give the cap head cap dining cap table a no caps french polish period" to enter the text shown here.

Insert Quotes and Emoticons

To insert double quotes, say "open quotes" and "close quotes." To insert single quotes, say "open single quotes" and "close single quotes." To enter standard emoticons, say "smiley face," "frown face," and "wink face."

For example, say "she said comma open quotes I want to go to Paris next summer exclamation point close quotes" to enter the text shown here.

Gather and Share Information with Siri

You can use Siri to research a wide variety of information online — everything from sports and movies to restaurants worth visiting or worth avoiding. You can also use Siri to perform hands-free calculations. When you need to share information quickly and easily, you can turn to Siri. By giving the right commands, you can quickly change your Facebook status or post on your wall. Similarly, you can send tweets on your Twitter account.

Find Information about Sports

Launch Siri and ask a question about sports. For example:

- "Siri, when's the next White Sox game?"
- "Did the Lakers win their last game?"
- "When's the end of the NBA season?"
- "Can you show me the roster for the Maple Leafs?"

Find Information about Movies

Launch Siri and ask a question about movies. For example:

- "Siri, where is the movie *Deliver Us from Evil* playing in Indianapolis?"
- "What's the name of Blake Lively's latest movie?"
- "Who's the star of *Transformers: Age of Extinction*?"
- "Is *Edge of Tomorrow* any good?"

Find a Restaurant

Launch Siri, and then tell Siri what type of restaurant you want. For example:

- "Where's the best Mexican food in Coeur d'Alene?"
- "Where can I get sushi in Albuquerque?"
- "Is there a brewpub in Minneapolis?"
- "Is there any dim sum within 50 miles of here?"

Address a Query to the Wolfram Alpha Computational Knowledge Engine

Launch Siri, and then say "Wolfram" and your query. For example:

- "Wolfram, what is the cube of 27?"
- "Wolfram, minus 20 centigrade in Kelvin."
- "Wolfram, tangent of 60 degrees."
- "Wolfram, give me the chemical formula of formaldehyde."

Update Your Facebook Status or Post a Comment on Your Wall

Launch Siri and give the appropriate command:

- "Update my Facebook status," and then give details when Siri prompts you.
- "Post on my Facebook wall," and then dictate the post when Siri prompts you.

If the post turns out to your liking, tap **Post**.

Send a Tweet

Launch Siri, and then say "Tweet" and the text of the tweet.

Tap **Add Location** if you want to add your current location to the tweet.

When you are satisfied with the tweet, tap **Send**.

Configure Siri to Work Your Way

To get the most out of Siri, spend a few minutes configuring Siri. You can set the language Siri uses and choose when Siri should give you voice feedback. You can also decide whether to use the Raise to Speak option, which activates Siri when you raise your iPhone to your face.

Most important, you can tell Siri which contact record contains your information, so that Siri knows your name, address, phone numbers, e-mail address, and other essential information.

Configure Siri to Work Your Way

1 Press the Home button.

The Home screen appears.

2 Tap **Settings**.

The Settings screen appears.

3 Tap **General**.

Note: When Siri is off, you can use the Voice Control feature to take actions such as dialing numbers and controlling music playback.

The General screen appears.

4 Tap **Siri**.

The Siri screen appears.

5 Set the **Siri** switch to On (◻).

6 Set the **Voice Activation** switch to On (◻) if you want to be able to activate Siri by saying "Hey Siri!" when your iPhone is plugged into power.

7 Tap **Language**.

The Language screen appears.

8 Tap the language you want to use.

9 Tap **Siri**.

The Siri screen appears.

10 Tap **Voice Gender**.

The Voice Gender screen appears.

11 Tap **Male** or **Female**.

12 Tap **Siri**.

13 Tap **Voice Feedback**.

The Voice Feedback screen appears.

14 Tap **Handsfree Only** or **Always**, as needed, to choose when to receive voice feedback.

15 Tap **Siri**.

The Siri screen appears.

16 Tap **My Info**.

The Contacts list appears.

17 Tap the contact record that contains your information.

TIP

Does Apple store the details of what I ask Siri?

Yes, but not in a way that will come back to haunt you. When you use Siri, your iPhone passes your input to servers in Apple's data center in North Carolina, USA, for processing. The servers analyze your request and tell Siri how to respond to it. Apple's data center stores the details of your request and may analyze them to determine what people use Siri for and work out ways of making Siri more effective. Apple does not associate your Siri data with other data Apple holds about you — for example, the identity and credit card data you used to pay for iTunes Match.

Using VoiceOver to Identify Items On-Screen

If you have trouble identifying the iPhone's controls on-screen, you can use the VoiceOver feature to read them to you. VoiceOver changes your iPhone's standard finger gestures so that you tap to select the item whose name you want it to speak, double-tap to activate an item, and flick three fingers to scroll.

VoiceOver can make your iPhone easier to use. Your iPhone also includes other accessibility features, which you can learn about in the next section, "Configure Other Accessibility Features."

Using VoiceOver to Identify Items On-Screen

1 Press the Home button.

The Home screen appears.

2 Tap **Settings**.

The Settings screen appears.

3 Tap **General**.

The General screen appears.

4 Tap **Accessibility**.

The Accessibility screen appears.

5 Tap **VoiceOver**.

Note: You cannot use VoiceOver and Zoom at the same time. If Zoom is on when you try to switch VoiceOver on, your iPhone prompts you to choose which of the two to use.

6 Tap the **VoiceOver** switch and move it to On (⬜ changes to ⬛).

7 Tap **VoiceOver Practice**.

A selection border appears around the button, and VoiceOver speaks its name.

8 Double-tap **VoiceOver Practice**.

9 Practice tapping, double-tapping, triple-tapping, and swiping. VoiceOver identifies each gesture and displays an explanation.

10 Tap **Done** to select the button, and then double-tap **Done**.

11 Swipe up with three fingers.

The screen scrolls down.

12 Tap **Speaking Rate** to select it, and then swipe up or down to adjust the rate.

13 Move the **Speak Hints** switch to On (⬜ changes to ⬛) if you want VoiceOver to speak hints about using VoiceOver.

14 Farther down the screen, tap **Typing Feedback** to select it, and then double-tap.

15 Tap and then double-tap the feedback type you want: **Nothing**, **Characters**, **Words**, or **Characters and Words**.

TIP

Is there an easy way to turn VoiceOver on and off?

Yes. You can set your iPhone to toggle VoiceOver on or off when you press the Home button three times in rapid sequence. At the bottom of the Accessibility screen, tap **Accessibility Shortcut** to display the Accessibility Shortcut screen. Tap **VoiceOver**, placing a check mark next to it, and then tap **Accessibility**.

Configure Other Accessibility Features

If you have trouble using your iPhone in its default configuration, you may do well to explore the other accessibility features that your iPhone offers apart from VoiceOver.

To help you see the screen better, iOS provides a full-featured zoom capability. After turning on zooming, you can display the Zoom Controller to give yourself easy control of zoom, choose the zoom region, and set the maximum zoom level. You can then triple-tap the screen to zoom in and out quickly.

Configure Other Accessibility Features

1 Press the Home button.

The Home screen appears.

2 Tap **Settings**.

The Settings screen appears.

3 Tap **General**.

The General screen appears.

Note: Apart from the accessibility features explained in this section, your iPhone supports physical accessibility features such as Switch Control and AssistiveTouch. Switch Control enables you to control your iPhone through a physical switch you connect to it. AssistiveTouch lets you use an adaptive accessory to touch the screen.

4 Tap **Accessibility**.

The Accessibility screen appears.

5 Tap **Zoom**.

The Zoom screen appears.

6 Set the **Zoom** switch to On (□ changes to ▣).

7 Set the **Follow Focus** switch to On (▣) to make the zoomed area follow the focus on screen.

8 Set the **Zoom Keyboard** switch to On (▣) to zoom the keyboard as well.

9 Set the **Show Controller** switch to On (▣).

Ⓐ The Zoom Controller appears.

10 Tap **Idle Visibility** and set the visibility percentage for the Zoom Controller when it is idle.

11 Tap **Zoom Region**.

The Zoom Region screen appears.

12 Tap **Full Screen Zoom** or **Window Zoom**, as needed.

13 Tap **Zoom**.

The Zoom screen appears.

14 Drag the **Maximum Zoom Level** slider to set the maximum zoom level, such as 8×.

15 Tap **Accessibility**.

The Accessibility screen appears.

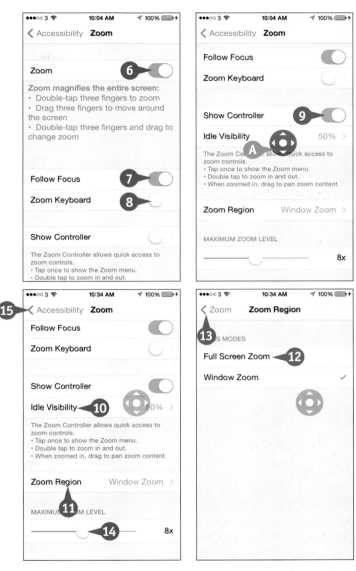

TIP

Is there an easy way to turn the Zoom feature on and off?

Yes. You can set your iPhone to toggle Zoom on or off when you press the Home button three times in rapid sequence. At the bottom of the Accessibility screen, tap **Accessibility Shortcut** to display the Accessibility Shortcut screen. Tap **Zoom**, placing a check mark next to it, and then tap **Accessibility**. You can also use the Home triple-press to toggle the VoiceOver feature, the Invert Colors feature, the Grayscale feature, the Switch Control feature, or the AssistiveTouch feature.

continued ▶

To make your iPhone's screen easier to read, you can invert the colors or switch the screen to grayscale. You can also increase the text size, make the text bold, and make iOS display the shapes around buttons so you can see exactly where they are. OS also includes a range of features that can help with hearing problems. You can connect a hearing aid, make the LED flash to warn you about alerts, and play mono audio instead of stereo audio.

Configure Other Accessibility Features (continued)

B You can set the **Invert Colors** switch to On (⬜) to invert the colors.

C You can set the **Grayscale** switch to On (⬜) to display colors in grayscale.

16 Tap **Speech**.

The Speech screen appears.

17 Set the **Speech Selection** switch, the **Speak Screen** switch, and the **Speak Auto-text** switch On (⬜) or Off (⬜), as needed.

18 Tap **Accessibility**.

The Accessibility screen appears.

19 Tap **Larger Text**.

The Larger Text screen appears.

20 Set the **Larger Accessibility Sizes** switch to On (⬜ changes to ⬜).

21 Drag the slider to set the text size.

22 Tap **Accessibility**.

The Accessibility screen appears.

D You can set the **Bold Text** switch to On (⬜) to make text appear bold.

E You can set the **Button Shapes** switch to On (⬜) to make shapes appear around buttons.

23 Tap **Increase Contrast**.

The Increase Contrast screen appears.

24 Set the **Reduce Transparency** switch, the **Darken Colors** switch, and the **Reduce White Point** switch to On (🔘) or Off (⬜), as needed to improve the contrast for your vision.

25 Tap **Accessibility**.

The Accessibility screen appears.

26 Set the **On/Off Labels** switch to On (🔘) if you want to display labels on the switches — I for On, O for Off.

27 Set the **LED Flash for Alerts** switch to On (🔘) to make the LED flash to warn you of alerts.

28 Set the **Mono Audio** switch to On (🔘) to get mono audio.

29 Set the **Phone Noise Cancellation** switch to On (🔘) to reduce ambient noise on calls.

30 Drag the slider to adjust the left-right audio balance.

31 Choose other options as needed in the Media, Learning, and Interaction sections.

TIPS

How do I set up a hearing aid with my iPhone?
Tap **Hearing Aids** on the Accessibility screen to display the Hearing Aids screen. Here you can pair a hearing aid that conforms to the Made for iPhone standard; for other hearing aids, work on the Bluetooth screen, as for other Bluetooth devices.

What does the Reduce Motion switch do?
Set the Reduce Motion switch to On (🔘) if you want to reduce the amount of movement that occurs when you tilt the iPhone when displaying a screen such as the Home screen, where the icons appear to float above the background.

Using Your iPhone with Your Mac

If you have a Mac, you can enjoy the impressive integration that Apple has built into iOS and OS X. Apple calls this integration Continuity. Continuity involves several features including Handoff, which enables you to pick up your work or play seamlessly on one device exactly where you have left it on another device. For example, you can start writing an e-mail message on your Mac and then complete it on your iPhone.

To use Continuity, your iPhone must be running iOS 8 or a later version, and your Mac must be running OS X 10.10, which is called Yosemite, or a later version. Your Mac must have Bluetooth 4.0 hardware. In practice, this includes a Mac mini or MacBook Air from 2011 or later, a MacBook Pro or iMac from 2012 or later, or a Mac Pro from 2013 or later.

Enabling Handoff

To enable your iPhone to communicate with your Mac, you need to enable the Handoff feature. Press the Home button to display the Home screen, tap **General** to display the General screen, and then tap **Handoff & Suggested Apps**. On the Handoff & Suggested Apps screen, set the **Handoff** switch to On (⬤), and then set the switches in the Suggested Apps list to On (⬤) or Off (▢), as needed.

Enable Handoff on Your Mac

You also need to enable Handoff on your Mac. To do so, click on the menu bar and then click **System Preferences** to open the System Preferences window. Click **General** to display the General pane. Click **Allow Handoff between this Mac and your iCloud devices** (▢ changes to ☑). You can then click **System Preferences** on the menu bar and click **Quit System Preferences** to quit System Preferences.

Make and Take Phone Calls on Your Mac

When you are using your Mac within Bluetooth range of your iPhone, Continuity enables you to make and take phone calls on your Mac instead of your iPhone. For example, when someone calls you on your iPhone, your Mac displays a call window automatically, and you can pick up the call on your Mac.

Send and Receive Text Messages from Your Mac

Your Mac can already send and receive messages via Apple's iMessage service, but when your iPhone's connection is available, your Mac can send and receive messages directly via Short Message Service (SMS) and Multimedia Messaging Service (MMS). This capability enables you to manage your messaging smoothly and tightly from your Mac.

Using Your iPhone in Your Car

If you take your iPhone everywhere with you, you will most likely want to use it in your car. You can choose from a wide range of technology for using your iPhone in your car. Your choices range from simply playing music through your existing stereo via a cable or radio transmitter to connecting the iPhone to a car unit that supports Apple's CarPlay standard.

With a CarPlay-compatible system, you can display your iPhone's content on your in-car device, enabling you to play music, make phone calls, view maps, hear and dictate messages, and take other actions.

Connect Your iPhone to Your Car Stereo via a Cable

If your car does not have a CarPlay-compatible system, and you are not able to add such a system, you can connect your iPhone to your car stereo via a cable so that you can play music from your iPhone through the car stereo. You can connect your iPhone's headphone socket to a standard

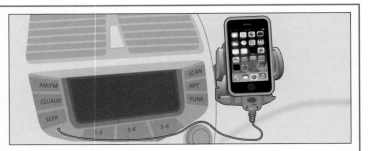

line-in socket on the stereo using a cable with 3.5mm connectors, which allows you to control the volume from the iPhone. Alternatively, you can use a Lightning-to–30-pin connector to get line-out audio from the iPhone, and then connect the 30-pin connector to the audio input.

You control the music from the iPhone, so it is helpful to have a mount or holder with which to secure the iPhone.

Connect Your iPhone to Your Car Stereo via a Radio Transmitter

If your car has neither a CarPlay-compatible system nor an audio input jack, you can play music from your iPhone through your car stereo by using a wireless transmitter. You connect the wireless transmitter to the iPhone, usually via the Lightning socket, and tune the radio on your car stereo to the

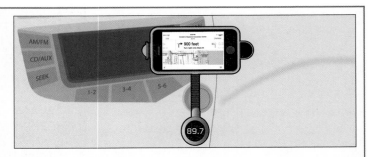

frequency on which the transmitter is broadcasting. Provided you pick a frequency with no nearby radio stations, you can get good reception and decent music quality.

With this arrangement, you control the music from the iPhone, so it is helpful to have a mount or holder to secure the iPhone. Some transmitters include stands for mounting the iPhone and electrical connections for charging the iPhone from your car's accessory socket.

Connect Your iPhone to Your Car's CarPlay Unit

If your vehicle has a CarPlay-compatible unit, you can connect your iPhone to it by inserting the iPhone in its dock. When you insert the iPhone, the CarPlay unit automatically detects the device and establishes communication with it. You can then use iPhone functions such as playing music, displaying maps, making hands-free phone calls, or having your messages read to you.

Play Music Through Your Car's Stereo

After connecting your iPhone to your CarPlay unit, you can play music from the iPhone through your car's stereo. The CarPlay unit mirrors the iPhone's screen, so you can easily see the music you are playing. You can control playback by using the controls built into the unit or built into your car — for example, using controls built into the steering wheel.

Display Maps on Your Car's Display

After connecting your iPhone to your CarPlay unit, you can use your iPhone's Maps app to navigate. For example, you can ask Siri for directions from one place to another, and then get turn-by-turn guidance for the journey.

CHAPTER 4

Setting Up Communications

In this chapter, you learn how to add your e-mail accounts to the Mail app and control how Mail displays your messages. This chapter also shows you how to control the way the iPhone displays your contacts, import contacts from a SIM card, and choose options for your calendars and notes.

●●●○○ 3 📶   4:59 PM   ⊿ 98% ▬
‹ Mail...   **Add Account**
☁️ iCloud
E🗷 Exchange
Google™
YAHOO!
Aol.
o☑ Outlook.com
Other

●●●○○ 3 📶   4:59 PM   ⊿ 98% ▬
Edit   **Calendars**   Done
Show All Calendars
EXCHANGE (WORK)
✓ ● Calendar   ⓘ
WORK ICLOUD ACCOUNT
All Work iCloud Account
✓ ● Home   ⓘ
● Work   ⓘ
ICLOUD
✓ All iCloud
✓ ● Me   ⓘ

Set Up Your Mail Accounts

Most likely, you set up your iCloud account while going through the setup routine for your iPhone. But if you have other e-mail accounts, you can set them up as explained in this section.

To set up an e-mail account, you need to know the e-mail address and password, as well as the e-mail provider. You may also need to know the addresses of the mail servers the account uses. For Microsoft Exchange, you must know the domain name as well.

Set Up Your Mail Accounts

1 Press the Home button.

The Home screen appears.

2 Tap **Settings**.

The Settings screen appears.

Note: If you have not yet set up an e-mail account on the iPhone, you can also open the Add Account screen by tapping **Mail** on the iPhone's Home screen.

3 Tap and drag up to scroll down until the fifth group of buttons appears.

4 Tap **Mail, Contacts, Calendars**.

The Mail, Contacts, Calendars screen appears.

5 Tap **Add Account**.

Note: This example uses a Google account. Setting up most other account types uses the same fields of information. For an iCloud account, you enter only the e-mail address and password.

The Add Account screen opens.

6 Tap the kind of account you want to set up.

The screen for setting up that type of account appears.

7 Tap **Name** and type your name as you want it to appear in messages you send.

8 Tap **Email** and type the e-mail address.

9 Tap **Password** and type the password.

10 Tap **Description** and type a descriptive name.

11 Tap **Next**.

The configuration screen for the account appears.

12 Make sure the **Mail** switch is set to On (⬛).

13 Set the **Contacts** switch, **Calendars** switch, **Notes** switch, and any other switches to On (⬛) or Off (☐), as needed.

14 Tap **Save**.

A The account appears on the Mail, Contacts, Calendars screen.

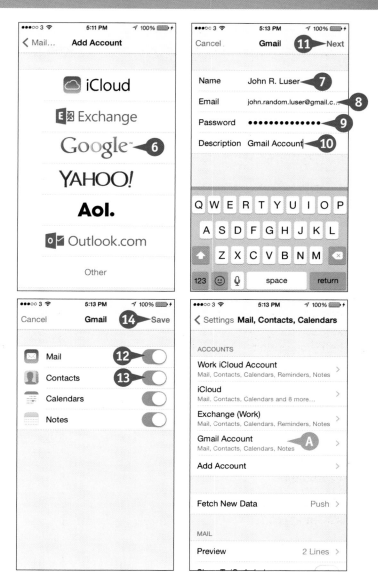

TIP

How do I set up a Hotmail account?

Hotmail is one of the services that Microsoft has integrated into its Outlook.com service. Tap the Outlook.com button on the Add Account screen, and then fill in your e-mail address, your password, and a descriptive name for the account on the Outlook screen that appears. Tap the **Next** button, wait while Mail verifies the account, and then set the **Mail** switch, **Contacts** switch, **Calendars** switch, and **Reminders** switch to On (⬛) or Off (☐), as needed.

91

Control How Your E-Mail Appears

Your iPhone's Mail app enables you to choose how many lines to include in message previews, decide whether to display the To and Cc label, and control whether Mail prompts you before deleting a message. To make messages easy to read, you can change the minimum font size. You can also choose whether to load remote images in messages; whether to mark e-mail addresses outside a particular domain, such as that of your company or organization; and whether to increase the indentation on messages you reply to or forward.

Control How Your E-Mail Appears

1 Press the Home button.

The Home screen appears.

2 Tap **Settings**.

The Settings screen appears.

3 Tap **Mail, Contacts, Calendars**.

The Mail, Contacts, Calendars screen appears.

4 Set the **Show To/Cc Label** switch to On (●) or Off (□), as needed.

5 Tap **Swipe Options**.

The Swipe Options screen appears.

6 Tap **Swipe Left**; tap **None**, **Mark as Read**, or **Flag**; and then tap **Back**.

7 Tap **Swipe Right**; tap **None**, **Mark as Read**, **Flag**, or **Archive**; and then tap **Back**.

8 Tap **Mail, Contacts, Calendars**.

9 Tap **Preview**.

The Preview screen appears.

10 Tap the number of lines you want to see in previews.

11 Tap **Mail, Contacts, Calendars**.

12 Tap **Flag Style** and then tap **Color** or **Shape** to control how message flags appear.

13 Set the **Ask Before Deleting** switch to On (🔘) or Off (⬜).

14 Set the **Load Remote Images** switch to On (🔘) or Off (⬜).

15 Tap **Mark Addresses**.

The Mark Addresses screen appears.

16 In the Mark Addresses Not Ending With box, type the domain name of your company or organization, such as surrealmacs.com.

17 Tap **Mail, Contacts, Calendars**.

The Mail, Contacts, Calendars screen appears.

18 Tap **Increase Quote Level**.

The Increase Quote Level screen appears.

19 Set the **Increase Quote Level** switch to On (🔘) or Off (⬜).

20 Tap **Mail, Contacts, Calendars**.

21 Tap **Settings**.

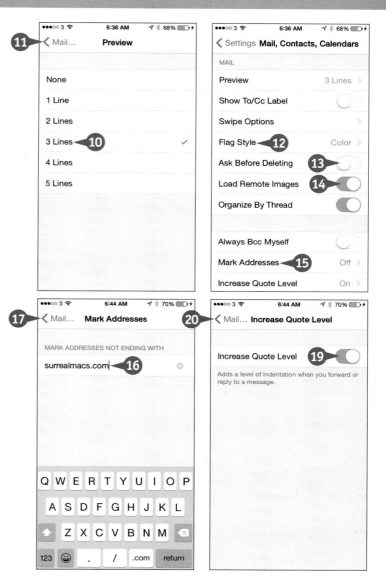

TIPS

Why turn off Load Remote Images?
Loading a remote image lets the sender know that you have opened the message. When Mail requests the remote image, the server that provides the image can log the date and time and your Internet connection's IP address, which reveals your approximate location.

What is Always Bcc Myself useful for?
Most e-mail services automatically put a copy of each message you send or forward into a folder with a name such as Sent. If your e-mail service does not use a Sent folder, set the **Always Bcc Myself** switch to On (🔘) to send a bcc copy of each message to yourself for your records.

Organize Your E-Mail Messages by Threads

The Mail app gives you two ways to view e-mail messages. You can view the messages as a simple list, or you can view them with related messages organized into *threads*, which are sometimes called *conversations*.

Having Mail display your messages as threads can help you navigate your Inbox quickly and find related messages easily. You may find threading useful if you tend to have long e-mail conversations, because threading reduces the number of messages you see at once.

Organize Your E-Mail Messages by Threads

Set Mail to Organize Your Messages by Thread

1 Press the Home button.

The Home screen appears.

2 Tap **Settings**.

The Settings screen appears.

3 Tap and drag up to scroll down until the fifth group of buttons appears.

4 Tap **Mail, Contacts, Calendars**.

The Mail, Contacts, Calendars screen appears.

5 Tap and drag up to scroll down the screen.

The Mail options appear.

6 Set the **Organize By Thread** switch to On (⬤).

Read Messages Organized into Threads

1 Press the Home button.

The Home screen appears.

2 Tap **Mail**.

The Mailboxes screen appears.

Note: If Mail displays the contents of a mailbox, tap ▤ to return to the Mailboxes screen.

3 Tap the mailbox you want to open.

The Inbox for the account appears.

Ⓐ Two chevrons on the right indicate a threaded message.

4 Tap the threaded message.

The Thread screen appears, showing the threaded message.

5 Tap the message you want to display.

Is there a quick way to enter my name and information at the end of a message?

Yes. You can create one or more e-mail signatures, which are sections of predefined text that Mail can insert at the end of messages. From the Home screen, tap **Settings**, and then tap **Mail, Contacts, Calendars**. Scroll down and tap **Signature** to display the Signature screen. Tap **All Accounts** to use the same signature for each account, or tap **Per Account** to use a different signature for each account. Then type the text to use.

Set Your Default E-Mail Account

If you set up two or more e-mail accounts on your iPhone, make sure that you set the right e-mail account to be the default account. The default account is the one from which the Mail app sends messages unless you choose another account, so choosing the appropriate account is important.

You can quickly set your default e-mail account on the Mail, Contacts, Calendars screen in the Settings app.

Set Your Default E-Mail Account

1 Press the Home button.

The Home screen appears.

2 Tap **Settings**.

The Settings screen appears.

3 Tap and drag up to scroll down until the fifth group of buttons appears.

4 Tap **Mail, Contacts, Calendars**.

The Mail, Contacts, Calendars screen appears.

5 Tap and drag up to scroll down until the fifth group of buttons appears.

6 Tap **Default Account**.

The Default Account screen appears.

7 Tap the account you want to make the default.

A A check mark appears next to the account you tapped.

8 Tap **Mail, Contacts, Calendars**.

Note: To change the e-mail account for a new message, tap and hold the **From** button, and then tap the address on the list that appears.

Control How Your Contacts Appear

To swiftly and easily find the contacts you need, you can set your iPhone to sort and display the contacts in your preferred order. Your iPhone can sort contacts either by first name or by last name. Whichever way you sort the contacts, your iPhone can display them in alphabetical order. By entering data only in the Company field for a business, you can make business names sort correctly whether you sort people's names by first name or last name.

Control How Your Contacts Appear

1 Press the Home button.

2 Tap **Settings**.

3 Tap **Mail, Contacts, Calendars**.

Ⓐ You can tap **Show in App Switcher** to display the Show in App Switcher screen, on which you can choose whether Phone Favorites and Recent contacts appear in the App Switcher.

4 Tap **Sort Order** or **Display Order** to display the Sort Order screen or the Display Order screen.

5 Tap **First, Last** or **Last, First**, as needed.

6 Tap **Mail, Contacts, Calendars**.

The Mail, Contacts, Calendars screen appears.

7 Tap **Short Name**.

The Short Name screen appears.

8 Set the **Short Name** switch to On (⬜).

9 Tap **First Name & Last Initial**, **First Initial & Last Name**, **First Name Only**, or **Last Name Only** to specify the format for short names.

10 Set the **Prefer Nicknames** switch to On (⬜) or Off (⬜), as needed.

11 Tap **Mail, Contacts, Calendars**.

The Mail, Contacts, Calendars screen appears.

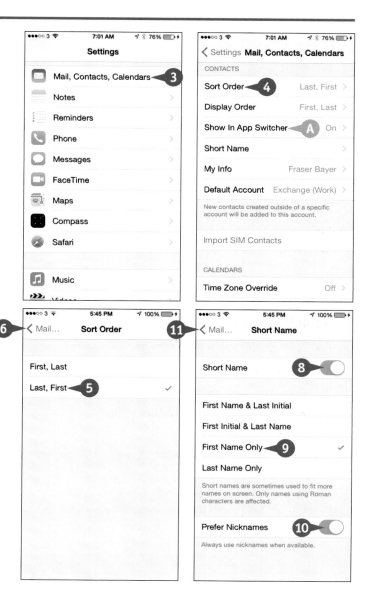

Import Contacts from a SIM Card

If you have stored contacts on a SIM card, you can import them into your iPhone. For example, you may have contacts stored on a SIM card from your previous cell phone. If the SIM card is the same size as the iPhone's SIM card, you can insert the SIM card in the iPhone temporarily and import the contacts. Another approach is to insert the iPhone's SIM card in an unlocked cell phone, copy the contacts to the SIM card, and then put the SIM card back in the iPhone.

Import Contacts from a SIM Card

1 Press the Home button.

The Home screen appears.

2 Tap **Settings**.

The Settings screen appears.

3 Tap and drag up to scroll down until the fifth group of buttons appears.

4 Tap **Mail, Contacts, Calendars**.

The Mail, Contacts, Calendars screen appears.

5 Tap and drag up to scroll down all the way to the bottom of the screen.

The bottom part of the Mail, Contacts, Calendars screen appears.

6 Tap **Import SIM Contacts**.

7 If the Import SIM Contacts to Account dialog appears, tap the account to use.

Your iPhone imports the contacts from the SIM.

8 Tap **Settings**.

Choose Default Alert Times for Calendar Events

B y synchronizing your calendars from your PC or Mac with your iPhone, you can keep details of your events in the palm of your hand.

To keep yourself on schedule, you can set default alert times to give you the warning you need before a regular event, an all-day event, or a birthday. You can set a different alert time for each type of event — for example, 15 minutes' notice for a regular appointment and a week's notice for a birthday.

Choose Default Alert Times for Calendar Events

1 Press the Home button.

2 On the Home screen, tap **Settings**.

The Settings screen appears.

3 Tap **Mail, Contacts, Calendars**.

The Mail, Contacts, Calendars screen appears.

4 Tap and drag up to the bottom of the screen.

5 Tap **Default Alert Times**.

The Default Alert Times screen appears.

6 Tap the event type to set the default alert time for. For example, tap **Events**.

The Events screen, Birthdays screen, or All-Day Events screen appears.

7 Tap the amount of time for the warning.

8 Tap **Back**.

9 On the Default Alert Times screen, set default alert times for other event types by repeating Steps **6** to **8**.

10 Tap **Mail, Contacts, Calendars**.

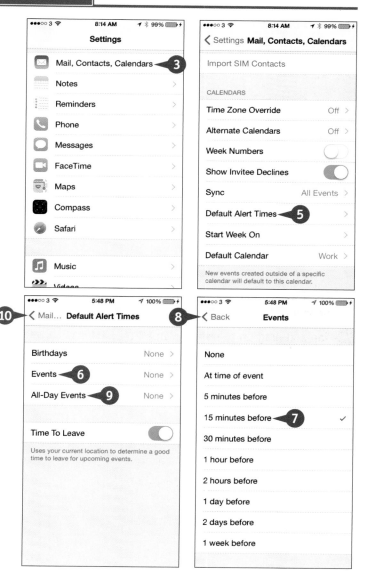

Choose Your Default Calendar and Time Zone

When you use multiple calendars on your iPhone, you should set your default calendar. This is the calendar that receives events you create outside any specific calendar. For example, if you have a Work calendar and a Home calendar, you can set the Home calendar as the default calendar.

If you travel to different time zones, you may need to use the Time Zone Override feature to specify the time zone in which to show event dates and times. Otherwise, Calendar uses the time zone for your current location.

Choose Your Default Calendar and Time Zone

1 Press the Home button.

The Home screen appears.

2 Tap **Settings**.

The Settings screen appears.

3 Tap and drag up to scroll down until the fifth group of buttons appears.

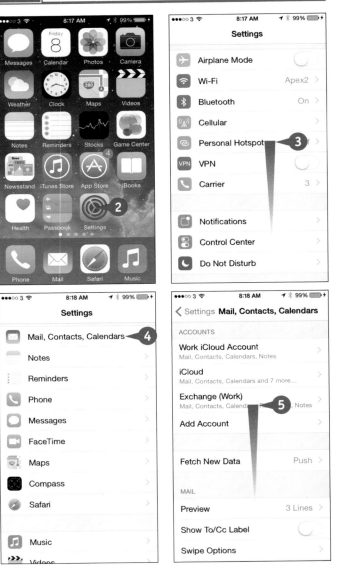

4 Tap **Mail, Contacts, Calendars**.

The Mail, Contacts, Calendars screen appears.

5 Tap and drag up to scroll down all the way to the bottom of the screen.

The bottom part of the Mail, Contacts, Calendars screen appears.

 Tap **Time Zone Override**.

The Time Zone Override screen appears.

⑦ Set the **Time Zone Override** switch to On ( ).

⑧ Tap **Time Zone**.

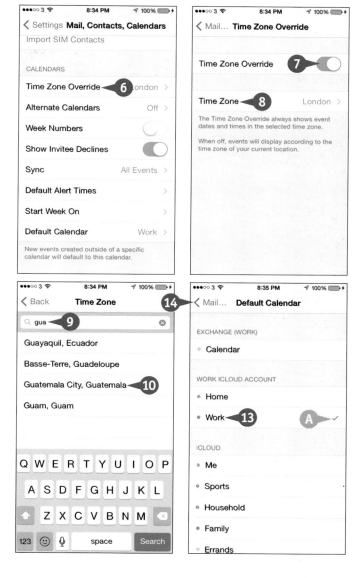

The Time Zone screen appears.

⑨ Type the first letters of a city in the time zone.

⑩ Tap the search result you want.

⑪ Tap **Mail, Contacts, Calendars**.

⑫ Tap **Default Calendar**.

The Default Calendar screen appears.

⑬ Tap the calendar you want to make the default.

Ⓐ A check mark appears next to the calendar.

⑭ Tap **Mail, Contacts, Calendars**.

TIP

Where do I control which calendars the Calendar app displays?
You choose the calendars in the Calendar app, not in the Settings app. Press the Home button to display the Home screen, tap **Calendar**, and then tap **Calendars**. On the Calendars screen, tap to place a check mark on each calendar you want shown. Tap to remove a check mark from a calendar you want to hide. Tap **Done** when you are finished.

Set Your Default Account for Notes

As described earlier in this chapter, you can set up multiple e-mail accounts on your iPhone. Each e-mail account can synchronize notes if the server offers this feature.

When you have set up multiple e-mail accounts with notes, you should set the default account for notes. The default account is the account in which your iPhone stores new notes unless you specify storing them elsewhere.

Set Your Default Account for Notes

1 Press the Home button.

The Home screen appears.

2 Tap **Settings**.

The Settings screen appears.

3 Tap and drag up to scroll down until the fifth group of buttons appears.

4 Tap **Notes**.

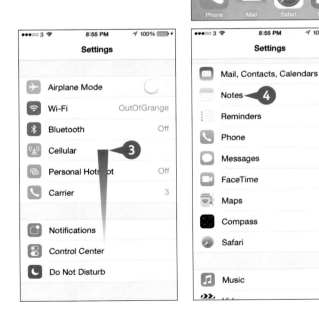

The Notes screen appears.

5 Tap **Default Account**.

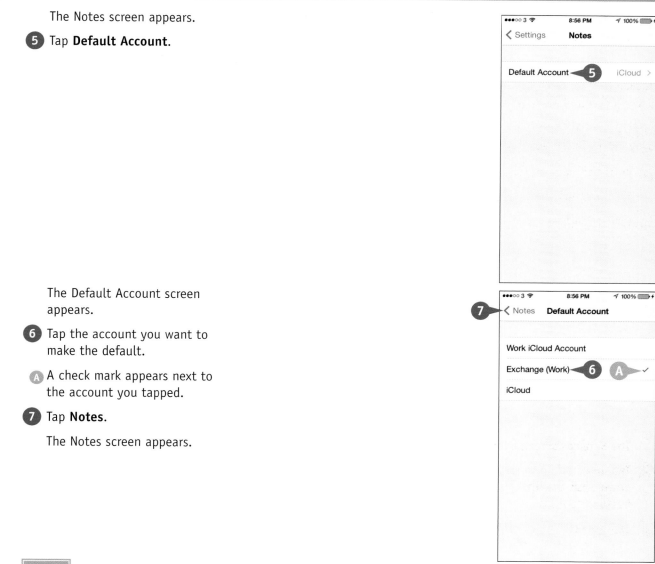

The Default Account screen appears.

6 Tap the account you want to make the default.

A A check mark appears next to the account you tapped.

7 Tap **Notes**.

The Notes screen appears.

TIP

Why does the Default Account setting not appear on the Notes screen on my iPhone?
The Default Account setting appears on the Notes screen in the Settings app when you have set up two or more e-mail accounts to synchronize notes. If you add multiple e-mail accounts to the iPhone, but set up only one account to synchronize notes, the Default Account setting does not appear because the only Notes account is the default account.

CHAPTER 5

Making Calls

You can make calls by holding the iPhone to your face, by using the speakerphone, or by using a headset. You can also make calls using Favorites and recent numbers, send and receive text and multimedia messages, and chat using the FaceTime feature.

Make Phone Calls

With your iPhone, you can make phone calls anywhere you have a connection to the cellular network. You can make a phone call by dialing the phone number using the iPhone's keypad, but you can place calls more easily by tapping the appropriate phone number for a contact, using the Recents screen, or using the Favorites list. When you need other people near you to be able to hear the phone call you are making, you can switch on your iPhone's speaker.

Make Phone Calls

Open the Phone App

1 Press the Home button.

The Home screen appears.

2 Tap **Phone**.

The Phone app opens and displays the screen you used last — for example, the Contacts screen.

 Your phone number appears at the top of the Contacts list for quick reference.

Dial a Call Using the Keypad

1 Tap **Keypad**.

The Keypad screen appears.

Note: On the Keypad screen, you can tap **Call** (📞) without dialing a number to display the last number dialed.

2 Tap the number keys to dial the number.

B You can tap **Add to Contacts** (⊕) to add this number to your Contacts list.

3 Tap **Call** (📞).

Your iPhone makes the call.

Dial a Call to a Contact

1 Tap **Contacts**.

The Contacts list appears.

2 Tap the contact you want to call.

The contact's info appears.

3 Tap **Call** (📞) on the phone number you want to call.

Your iPhone makes the call.

Note: You can also place a call to a phone number that the iPhone has identified — for example, by tapping an underlined phone number on a web page.

End a Phone Call

1 Tap **End** (📞).

Your iPhone ends the call.

The Call Ended screen appears for a moment.

Your iPhone then displays the screen from which you placed the call.

TIPS

Can I use the iPhone as a speaker phone?
Yes. Tap **Speaker** on the screen that appears while you are making a phone call. The iPhone starts playing the phone call through the speaker on the bottom instead of the small speaker at the top. Tap **Speaker** again to switch off the speaker.

What is Dial Assist?
Dial Assist is a feature that automatically determines the correct local prefix or international prefix when you place a call. To turn Dial Assist on or off, tap **Settings** on the Home screen, tap **Phone**, and then set the **Dial Assist** switch to On (🔘) or Off (⬜).

Using the Headset to Make and Take Calls

Your iPhone includes a headset that you can use not only for listening to music but also for making and taking phone calls. The control box on the headset's wire includes a microphone, a clicker switch for answering and hanging up phone calls, and Volume Up and Volume Down buttons.

Using the headset is convenient not only when you are out and about but also when you are listening to music. Your iPhone automatically pauses the music when you receive a phone call.

Using the Headset to Make and Take Calls

Make a Call Using the Headset

1 Connect the headset to your iPhone if it is not already connected.

Note: You can dial a call by activating Siri and speaking the number or the contact's name. See Chapter 3 for instructions on using Siri.

2 Press the Home button.

The Home screen appears.

3 Tap **Phone**.

The Phone app opens.

4 Dial the call as usual using one of the techniques described in this chapter. For example, tap **Contacts**, tap the contact, and then tap **Call** (📞) on the button for the appropriate phone number.

5 If you need to change the volume, press the Volume Up button or the Volume Down button on the headset control box.

6 Press the clicker button on the headset when you are ready to end the call.

Take a Call Using the Headset

1 Connect the headset to your iPhone if it is not already connected.

When you receive an incoming call, the phone ring plays in the headset and the screen comes on if it is off.

The screen shows the caller's name and phone details — for example, Mobile, Work, "other," or the phone number.

Note: If you are listening to music when you receive a call, your iPhone automatically fades and pauses the music. The same goes for video.

2 Press the clicker button on the headset to take the call.

A The screen shows the caller's name and the call's duration.

3 If you need to change the volume, press the Volume Up button or the Volume Down button on the headset control box.

4 Press the clicker button on the headset when you are ready to end the call.

The Call Ended screen appears briefly.

The previous screen then reappears.

How do I access the phone controls during a call I accepted with the headset?
To access the phone controls while the iPhone is locked, tap and drag the **slide to unlock** prompt to the right. The Home screen appears with a green bar at the top. Tap this bar to display the call screen.

Using a Wireless Headset or Car Kit

Instead of using the headset that came with your iPhone, you can use a Bluetooth headset. Similarly, you can use a car kit with a Bluetooth connection when using your iPhone in your vehicle.

You must first pair the Bluetooth headset or car kit with your iPhone, as discussed in Chapter 6.

Using a Wireless Headset or Car Kit

1 Turn on the wireless headset or connection, and make sure it works.

2 Press the Home button.

   The Home screen appears.

3 Tap **Phone**.

   The Phone app opens.

4 Dial the call as usual using one of the techniques described in this chapter. For example, tap **Contacts**, tap the contact, and then tap **Call** (📞) next to the appropriate phone number.

Note: You can also tell Siri to place the call for you.

   Your iPhone places the call.

5 Tap **audio**.

   The Audio dialog opens.

6 Tap the headset or other device you want to use.

   The Audio dialog closes.

Note: If you are playing audio or video on a Bluetooth headset when you receive a call, your iPhone automatically pauses the audio or video and plays the ringtone on the headset.

Mute a Call or Put a Call on Hold

When you are on a call, you may need to mute your iPhone's microphone so that you can confer with people near you without the person at the other end of the phone call hearing.

You may also need to put a call on hold so that you can make another call or take a break from the call.

Mute a Call or Put a Call on Hold

1 Establish the phone call as usual. For example, call a contact.

2 Tap **mute**.

The Mute button reverses its colors and the iPhone mutes the call.

3 When you are ready to unmute the call, tap **mute** again.

4 To put the call on hold, tap and hold **mute** for several seconds.

The Hold button appears in place of the Mute button.

5 When you are ready to take the call off hold, tap **hold**.

Note: After placing a call on hold, you can make another call if necessary.

Make a Conference Call

As well as making phone calls to one other phone at a time, your iPhone can make conference calls to multiple phones. To make a conference call, you call the first participant, and then add each other participant in turn.

During a conference call, you can talk in private to individual participants. You can also drop a participant from the call.

Make a Conference Call

1 Press the Home button.

2 Tap **Phone**.

3 Tap **Contacts**.

4 Tap the contact you want to call first.

5 Tap the phone number to use.

Note: You can also add a contact to the call by using Favorites, Recents, or Keypad.

Your iPhone establishes the call.

6 Tap **add call**.

The Contacts screen appears.

7 Tap the contact you want to add.

The contact's record appears.

8 Tap **Call** (📞) on the button for the phone number to use.

A The iPhone places the first call on hold and makes the new call.

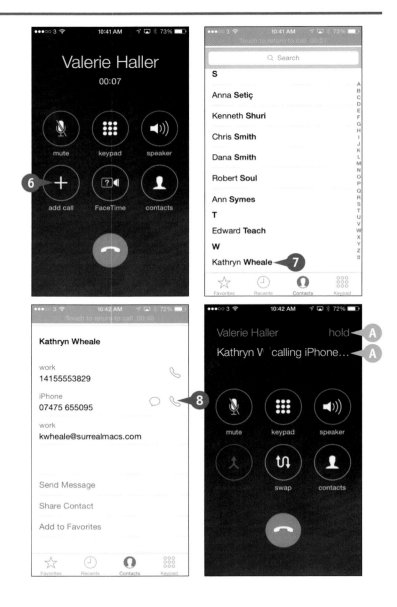

9 Tap **merge calls**.

The iPhone merges the calls and displays the participants' names at the top of the screen. You can now speak to both participants.

B You can add further participants by tapping **add call**, specifying the contact or number, and then merging the calls.

10 To speak privately to a participant, tap 🛈.

The Conference screen appears, showing a list of the participants.

11 Tap **Private** next to the participant.

The iPhone places the other callers on hold.

12 When you are ready to resume the conference call, tap **merge calls**.

The iPhone merges the calls, and all participants can hear each other again.

13 When you finish the call, tap **End** (⬤).

The iPhone ends the call.

How do I drop a participant from a conference call?

Tap 🛈 to display the Conference screen, and then tap **End** next to the participant you want to drop.

How many people can I add to a conference call?

This depends on your carrier, not on your iPhone. Ask your carrier what the maximum number of participants can be.

Y ou can dial phone numbers easily from your Contacts list, but you can save further time and effort by using the Favorites and Recents features built into the Phone app.

Favorites are phone numbers that you mark as being especially important to you. Recents are phone numbers you have called and received calls from recently.

Save Time with Call Favorites and Recents

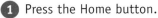

Add a Contact to Your Favorites List

1 Press the Home button.

The Home screen appears.

2 Tap **Phone**.

The Phone app opens.

3 Tap **Contacts**.

The Contacts list appears.

4 Tap the contact you want to add.

The contact's record appears.

5 Tap **Add to Favorites**.

The Add to Favorites dialog opens.

6 Tap the phone number or e-mail address you want to add to your Favorites list.

A You can tap **FaceTime** to create a favorite for FaceTime video calling.

B You can tap **FaceTime Audio** to create a favorite for audio-only calls with FaceTime.

Call a Favorite

1 In the Phone app, tap **Favorites**.

The Favorites list appears.

2 Tap the Favorite you want to call.

Your iPhone places the call.

C To display the contact's record, tap 🛈 instead of tapping the contact's button. You can then tap a different phone number for the contact if necessary.

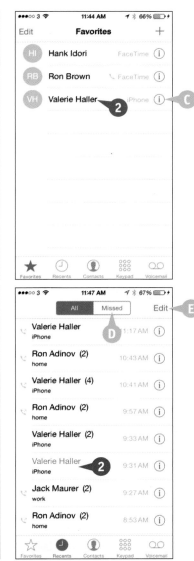

Call a Recent

1 In the Phone app, tap **Recents**.

The Recents screen appears. Red entries indicate calls you missed.

D Tap **Missed** if you want to see only recent calls you missed.

2 Tap the recent you want to call.

Your iPhone places the call.

E If you want to clear the Recents list, tap **Edit** and **Clear**. In the dialog that opens, tap **Clear All Recents**.

TIP

How do I remove a contact from my Favorites?

Tap **Favorites** to display the Favorites list, and then tap **Edit**. Tap ⊖ next to the contact. You can also rearrange your favorites by tapping ▭ and dragging up or down. Tap **Done** when you have finished changing your favorites.

Send Text and Multimedia Messages

Whenen you need to communicate quickly with another phone user, but do not need to speak to him, you can send an instant message. Your iPhone can send instant messages using the Short Message Service, abbreviated to SMS; the Multimedia Messaging Service, MMS; or Apple's iMessage service. An SMS message consists of only text, whereas an MMS message can contain text, videos, photos, sounds, or other data. An iMessage can contain text, multimedia content, or both. The Messages app automatically chooses the appropriate type — SMS, MMS, or iMessage — for the messages you create and the ways you send them.

Send Text and Multimedia Messages

1 Press the Home button.

The Home screen appears.

2 Tap **Messages**.

The Messages screen appears.

3 Tap **New Message** (⬜).

Note: Before sending an SMS or MMS message, make sure the recipient's phone number can receive such messages. Typically, you do not receive an alert if the message cannot be delivered.

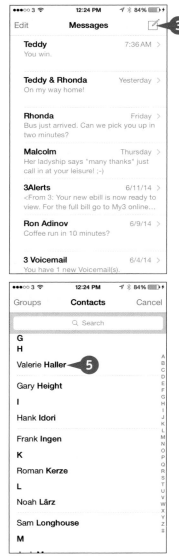

The New Message screen appears.

4 Tap ⊕.

The Contacts list appears.

5 Tap the contact to whose phone you want to send the message.

Note: If the contact's record contains only one phone number, the iPhone may add the contact's name to the New Message screen without displaying the contact's record.

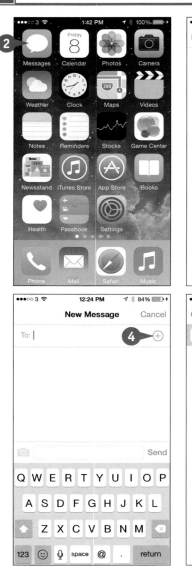

The contact's record opens.

6 Tap the phone number to use.

The contact's name appears in the To field of the New Message screen.

7 Tap in the text field, and then type your message.

8 To add a photo, tap .

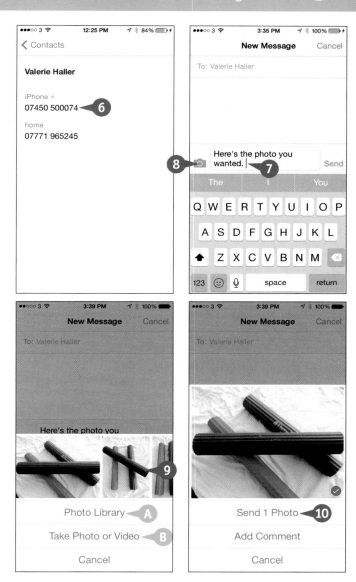

A dialog opens.

9 Tap a recent photo to add it. Scroll left to view other photos if necessary.

Ⓐ You can tap **Photo Library** to select a photo from your photo library.

Ⓑ You can tap **Take Photo or Video** to take a photo or video with your iPhone's camera.

10 Tap **Send 1 Photo**.

Note: You can send multiple photos with a message.

Messages sends the message and the photo.

TIPS

How can I respond quickly to an instant message?

When Messages displays a notification for an instant message, tap the notification to display the Text Message box. You can then type a reply and tap **Send** to send it.

Is there another way to send a photo or video?

Yes. You can start from the Camera app or the Photos app. Select the photo or video you want to share, and then tap **Share** (⬆). On the Share sheet, tap **Message**. Your iPhone starts an MMS message containing the photo or video. You can then address and send the message.

Manage Your Instant Messages

essages is great for communicating quickly and frequently with your nearest and dearest and with your colleagues, so it may not take long before the interface is so full of messages that it becomes hard to navigate.

To keep your messages under control, you can forward messages to others and delete messages you do not need to keep. You can either delete messages from a conversation, leaving the conversation's other messages, or delete the entire conversation.

Manage Your Instant Messages

Delete an Entire Conversation

1 Press the Home button.

The Home screen appears.

2 Tap **Messages**.

The Messages screen appears.

3 Tap **Edit**.

The Messages screen switches to Edit mode.

4 Tap ☑ for the conversation you want to delete.

The Delete button appears.

5 Tap **Delete**.

Messages deletes the conversation.

A You can also delete a conversation by swiping it to the left and then tapping **Delete**.

6 When you finish deleting conversations, tap **Done**.

Messages turns off Edit mode.

Forward or Delete One or More Messages from a Conversation

1 On the Messages screen, tap the conversation that contains the message or messages you will forward.

The conversation appears.

2 Tap and hold a message.

A pop-up menu appears.

3 Tap **More**.

A selection button (☐) appears to the left of each message.

4 Tap ☐ (☐ changes to ☑) for each message you want to affect.

5 Tap **Forward** (⬛).

Messages starts a new message containing the message or messages you selected.

Note: Instead of forwarding the messages, you can tap **Delete** (🗑) to delete them from the conversation. Alternatively, tap **Delete All** to delete all the messages.

6 Address the message.

7 Type any extra text needed.

8 Tap **Send** to send the message.

TIP

Can I resend a message?

Yes, you can resend a message in either of these ways:

- If a red icon with an exclamation point appears next to the message, the message has not been sent. Tap the icon to try sending the message again.

- If the message has been sent, you can forward it as described in this section. Alternatively, tap and hold the message text, and then tap **Copy** to copy it. Tap and hold in the message text field, and then tap **Paste** to paste the text. Tap **Send** to send the message.

Chat Face-to-Face Using FaceTime

By using your iPhone's FaceTime feature, you can enjoy video chats with any of your contacts who have an iPhone 4 or later, an iPad 2 or later, an iPad mini, a fourth-generation or later iPod touch, or the FaceTime for OS X application.

To make a FaceTime call, you and your contact must both have Apple IDs. Your iPhone must be connected to either a wireless network or the cellular network. Using a wireless network is preferable because you typically get better performance and do not use up your cellular data allowance.

Chat Face-to-Face Using FaceTime

Receive a FaceTime Call

1 When your iPhone receives a FaceTime request, and the screen shows who is calling, aim the camera at your face, and then drag the **slide to answer** slider.

Note: If your iPhone is unlocked, tap **Answer** to answer.

The Connecting screen appears.

When the connection is established, your iPhone displays the caller full screen, with your video inset.

2 Start your conversation.

3 Tap the screen.

The controls appear.

4 If you need to mute your microphone, tap **Mute** (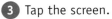).

A The background behind the Mute icon turns gray, and the Mute icon appears on your inset video.

5 Tap **Mute** (📷) when you want to turn muting off again.

6 Tap **End** (📷) when you are ready to end the FaceTime call.

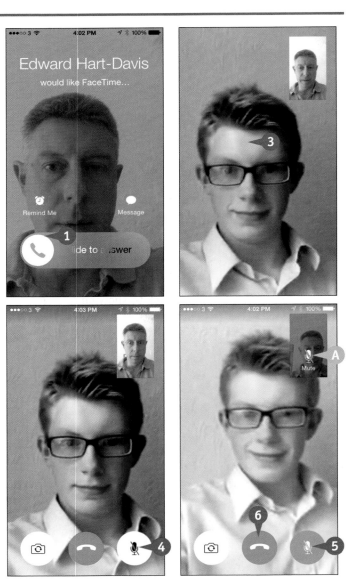

120

Make a FaceTime Call

1 Press the Home button.

The Home screen appears.

2 Tap **Phone**.

The Phone app opens.

3 Tap **Contacts**.

The Contacts list appears.

4 Tap the contact you want to call with FaceTime.

The contact's record opens.

5 Tap  on the FaceTime button.

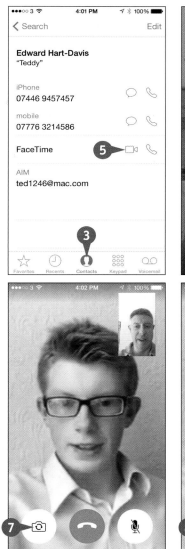

The Phone app starts a FaceTime call, showing your video preview.

6 When your contact answers, smile and speak.

7 If you need to show your contact something using the rear-facing camera, tap **Switch Cameras** (▣).

B Your inset video shows the picture that is being sent to your contact.

8 When you need to switch back to showing yourself, tap **Switch Cameras** (▣).

9 When you are ready to end the call, tap **End** (▬).

TIP

Are there other ways of starting a FaceTime call?

Yes. You can start a FaceTime call in these ways:

- During a phone call, tap ▣.
- In the Contacts app, tap the contact to display the contact record, and then tap ▣.
- Ask Siri to call a contact via FaceTime. For example, press and hold the Home button to summon Siri, and then say "FaceTime John Smith."

CHAPTER 6

Networking and Social Networking

You can control which cellular and wireless networks your iPhone uses and enjoy social networking wherever you go.

Turn Cellular and Wi-Fi Access On and Off

Normally, you will want to keep your iPhone connected to the cellular network so that you can make or receive phone calls and access the Internet. But when you do not need or may not use the cellular network, you can turn on the iPhone's Airplane Mode feature to cut off all connections.

Turning on Airplane Mode turns off Wi-Fi connections as well, but you can also turn Wi-Fi on and off separately when you need to.

Turn Cellular and Wi-Fi Access On and Off

1 Press the Home button.

The Home screen appears.

2 Tap **Settings**.

The Settings screen appears.

3 To turn Airplane Mode on, set the **Airplane Mode** switch to On (⬜).

Note: When your iPhone has a wireless network connection, it uses that connection instead of the cellular connection. This helps keep down your cellular network usage and often gives a faster connection.

A The iPhone turns off all cellular and Wi-Fi connections. An airplane icon appears in the status bar.

4 To turn on Wi-Fi, tap **Wi-Fi**.

The Wi-Fi screen appears.

5 Set the **Wi-Fi** switch to On (⬜).

The list of available networks appears, and you can connect as described in the section "Connect to Wi-Fi Networks," later in this chapter.

Monitor Your Cellular Network Usage

Most iPhone contracts include a certain amount of cellular network usage every month. If you use your iPhone extensively, you may need to monitor your usage of the cellular network to avoid incurring extra charges.

Monitor Your Cellular Network Usage

1 Press the Home button.

The Home screen appears.

2 Tap **Settings**.

The Settings screen appears.

3 Tap **Cellular**.

The Cellular screen appears.

Ⓐ The readouts in the Call Time area show the amount of time you have spent making calls in the current billing period and your phone's lifetime.

Ⓑ The readouts in the Cellular Data Usage area show your cellular data usage for the current period and how much roaming data you have used.

Note: To reset your usage statistics, tap **Reset Statistics** at the bottom of the Cellular screen.

Control Cellular Data and Background Refresh

To control your iPhone's use of cellular data, you can turn cellular data on and off on the Cellular screen in the Settings app.

You can decide which apps can use cellular data. You can consult the readouts on the Cellular screen to find out which apps and services use the most data, and then turn off greedy apps. You can also use the Background App Refresh feature to control which apps refresh their content via Wi-Fi or cellular connections when running in the background rather than the foreground.

Control Cellular Data and Background Refresh

1 Press the Home button.

The Home screen appears.

2 Tap **Settings**.

The Settings screen appears.

3 Tap **Cellular**.

The Cellular screen appears.

4 If you need to turn cellular data off altogether, set the **Cellular Data** switch to Off (☐).

Ⓐ You can set the **Enable 4G** switch or **Enable LTE** switch to On (☐) to enable 4G or LTE cellular service where it is available.

5 Set each app's switch to On (☐) or Off (☐), as needed.

Note: If you set the **Cellular Data** switch to Off (☐), the app switches are dimmed and unavailable.

6 To see which system services have been
using cellular data, tap **System Services**.

The System Services screen appears.

7 Browse the list to identify any services
that hog cellular data.

8 Tap **Cellular**.

The Cellular screen appears.

9 Tap **Settings**.

The Settings screen appears.

10 Tap **General**.

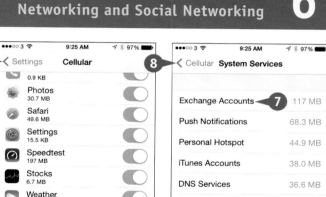

The General screen appears.

11 Tap **Background App Refresh**.

The Background App Refresh screen
appears.

12 Set the **Background App Refresh** switch
to On (⬛) or Off (⬜), as needed.

13 Set each individual app switch to On (⬛)
or Off (⬜), as needed.

14 Tap **General**.

The General screen appears.

15 Tap **Settings**.

The Settings screen appears.

TIP

Which apps should I allow to use Background App Refresh?
Normally, you should restrict Background App Refresh to those apps for which it is important to have
updated information immediately available each time you access the app. For example, if you use your
iPhone for navigation, getting updated map and GPS information in the background is a good idea, whereas
updating magazine subscriptions is usually a waste of cellular data.

Connect Your iPhone to a Different Carrier

Your iPhone's SIM card makes it connect automatically to a particular carrier's network, such as the AT&T network or the Verizon network. When you go outside your carrier's network, you can connect the iPhone manually to a different carrier's network. For example, if you travel to the United Kingdom, you can connect your iPhone to carriers such as O2, Vodafone, Three, or EE.

Connect Your iPhone to a Different Carrier

1 Press the Home button.

The Home screen appears.

2 Tap **Settings**.

The Settings screen appears.

3 Tap **Carrier**.

Note: To connect to a different carrier's network, you may need to set up an account with that carrier or pay extra charges to your standard carrier.

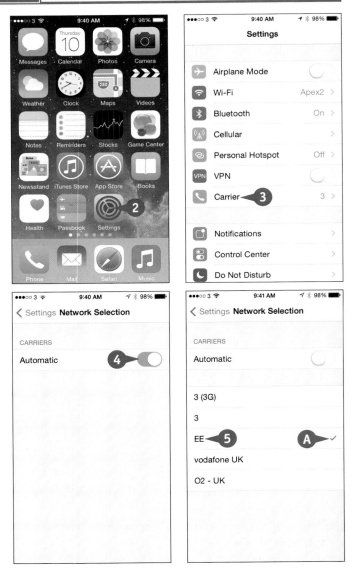

The Network Selection screen appears.

4 Set the **Automatic** switch to Off (☐).

The list of available carriers appears.

5 Tap the carrier you want to use.

A A check mark appears next to the carrier.

Note: When you want to switch back to your regular carrier, set the **Automatic** switch on the Network Selection screen to On (☐).

Turn Data Roaming On or Off

When you need to use your iPhone in a location where your carrier does not provide Internet service, you can turn on data roaming, which enables you to access the Internet using other carriers' networks. You can incur extra charges when using data roaming, especially when you use it in another country, so it is wise to keep data roaming turned off and turn it on only when you need it. Normally, you will want to use data roaming only when no wireless network connection is available.

Turn Data Roaming On or Off

1 Press the Home button.

The Home screen appears.

2 Tap **Settings**.

The Settings screen appears.

3 Tap **Cellular**.

The Cellular screen appears.

A You can also turn off cellular data altogether by setting the **Cellular Data** switch to Off (☐). Do this when you need to ensure all apps use Wi-Fi rather than cellular connections.

4 Set the **Data Roaming** switch to On (▣).

Note: When you need to turn data roaming off again, set the **Data Roaming** switch on the Cellular screen to Off (☐).

Connect Bluetooth Devices to Your iPhone

To extend your iPhone's functionality, you can connect devices to it that communicate using the wireless Bluetooth technology.

For example, you can connect a Bluetooth headset and microphone so that you can listen to music and make and take phone calls. Or you can connect a Bluetooth keyboard so that you can quickly type e-mail messages, notes, or documents.

Connect Bluetooth Devices to Your iPhone

Set Up a Bluetooth Device

1 Press the Home button.

The Home screen appears.

2 Tap **Settings**.

The Settings screen appears.

3 Tap **Bluetooth**.

The Bluetooth screen appears.

4 Set the **Bluetooth** switch to On (⬜).

The iPhone scans for Bluetooth devices.

5 Turn on the Bluetooth device and make it discoverable.

Note: Read the Bluetooth device's instructions to find out how to make the device discoverable via Bluetooth.

A Devices marked "Not Connected" are already paired with your iPhone. You can tap a device to connect it.

6 Tap the device's button.

B For a device such as a keyboard or a computer, the Bluetooth Pairing Request dialog opens.

7 Type the code on the device.

The iPhone pairs with the device and then connects to it.

C The Devices list shows the device as Connected. You can start using the device.

Choose the Device for Playing Audio or Taking a Call

1 Tap at the bottom of the screen and swipe up. This example uses the Music app.

Control Center opens.

2 Tap **AirPlay**.

The AirPlay dialog opens.

3 Tap the device you want to use.

4 Tap **Done**.

The AirPlay dialog closes.

5 Tap the app above Control Center.

Control Center closes.

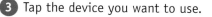

TIP

How do I stop using a Bluetooth device?

When you no longer need to use a particular Bluetooth device, tell your iPhone to forget it. Press the Home button, and then tap **Settings**. Tap **Bluetooth**, and then tap the device's info button ([ⓘ]). On the device's screen, tap **Forget this Device**, and then tap **Forget Device** in the confirmation dialog.

Share Items via AirDrop

AirDrop enables you to share files swiftly and easily with iOS devices near your iPhone and Macs running OS X 10.10, Yosemite, or later versions. For example, you can use AirDrop to share a photo, a contact record, or an item from Passbook. You can use AirDrop in any app that displays a Share button (⬆).

You can turn AirDrop on when you need it and off when you do not. When AirDrop is on, you can choose between accepting items only from your contacts or from everyone.

Share Items via AirDrop

Turn AirDrop On or Off

1 Swipe up from the bottom of the screen.

Control Center opens.

A The readout shows AirDrop's status: *AirDrop*, indicating the feature is off; *AirDrop: Contacts Only*; or *AirDrop, Everyone*.

2 Tap **AirDrop**.

Note: AirDrop uses Wi-Fi or Bluetooth to transfer files wirelessly without the devices having to be on the same wireless network.

The AirDrop dialog opens.

3 Tap **Off**, **Contacts Only**, or **Everyone**, as needed.

The AirDrop dialog closes.

B The AirDrop readout shows the AirDrop setting you chose.

4 Tap the screen above Control Center.

Control Center closes.

Share an Item via AirDrop

1 Open the app that contains the item. For example, tap **Photos** on the Home screen.

2 Navigate to the item you want to share. For example, tap a photo to open it.

3 Tap **Share** (⬆).

The Share sheet appears.

C In some apps, you can select other items to share at the same time. For example, in Photos, you can select other photos.

4 In the AirDrop area, tap the contact or device you want to send the item to.

Receive an Item via AirDrop

D When someone tries to send you an item via AirDrop, your iPhone displays a pop-up message.

E Your iPhone receives the item, stores it in the appropriate app, and displays it if possible. For example, when you receive a photo, the Photos app opens and displays the photo so that you can enjoy it, edit it, delete it, or all three.

Which devices can use AirDrop?
AirDrop works on the iPhone 6 and iPhone 6 Plus, iPhone 5s, iPhone 5c, iPhone 5, fifth-generation iPad, fourth-generation iPad, iPad mini, and fifth-generation iPod touch. Earlier iOS devices do not have the wireless hardware needed for AirDrop.

Does AirDrop pose a security threat to my iPhone and data?
AirDrop encrypts files so it can transfer them securely. When using AirDrop, you choose which files — if any — you want to share from your iPhone; other iOS devices cannot use AirDrop to grab files from your iPhone. Similarly, when someone tries to send you a file via AirDrop, you can choose whether to accept or reject it.

Share Internet Access Using Personal Hotspot

Your iPhone can not only access the Internet itself from anywhere it has a suitable connection to the cellular network, but it can also share that Internet access with your computer and other devices. This feature is called Personal Hotspot.

For you to use Personal Hotspot, your iPhone's carrier must permit you to use it. Most carriers charge an extra fee per month on top of the standard iPhone charge.

Share Internet Access Using Personal Hotspot

Set Up Personal Hotspot

1 Press the Home button.

The Home screen appears.

2 Tap **Settings**.

The Settings screen appears.

3 Tap **Personal Hotspot**.

The Personal Hotspot screen appears.

4 Tap **Wi-Fi Password**.

The Wi-Fi Password screen appears.

5 Tap 🔘 to clear the default password.

6 Type the password you want to use.

7 Tap **Done**.

The Personal Hotspot screen appears again.

8 Set the **Personal Hotspot** switch to On (■).

The Personal Hotspot screen shows the message Now Discoverable and displays information for connecting computers and devices to the hotspot.

Note: When Personal Hotspot is active — when a computer or device is using the connection — Personal Hotspot appears in a blue bar across the lock screen and the Home screen to remind you. The bar shows the number of connections.

You can now connect your PC or Mac to the iPhone's Internet connection.

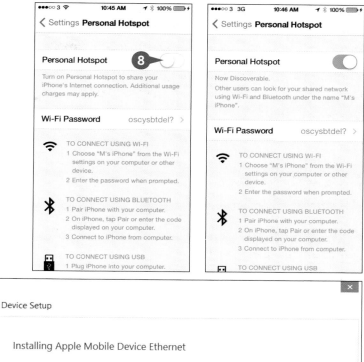

Connect a PC to Personal Hotspot via USB

1 Turn on Personal Hotspot on your iPhone as described earlier.

2 Connect the iPhone to the PC via USB.

Windows detects the iPhone's Internet connection as a new network connection and installs software for it.

Ⓐ If the Device Setup dialog box remains open after the software installation finishes, click **Close**.

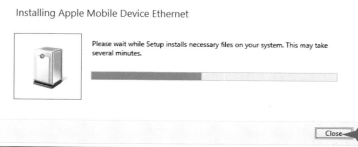

Which devices can I connect to Personal Hotspot?	**Should I use USB or Wi-Fi to connect my computer to Personal Hotspot?**
You can connect almost any Wi-Fi–capable computer or device to Personal Hotspot. Personal Hotspot works like other wireless access points, which makes it easy to connect your devices.	If your PC or Mac is close to the iPhone, using the USB cable is usually easiest. But Wi-Fi gives you greater range and allows you to connect multiple computers to Personal Hotspot at once.

continued ►

You can connect up to five computers or other devices, such as iPads or other tablet computers, to the Internet by using Personal Hotspot on your iPhone. Because the devices share the connection, the more devices you use, the slower the connection speed will appear to be on each device. Connecting more devices also typically increases the amount of data transferred across the iPhone's Internet connection and so consumes your data allowance faster.

Share Internet Access Using Personal Hotspot (continued)

Normally, Windows begins using the tethered USB connection automatically. If not, you can open Network and Sharing Center and configure the network settings manually.

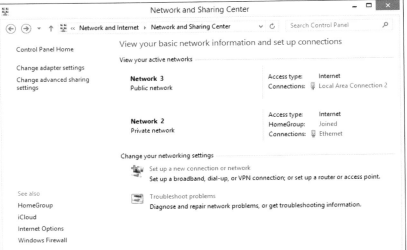

Connect a Mac via Personal Hotspot via USB

1 Turn on Personal Hotspot on your iPhone as described earlier.

2 Connect the iPhone to the Mac via USB.

Note: If your Mac displays the A New Network Interface Has Been Detected dialog, click **Network Preferences** to open Network Preferences.

3 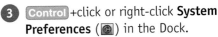+click or right-click **System Preferences** () in the Dock.

The System Preferences context menu opens.

4 Click **Network**.

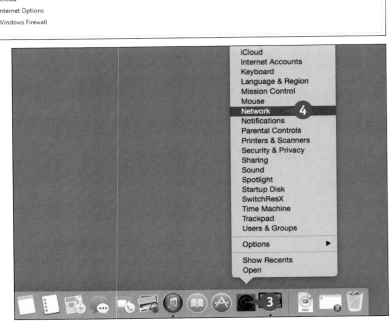

The Network preferences pane of System Preferences opens.

5 Click **iPhone USB**.

6 Click **Apply**.

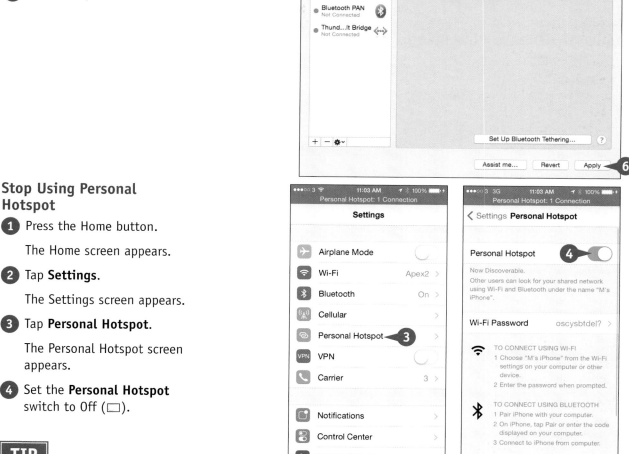

Stop Using Personal Hotspot

1 Press the Home button.

The Home screen appears.

2 Tap **Settings**.

The Settings screen appears.

3 Tap **Personal Hotspot**.

The Personal Hotspot screen appears.

4 Set the **Personal Hotspot** switch to Off (☐).

TIP

Can I use Personal Hotspot as my main Internet connection?
Yes. But make sure that your data plan provides enough data for your computer use as well as your iPhone use. If it does not, you may incur extra charges, and you will do better to use Personal Hotspot only when your main Internet connection is not available.

The Internet connection speeds you get from a connection to your iPhone's Personal Hotspot are usually slower than a broadband Internet connection such as a DSL or cable connection. But if your Internet use is light, you may find these speeds adequate.

Connect to Wi-Fi Networks

Your iPhone can connect to the Internet via either the cell phone network or a Wi-Fi network. To conserve your data allowance, use a Wi-Fi network instead of the cell phone network whenever you can.

The first time you connect to a Wi-Fi network, you must provide the network's password. After that, the iPhone stores the password, so you can connect to the network without entering the password again.

Connect to Wi-Fi Networks

Connect to a Network Listed on the Wi-Fi Screen

1 Press the Home button.

The Home screen appears.

2 Tap **Settings**.

The Settings screen appears.

3 Tap **Wi-Fi**.

The Wi-Fi screen appears.

4 If Wi-Fi is off, set the **Wi-Fi** switch to On (🔲).

The Choose a Network list appears. A lock icon (🔒) indicates the network has security such as a password.

5 Tap the network you want to connect to.

Note: If the network does not have a password, your iPhone connects to it without prompting you for a password.

The Enter Password screen appears.

6 Type the password.

7 Tap **Join**.

Your iPhone connects to the wireless network.

A The Wi-Fi screen appears again, showing a check mark next to the network the iPhone has connected to.

Connect to a Network Not Listed on the Wi-Fi Screen

1 On the Wi-Fi screen, tap **Other**.

The Other Network screen appears.

2 Type the network name.

3 Tap **Security**.

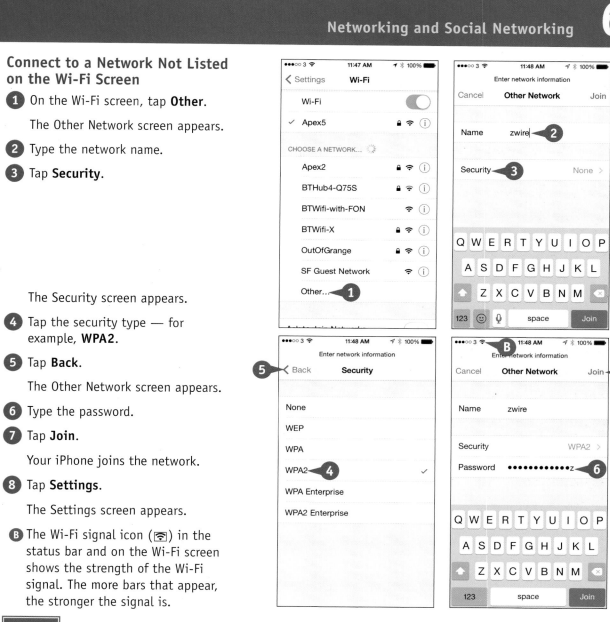

The Security screen appears.

4 Tap the security type — for example, **WPA2**.

5 Tap **Back**.

The Other Network screen appears.

6 Type the password.

7 Tap **Join**.

Your iPhone joins the network.

8 Tap **Settings**.

The Settings screen appears.

Ⓑ The Wi-Fi signal icon (📶) in the status bar and on the Wi-Fi screen shows the strength of the Wi-Fi signal. The more bars that appear, the stronger the signal is.

TIPS

What does the Ask to Join Networks switch control?
Your iPhone automatically connects to networks it "knows" — those it has connected to before. Set the **Ask to Join Networks** switch to On (🔘) if you want your iPhone to prompt you when unknown networks are available.

How do I stop using a particular wireless network?
Tap the info button (ⓘ) to the right of the network's name on the Wi-Fi screen. On the network's screen, tap **Forget this Network**. In the dialog that opens, tap **Forget**.

Log In to Wi-Fi Hotspots

When you are in town or on the road, you can log in to Wi-Fi hotspots to enjoy fast Internet access without using your iPhone's data allowance.

You can find Wi-Fi hotspots at many locations, including coffee shops and restaurants, hotels, and airports. Some municipal areas, and even some parks and highway rest stops, also provide public Wi-Fi. Some Wi-Fi hotspots charge for access — and prompt you to provide a means of payment — whereas others are free to use.

Log In to Wi-Fi Hotspots

1 Press the Home button.

The Home screen appears.

2 Tap **Settings**.

The Settings screen appears.

3 Tap **Wi-Fi**.

The Wi-Fi screen appears.

4 If Wi-Fi is off, set the **Wi-Fi** switch to On (⬜).

The list of wireless networks appears.

5 Tap the Wi-Fi hotspot you want to join.

Ⓐ The progress symbol appears while the iPhone attempts to connect to the hotspot.

Ⓑ The Wi-Fi screen displays a check mark next to the hotspot.

❻ Press the Home button.

The Home screen appears.

❼ Tap **Safari**.

Note: You may find that Safari opens automatically and displays the login screen for the hotspot.

The login screen for the hotspot appears.

❽ Type your user name and password.

❾ Tap the button to log in.

You can then use the Internet. For example, you can browse the web using Safari or send and receive e-mail using Mail.

TIP

What precautions should I take when using Wi-Fi hotspots?

The main danger is that you may connect to a malevolent network. To stay safe, connect only to hotspots provided by reputable establishments — for example, national hotel or restaurant chains — instead of hotspots run by unknown operators.

When you finish using a Wi-Fi hotspot that you do not plan to use again, tell the iPhone to forget the network using the technique described in the previous section, "Connect to Wi-Fi Networks."

Set Up Your Social Network Accounts

Your iPhone has built-in support for several types of social networks, including Facebook, Twitter, Flickr, and Vimeo. iOS makes it easy to post updates, photos, and videos to your accounts on these social networks. For example, you can quickly create a Facebook post or a Twitter tweet from the Notifications screen, or you can share a photo from the Photos app or the Camera app.

Before you can use a social network, you must enter the details of your account, as described in this section.

Set Up Your Social Network Accounts

Open the Settings App and Set Up Your Twitter Account

 Press the Home button.

The Home screen appears.

 Tap **Settings**.

The Settings screen appears.

 Tap **Twitter**.

The Twitter screen appears.

4 Type your username.

Note: To create a new Twitter account, tap **Create New Account** and follow the resulting screens.

5 Type your password.

6 Tap **Sign In**.

Twitter verifies your username and password, and then sets up your account on the iPhone.

 You can tap **Update Contacts** to add Twitter usernames and photos to your Contacts.

7 Tap **Settings**.

The Settings screen appears.

Set Up Your Facebook Account

1 On the Settings screen, tap **Facebook**.

2 On the Facebook screen, type your username.

Note: To create a new Facebook account, tap **Create New Account** and follow the resulting screens.

3 Type your password.

4 Tap **Sign In**.

5 On the information screen, tap **Sign In**.

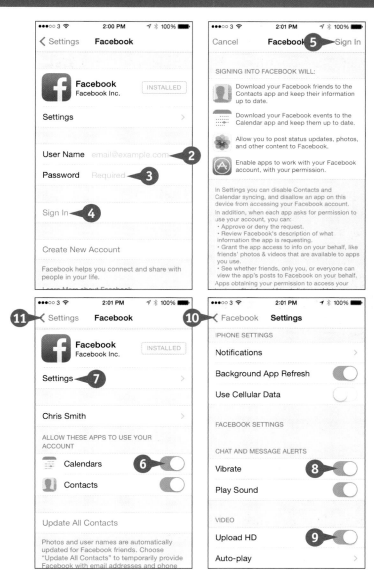

6 Set the **Contacts** switch and **Calendars** switch to On (⬛) or Off (⬜), as needed.

7 Tap **Settings**.

8 Set the **Vibrate** switch and **Play Sound** switch to control which chat and message alerts you get.

9 Set the **Upload HD** switch to On (⬛) or Off (⬜), as needed.

10 Tap **Facebook**.

The Facebook screen appears.

11 Tap **Settings**.

The Settings screen appears.

TIP

How do I set up my Flickr account and Vimeo account?
To set up a Flickr account or Vimeo account, tap **Flickr** or **Vimeo** on the Settings screen. If the Install button appears, the app is not yet installed, so you need to tap **Install** to install it. You can then return to the Settings app, type your username and password, and tap **Sign In**.

Share Your Updates Using Twitter

Your iPhone's apps are fully integrated with Twitter, the online microblogging service. If you need to send a short textual tweet, you can use the Twitter app, creating the tweet from within the app itself. If you need to send a photo, you can start from the Photos app, and create a tweet in moments.

Share Your Updates Using Twitter

Send a Text Tweet

1 Press the Home button.

The Home screen appears.

2 Tap **Twitter**.

Note: If Twitter does not appear on the Home screen, tap **Settings**, tap **Twitter**, and then tap **Install**.

The Twitter app opens.

3 Tap **New Tweet** ().

The New Tweet screen appears.

4 Type the text of the tweet.

Note: You can also tap the microphone icon () to activate Siri, and then dictate the text of the tweet.

5 Tap if you want to add your location to the tweet.

6 Tap **Tweet**.

Twitter posts the tweet to your Twitter account.

Send a Photo Tweet

1 From the Home screen, tap **Photos**.

The Photos app opens.

2 Navigate to the photo you want to tweet. For example, tap **Camera Roll**.

3 Tap the photo to display it.

4 Tap **Share** (⬆️).

The Share sheet appears.

5 Tap **Twitter**.

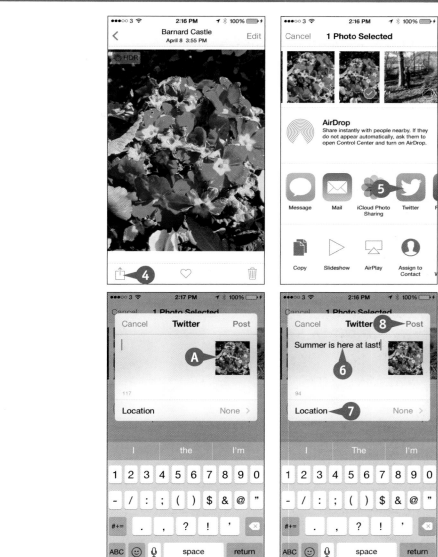

A The Twitter dialog opens, showing the tweet with the photo attached.

6 Type the text of the tweet.

7 Tap **Location** if you want to add the location to the tweet. In the Location dialog, check that the location is correct, and then tap Twitter to return to the Twitter dialog.

8 Tap **Post**.

Your iPhone posts the tweet.

TIP

How do I read other people's tweets?

To read other people's tweets, use the Twitter app. Press the Home button to display the Home screen, tap **Twitter**, and then tap **Home** to catch up on tweets from the Twitter accounts you are following.

Post Updates on Facebook

If you have an account on Facebook, the world's biggest social network, you can post updates directly from your iPhone with a minimum of fuss.

You can work either from within the Facebook app or from apps that contain content suitable for Facebook posts. For example, you can post a photo from the Photos app to Facebook, as described in this section.

Post Updates on Facebook

Post an Update Using the Facebook App

 Press the Home button.

The Home screen appears.

 Tap **Facebook**.

Note: If Facebook does not appear on the Home screen, tap **Settings**, tap **Facebook**, and then tap **Install**.

The Facebook app opens.

③ Tap **Status**.

The Update Status screen appears.

④ Type your update.

⑤ Tap **Post**.

Ⓐ The update appears on your screen.

146

Post a Photo Update

1. In the Photos app, navigate to the photo you want to post. For example, tap **Moments** and then tap the moment that contains the photo.

2. Tap the photo to display it.

3. Tap **Share** (□).

   The Share sheet appears.

4. Tap **Facebook**.

   The Facebook dialog opens.

5. Type the text for the update.

6. Tap **Album**.

   The Album screen appears.

7. Tap the album to which you want to assign the photo.

8. To add the location, tap **Location**, select the location in the Location dialog, and then tap **Facebook** to return to the Facebook dialog.

9. Tap **Audience**.

   The Audience dialog appears.

10. Tap the Facebook audience to share the post with, such as **Your friends**.

11. In the Facebook dialog, tap **Post**.

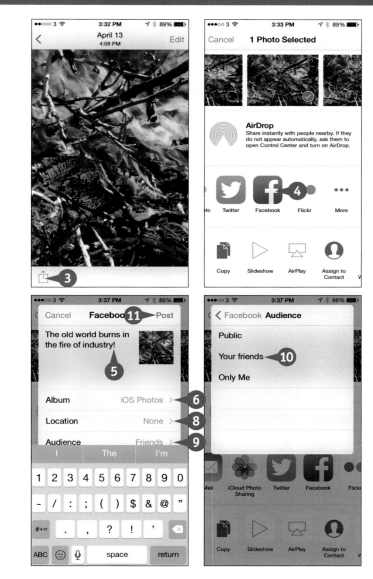

TIP

From what other apps can I post updates to Facebook?

You can post updates to Facebook from any app to which the developer has added Facebook integration. For example, you can post a location from the Maps app or a lecture from iTunes U to Facebook.

To see whether you can post updates to Facebook from an app, tap **Share** (□) from the app. If Facebook appears on the Share sheet, you can post an update to Facebook.

Share Photos on Flickr

You can easily share photos from your iPhone to your account on the Flickr photo-sharing service. You can post either a single photo or multiple photos. Flickr adds the photos to your Photostream, making them available instantly.

When posting photos to Flickr, you can choose the audience for them. For example, you may want to give some photos a Public audience, while restricting others to Family or Friends. You may prefer to keep some photos to yourself by using the Only Me audience.

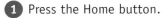

Share Photos on Flickr

1 Press the Home button.

The Home screen appears.

2 Tap **Photos**.

The Photos screen appears.

3 Navigate to the item that contains the photo or photos you want to share. For example, tap **Albums** and then tap the album that contains the photo.

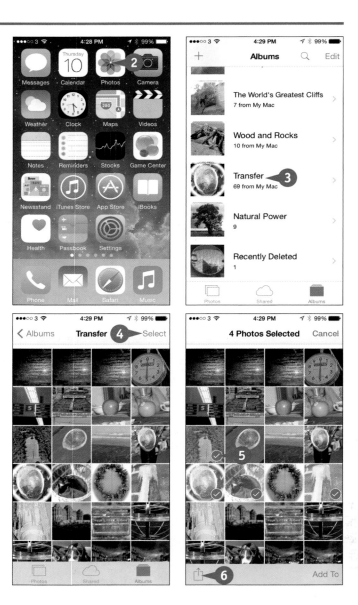

4 Tap **Select**.

Note: If you want to share a single photo, you can tap the photo to open it, and then tap **Share** (⬆).

The Photos app displays selection controls.

5 Tap each photo you want to share (☑ appears on each selected photo).

6 Tap **Share** (⬆).

The Share sheet appears.

7 Tap **Flickr**.

Note: You may need to scroll the list of apps to the left to see Flickr.

The Flickr dialog opens.

8 Type the accompanying text for the photo or photos.

9 Tap **Audience**.

The Audience dialog opens.

10 Tap the audience you want for the photos. For example, tap **Family**.

11 Tap **Flickr**.

The Flickr dialog appears.

12 Tap **Post**.

Your iPhone posts the photos to your Flickr Photostream.

TIP

Can I upload photos to Flickr from other apps?
You can upload photos to Flickr from any app whose Share sheet displays the Flickr icon. The easiest way to find out if an app supports uploading to Flickr is to select an item in the app and tap **Share** (🔳) to display the Share sheet.

Sign In to Game Center

Game Center is a social gaming feature included in iOS — the operating system for the iPhone, iPad, and iPod touch — and in recent versions of OS X, including OS X version 10.10, which is called Yosemite. Game Center enables you to take part in a wide range of single-player and multiplayer games.

To start using Game Center, you sign in using your Apple ID. If you do not yet have an Apple ID, you can create one for free within minutes by tapping **Create New Apple ID** at the bottom of the Game Center setup screen.

Sign In to Game Center

1 Press the Home button.

The Home screen appears.

2 Tap **Game Center**.

The Game Center screen appears.

3 Type your Apple ID.

4 Type your password.

5 Tap **Go** on the keyboard.

The Create a Nickname screen appears.

6 Type the nickname you want to use for Game Center.

Note: Your nickname must be unique within Game Center. If it is not, the setup routine prompts you to choose another nickname.

7 Tap **Next**.

The Privacy screen appears.

8 Set the **Public Profile** switch to On (▢) if you want everyone to be able to see you. Set this switch to Off (▢) if you want to be hidden from other players.

9 Tap **Next**.

The Friend Recommendations screen appears.

10 Set the **Contacts** switch to On (◉) if you want to upload your iCloud contacts to Game Center and get personalized friend recommendations. Otherwise, set this switch to Off (□).

11 Set the **Facebook** switch to On (◉) if you want to upload your Facebook contacts to Game Center so you can get personalized friend recommendations. Otherwise, set this switch to Off (□).

12 Tap **Done**.

The Me screen appears.

13 Tap **add photo**.

A dialog opens.

14 Tap **Choose Photo** or **Take Photo**, as appropriate, and follow the prompts to select or take a suitable photo.

15 Tap **Enter status**.

16 Type the status you want.

17 Tap **Done**.

You can now start using Game Center as explained in the next section, "Add and Play Games with Game Center."

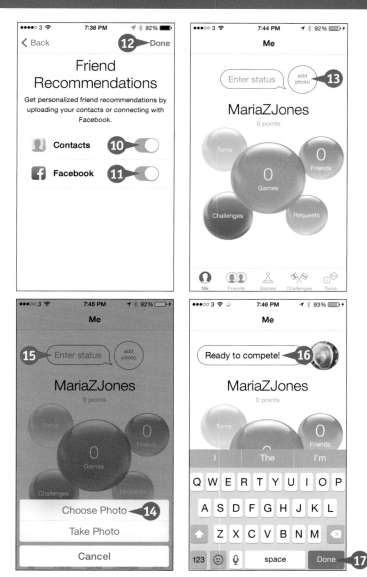

TIPS

Should I set the Public Profile switch to On or Off?

Generally it is better to err on the side of caution and set the Public Profile switch to Off (□) while you are coming to grips with Game Center. After you have explored Game Center, you can decide whether to make yourself publicly visible on it.

Should I upload my Facebook and iCloud contacts to Game Center?

Uploading your contacts can be a great way to get started quickly with Game Center. But here, too, you may prefer to take a gradual approach and explore Game Center before uploading your contacts.

Add and Play Games with Game Center

After setting up your account, as explained in the previous section, "Sign In to Game Center," you can play games with Game Center.

If your iPhone already contains games that work with Game Center, the games will be ready to play when you launch Game Center. You can add further games by opening the App Store app from Game Center and downloading either free or purchased games.

Add and Play Games with Game Center

1 Press the Home button.

The Home screen appears.

2 Tap **Game Center**.

Game Center logs you in.

The Me screen appears.

3 Tap **Games**.

A From the Me screen, you can also tap **Games** to reach the Games screen.

The Games screen appears.

B The Recommended list shows games you do not have.

Note: In the Recommended list, "Based on" means that the recommendation is based on a game you have, not that the recommended game is based on the game mentioned.

C The My iOS Games list shows the games you have.

D To launch a game you have, you can tap it in the My iOS Games list.

4 Tap a game that interests you.

The game's screen appears.

5 Tap **Free App** or the price button if you want to buy the game.

The iTunes Store screen appears, showing the game's information.

6 Tap **Free**.

The Install button appears.

7 Tap **Install**.

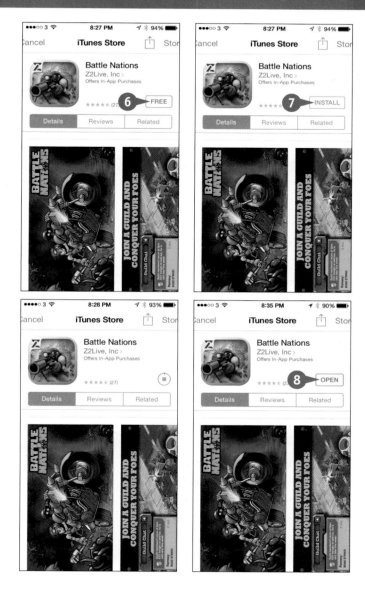

Your iPhone downloads and installs the app.

8 After the installation finishes, tap **Open**.

The game launches, and you can start playing it.

How can I tell which games work with Game Center?
All the games you can access through Game Center work with Game Center. When you are browsing games in the App Store, tap **Details** and scroll down to the Supports area. Make sure the Game Center name appears in this area, indicating that the game works with Game Center.

Add Friends and Play Games with Them

To get the most out of Game Center, you can add friends to your Friends list and challenge them to play games with you. Similarly, other people can invite you to be friends and to play games. When other people send you invitations, you respond accordingly.

Add Friends and Play Games with Them

Send a Friend Request

1. Press the Home button.

   The Home screen appears.

2. Tap **Game Center**.

   Game Center logs you in.

   The Me screen appears.

3. Tap **Friends**.

   The Friends screen appears.

Ⓐ You can tap a friend recommendation to add that person.

4. Tap **Add** (⊞).

   The Friend Request screen appears.

5. Enter the friend's e-mail address. You can tap ⊕ to choose from your contacts.

6. Type a message. Usually, it is a good idea to write something to help your friend identify you.

7. Tap **Send**.

Note: When your friend accepts the request, Game Center notifies you and adds the friend as a Game Center friend.

154

Send a Challenge

1 In Game Center, tap **Friends**.

The Friends screen appears.

2 Tap the friend you want to challenge.

The Info screen for the friend appears.

3 Tap the **Games** balloon.

The list of games appears.

B The Games in Common list shows the games that you and the friend have in common.

4 Tap the game for the challenge.

5 Tap your friend's score or achievement.

The Challenge dialog opens.

6 Tap **Send a Challenge**.

7 Tap the challenge you want to send. The challenges available depend on the game.

The Challenge screen appears.

8 Type a message.

9 Tap **Send**.

Game Center sends the challenge.

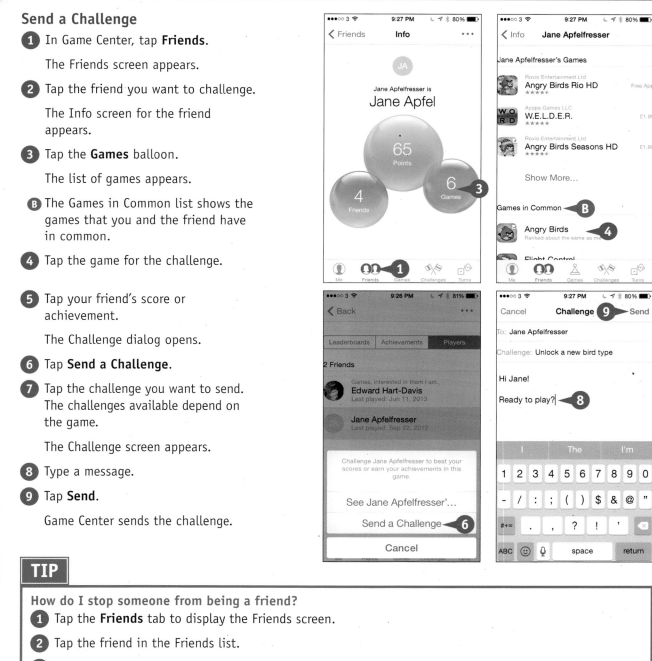

TIP

How do I stop someone from being a friend?

1 Tap the **Friends** tab to display the Friends screen.

2 Tap the friend in the Friends list.

3 Tap ⋯.

4 Tap **Unfriend** in the dialog that opens.

CHAPTER 7

Working with Apps

iOS enables you to customize the Home screen, putting the icons you need most right at hand and organizing them into folders. You can switch instantly among the apps you are running, find the apps you need on Apple's App Store, and update and remove apps. You can also install apps provided by an administrator and work easily with text.

Customize the Home Screen

From the Home screen, you run the apps on your iPhone. You can customize the Home screen to put the apps you use most frequently within easy reach. You can create further Home screens as needed and move the app icons among them. You can customize the Home screen by working on the iPhone, as described here. If you synchronize your iPhone with a computer, you can use iTunes instead. This is an easier way to make extensive changes, such as changing the order of the Home screens.

Customize the Home Screen

Unlock the Icons for Customization

 Press the Home button.

The Home screen appears.

2 Tap and drag left or right to display the Home screen you want to customize.

A You can also tap the dots to move from one Home screen to another.

3 Tap and hold the icon you want to move.

Note: You can tap and hold any icon until the apps start jiggling. Usually, it is easiest to tap and hold the icon you want to move, and then drag that icon.

The icons start to jiggle, indicating that you can move them.

Move an Icon within a Home Screen

1 After unlocking the icons, drag the icon to where you want it.

The other icons move out of the way.

2 When the icon is in the right place, drop it.

B The icon stays in its new position.

158

Move an Icon to a Different Home Screen

 After unlocking the icons, drag the icon to the left edge of the screen to display the previous Home screen or to the right edge to display the next Home screen.

The previous Home screen or next Home screen appears.

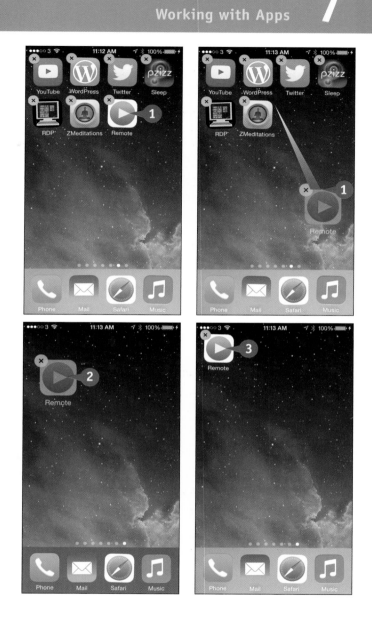

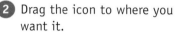 Drag the icon to where you want it.

If the Home screen contains other icons, they move out of the way as needed.

3 Drop the icon.

The icon stays in its new position.

Stop Customizing the Home Screen

 Press the Home button.

The icons stop jiggling.

TIP

How can I put the default apps back on the Home screen?
Press the Home button, tap **Settings**, and then tap **General**. Tap and drag up to scroll down the screen, and then tap **Reset**. On the Reset screen, tap **Reset Home Screen Layout**, and then tap **Reset Home Screen** in the dialog that opens. Press the Home button to return to the Home screen.

Organize Apps with Folders

To organize the Home screen, you can arrange the items into folders. The iPhone's default Home screen layout includes a folder named Extras, which contains items such as the Contacts app and the Compass app, but you can create as many other folders as you need. Like the Home screen, each folder can have multiple pages, so you can put many apps in a folder.

You create a folder by dragging one icon onto another icon. Doing this creates a folder containing both items. You can then rename the folder and add more apps to it.

Organize Apps with Folders

Create a Folder

1 Display the Home screen that contains the item you want to put into a folder.

2 Tap and hold the item until the icons start to jiggle.

Note: When creating a folder, you may find it easiest to first put both items you will add to the folder on the same screen.

3 Drag the item to the other icon you want to place in the folder you create.

The iPhone creates a folder, puts both icons in it, and assigns a default name based on the genre.

4 Tap in the folder name box.

The keyboard appears.

5 Type the name for the folder.

6 Tap outside the folder.

The iPhone applies the name to the folder.

7 Press the Home button.

The icons stop jiggling.

Open an Item in a Folder

 Display the Home screen that contains the folder.

2 Tap the folder's icon.

The folder's contents appear, and the items outside the folder fade.

3 If necessary, drag left or right or tap a dot to navigate to another page in the folder.

4 Tap the item you want to open.

The item opens.

Add an Item to a Folder

1 Display the Home screen that contains the item.

2 Tap and hold the item until the icons start to jiggle.

3 Drag the icon on top of the folder and drop it there.

Note: If the folder is on a different Home screen from the icon, drag the icon to the left edge to display the previous Home screen or to the right edge to display the next Home screen.

The item goes into the folder.

4 Press the Home button to stop the icons jiggling.

TIPS

How do I take an item out of a folder?
Tap the folder to display its contents, and then tap and hold the item until the icons start to jiggle. Drag the item out of the folder, drag it to where you want it on the Home screen, and then drop it.

How do I create another page in a folder?
Open the folder, and then tap and hold an item until the icons start jiggling. Drag the item to the right of the screen. A new page appears automatically.

Switch Quickly from One App to Another

You can run many apps on your iPhone at the same time, switching from one app to another as needed.

The most straightforward way of switching from one app to another is to press the Home button to display the Home screen, and then tap the icon for the app you want to start using. But the iPhone also has an app-switching screen that enables you to switch quickly from one running app to another running app. From the app-switching screen, you can also easily close one or more running apps.

Switch Quickly from One App to Another

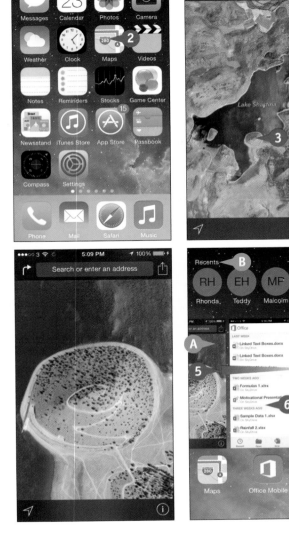

1 Press the Home button.

The Home screen appears.

2 Tap the app you want to launch.

The app's screen appears.

3 Start using the app as usual.

4 Press the Home button twice in quick succession.

A The app-switching screen appears.

B The Recents list at the top of the app-switching screen enables you to quickly get in touch with a contact with whom you have communicated recently.

5 Tap and drag left to scroll until you see the app you want.

Note: The last app you used appears on the left side of the app-switching screen. To its left is the Home screen. To its right are the apps you have used most recently.

6 Tap the app.

The app appears.

7 When you are ready to switch back, press the Home button twice in quick succession.

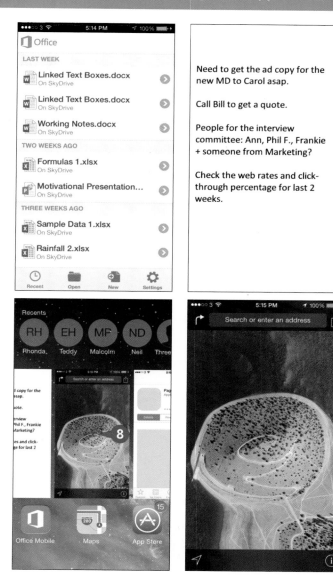

The app-switching screen appears.

8 Scroll left or right as needed, and then tap the app to which you want to return.

The app appears, ready to resume from where you stopped using it.

TIP

How do I stop an app that is not responding?

If an app stops responding, you can quickly close it from the app-switching screen. Press the Home button twice to open the app-switching screen. Scroll to the problem app, and then drag it upward so it disappears off the screen. Tap the app you want to use or press the Home button to return to the Home screen.

You can use this move to close any app that you no longer want to use, whether or not it has stopped responding.

Find Apps on the App Store

The iPhone comes with essential apps, such as Safari for surfing the web, Mail for e-mail, and Calendar for keeping your schedule. But to get the most out of your iPhone, you will likely need to add other apps.

To get apps, you use the App Store, which provides apps that Apple has approved as correctly programmed, suitable for purpose, and free of malevolent code. Before you can download any apps, including free apps, you must create an App Store account.

Find Apps on the App Store

1 Press the Home button.

The Home screen appears.

2 Tap **App Store**.

The App Store screen appears.

3 Tap **Categories**.

The Categories screen appears.

4 Tap the category you want to see.

The category's screen appears, showing the Best New Apps list.

5 Tap and drag to see additional apps in a list, or tap and drag up to see other lists. Then tap **See All** to display your chosen list.

The screen shows the list you chose.

6 Tap the app you want to view.

The app's screen appears.

Note: To understand what an app does and how well it does it, look at the app's rating, read the description, and read the user reviews. Swipe the images to see screen captures from the app.

7 Tap the price button or the **Free** button.

The price button or Free button changes to an Install button.

8 Tap **Install**.

9 If the iPhone prompts you to sign in, type your password and tap **OK**.

Note: If you have not created an App Store account already, the iPhone prompts you to create one now.

The iPhone downloads and installs the app.

10 Tap **Open** to launch the app.

TIP

Why does the App Store not appear on the Home screen or when I search for it?

If the App Store does not appear on the Home screen, and if searching for it does not show a result, the iPhone has restrictions applied that prevent you from installing apps. You can remove these restrictions if you know the restrictions passcode. Press the Home button, tap **Settings**, and then tap **General**. Scroll down, and then tap **Restrictions**. Type the passcode on the Enter Passcode screen, and then tap the **Installing Apps** switch and move it to On (☐ changes to ☑).

Update and Remove Apps

To keep your iPhone's apps running smoothly, you should install app updates when they become available. Most updates for paid apps are free, but you must often pay to upgrade to a new version of the app. You can download and install updates using either the iPhone itself or iTunes on your computer.

When you no longer need an app you have installed on your iPhone, you can remove it. You can remove the app from your iPhone by working either on the iPhone itself or in iTunes on your computer. You cannot remove the built-in apps.

Update and Remove Apps

Update an App

1 Press the Home button.

The Home screen appears.

 The badge on the App Store icon shows the number of available updates.

2 Tap **App Store**.

The App Store screen appears.

3 Tap **Updates**.

The Updates screen appears.

4 Tap **Update All** to apply all the available updates now.

B You can tap **Update** to update a single app.

C You can tap **Purchased** to view the list of apps you have purchased.

From the Purchased screen, you can update individual apps or install apps you have bought but not yet installed on this iPhone.

Remove an App from the iPhone

1 Press the Home button.

The Home screen appears.

2 Display the Home screen that contains the app you want to delete.

3 Tap and hold the item until the icons start to jiggle.

4 Tap ⊠ on the icon.

The Delete dialog appears.

5 Tap **Delete**.

The iPhone deletes the app, and the app's icon disappears.

6 Press the Home button.

The icons stop jiggling.

TIPS

How do I update an app using iTunes?

In iTunes, click **Apps** (🎵). In the bar at the top of the iTunes window, click **Updates**, and then click **Update All Apps**. In the Sign In to Download from the iTunes Store dialog, type your password and click **Sign In**. On the My App Updates screen, click **Download All Free Updates**, connect your iPhone, and then click **Sync** to start synchronization.

How do I remove an app from my iPhone using iTunes?

Connect your iPhone to your computer, and then click **iPhone** (🔲) on the navigation bar. Click **Apps**, locate the app in the list, and then click **Remove**. Click **Sync** to start synchronization.

Install an App Provided by an Administrator

If you use an iPhone administered by a company or organization, an administrator may provide apps for you to install using iTunes. You will usually copy the app's file from a network drive, but you may also receive it attached to an e-mail message.

To install the app, you add it to iTunes on your PC or Mac, and then sync the iPhone with iTunes.

Install an App Provided by an Administrator

1 With iTunes active on your computer, click **File** in the menu bar.

2 Click **Add File to Library** in Windows or **Add to Library** on a Mac.

The Add To Library dialog opens.

Note: If you receive the app's file attached to an e-mail message, save it to a folder, and then use the Add To Library dialog to add it to iTunes. In Mail on a Mac, you can simply double-click an attached app's file to add it to iTunes.

3 Open the folder that contains the app's file.

4 Click the app's file.

5 Click **Open**.

A iTunes adds the app to the apps list.

6 Connect your iPhone to the PC or Mac via the USB cable.

Note: You can also install an app provided by an administrator by syncing wirelessly.

7 Click **iPhone** () on the navigation bar.

The iPhone's control screens appear.

8 Click **Apps**.

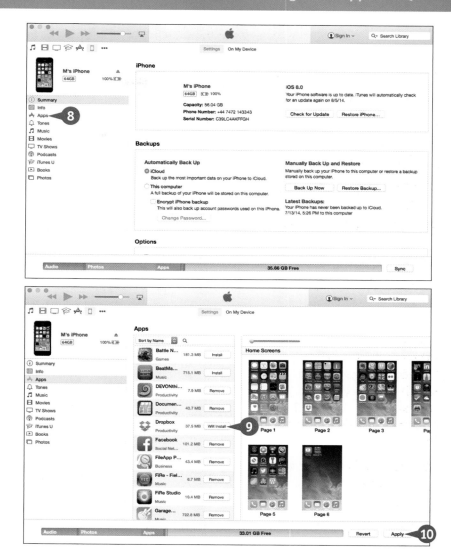

The Apps screen appears.

9 Click **Install**. Install changes to Will Install.

Note: You can also click **Automatically sync new apps** (☐ changes to ☑) below the Apps list to make iTunes automatically sync all new apps.

10 Click **Apply**. If you have not made changes, this button is named Sync.

iTunes installs the app on your iPhone.

Is there another way to add an app's file to iTunes?

Yes. You can quickly add an app's file to iTunes by dragging the app's file from a Windows Explorer window or a Finder window to the main part of the iTunes window — for example, the part that shows the music when iTunes is in Music view. On a Mac, you can also add the app to iTunes by dragging the app's file to the iTunes icon on the Dock and dropping it there.

Cut, Copy, and Paste Text

You can type text easily on your iPhone's keyboard or dictate it using Siri, but if the text already exists, you can copy the text and paste it instead. For example, you can copy text from a note and paste it into an e-mail message you are composing.

If the text is in a document you can edit, you can cut the text from the document instead of copying it. If the text is in a document you cannot edit, you can copy the text but not cut it. The technique depends on whether you can edit the document.

Cut, Copy, and Paste Text

Select and Copy Text You Cannot Edit

Note: An example of text you cannot edit is a web page you open in Safari.

1 Tap and hold in the section of text you want to copy.

A selection highlight with handles appears around the text. The Copy button appears above the selection.

2 Drag the handles of the selection highlight around the text that you want.

3 Tap **Copy**.

Your iPhone places the text on the Clipboard, a hidden storage area.

Select and Copy Text You Can Edit

Note: An example of text you can edit is a note you create in Notes or a message you compose in Mail.

1 Tap and hold until you see the magnifying glass and then release.

A bar appears containing the Select button and Select All button.

2 Tap **Select**.

Note: Tap **Select All** to select all the text.

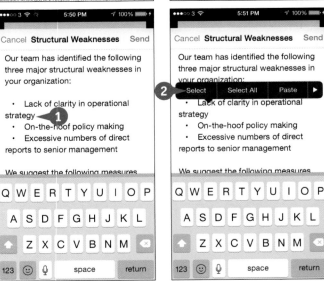

Blue selection handles appear around the current word, and further options appear on the selection bar.

③ Tap and drag the selection handles around the text that you want.

④ Tap **Copy** or **Cut**, as needed.

Note: This example uses Copy instead of Cut.

Paste the Content You Have Copied or Cut

① Open the app in which you want to paste the text.

Note: This example shows text being pasted into a new note in the Notes app.

② Tap where you want to paste the text.

③ Tap **Paste**.

Ⓐ Your iPhone inserts the copied text in the document.

TIPS

How many items can I store on the Clipboard?

You can store only one item on the Clipboard at a time. Each item you cut or copy replaces the existing item on the Clipboard. But until you replace the existing item on the Clipboard, you can paste it as many times as needed.

Can I transfer the contents of the Clipboard to my computer?

You cannot transfer the Clipboard's contents directly to your computer, but you can easily transfer them indirectly. For example, paste them into an e-mail message and send it to yourself, or paste them into a note in the Notes app and sync your devices.

Bold, Italicize, Underline, and Replace Text

Some apps enable you to add text formatting such as boldface, underline, and italics to text to make parts of it stand out. For example, you can apply formatting in e-mail messages you create using the Mail app and in various apps for creating word-processing documents.

To apply formatting, you first select the text, and then choose options from the pop-up formatting bar. Some apps also offer other text commands, such as replacing a word or phrase from a menu of suggestions.

Bold, Italicize, Underline, and Replace Text

Apply Bold, Italics, and Underline

1 Tap and hold the text to which you want to apply bold, italics, or underline.

A pop-up bar of text options appears.

2 Tap **Select**.

Part of the text is highlighted, and handles appear.

3 Drag the handles to select the text that you want to bold, italicize, or underline.

4 Tap the **B**_I_U button in the pop-up bar.

The pop-up bar displays formatting options.

5 Tap **Bold**, **Italics**, or **Underline**, as needed.

The text takes on the formatting you chose.

6 Tap outside the selected text to deselect it.

Replace Text with Suggested Words

1 Double-tap the word you want to replace.

Note: You can tap and hold anywhere in the word, and then tap **Select** on the pop-up formatting bar to select the word.

Selection handles appear around the word.

The pop-up formatting bar appears.

2 Tap ▶.

The pop-up formatting bar displays other buttons.

3 Tap **Replace**.

The pop-up formatting bar displays suggested replacement words.

4 Tap the word with which you want to replace the selected word.

Your iPhone replaces the word.

What does the Quote Level button on the pop-up formatting bar in Mail do?
Tap the **Quote Level** button when you need to increase or decrease the quote level of your selected text. When you tap Quote Level, the pop-up formatting bar displays an Increase button and a Decrease button. Tap **Increase** to increase the quote level, indenting the text more and adding a colored bar to its left, or **Decrease** to decrease the quote level, reducing the existing indent and removing a colored bar.

CHAPTER 8

Browsing the Web and E-Mailing

Your iPhone is fully equipped to browse the web and send e-mail via a Wi-Fi connection or cellular network.

Browse the Web with Safari

Your iPhone comes equipped with the Safari app, which enables you to browse the web. You can quickly go to a web page by entering its address in the Address box or by following a link.

Although you can browse quickly by opening a single web page at a time, you may prefer to open multiple pages and switch back and forth among them. Safari makes this easy to do.

Browse the Web with Safari

Open Safari and Navigate to Web Pages

1 Press the Home button.

The Home screen appears.

2 Tap **Safari**.

Safari opens and loads the last web page that was shown.

3 Tap the Address box.

Safari selects the current contents of the Address box, and the keyboard appears.

4 Tap ⊗ if you need to delete the contents of the Address box.

5 Type the address of the page you want to open.

A You can also tap a search result that Safari displays below the Address box.

6 Tap **Go**.

Safari displays the page.

7 Tap a link on the page.

Safari displays that page.

B After going to a new page, tap ◁ to display the previous page. You can then tap ▷ to go forward again to the page you just went back from.

Open Multiple Pages and Navigate Among Them

1 Tap **Pages** (▢).

Safari displays the list of open pages, each bearing a Close button (✖).

2 Tap **New Page** (➕).

C You can tap a device name to see the web pages open on that device.

Note: In landscape orientation, the iPhone 6 displays a tab bar at the top of the screen. Tap the tab for the page you want to view.

Safari opens a new page and displays your bookmarks.

3 Tap the Address box, and then go to the page you want.

Note: You can also go to a page by using a bookmark, as described in the next section, "Access Websites Quickly with Your Bookmarks."

The page appears.

4 To switch to another page, tap **Pages** (▢).

Safari displays the list of pages.

5 Tap the page you want to see.

D You can tap the **Close** button (✖) to close a page.

How do I search for information?

Tap the Address box to select its current contents, and then type your search terms. Safari searches as you type; you can type further to narrow down the results, and stop as soon as you see suitable results. Tap the result you want to see, and then tap a link on the results page that Safari opens.

How can I return to a tab I closed by mistake?

Tap **Pages** (▢) to display the list of open pages, and then tap and hold **New Page** (➕). On the Recently Closed Tabs screen, tap the tab you want to reopen.

Access Websites Quickly with Your Bookmarks

Typing web addresses can be laborious, even with the help that the iPhone's keyboard adds, so you will probably want to use bookmarks to access websites you visit often.

By syncing your existing bookmarks from your computer or online account, as described in Chapter 1, you can instantly provide your iPhone with quick access to the web pages you want to visit most frequently. You can also create bookmarks on your iPhone, as discussed in the next section, "Create Bookmarks."

Access Websites Quickly with Your Bookmarks

Open the Bookmarks Screen

1 Press the Home button.

The Home screen appears.

2 Tap **Safari**.

Safari opens.

3 Tap **Bookmarks** ().

The Bookmarks screen appears.

Explore Your History

1 On the Bookmarks screen, tap **History**.

A list of the web pages you have recently visited appears.

Ⓐ You can tap a day to display the list of web pages you visited on that day.

2 Tap **Bookmarks** to return to the Bookmarks screen.

Explore a Bookmarks Category

1. On the Bookmarks screen, tap the bookmarks folder or category you want to see. This example uses the **Shopping** folder.

   The contents of the folder or category appear. For example, the contents of the Shopping folder appear.

2. Tap ◁ one or more times to go back.

Open a Bookmarked Page

1. When you find the bookmark for the web page you want to open, tap the bookmark.

B. The web page opens.

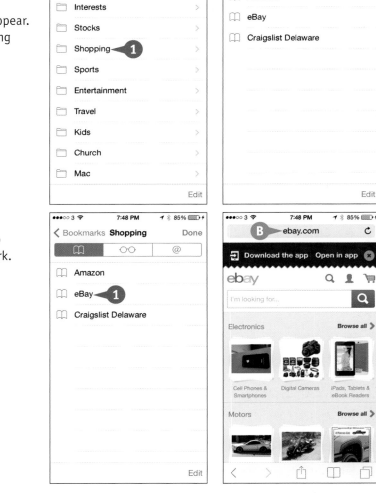

How can I quickly access a website?
Creating a bookmark within Safari — as discussed in the next section, "Create Bookmarks" — is good for sites you access now and then. But if you access a site frequently, create an icon for it on your Home screen. Open the site in Safari. Tap **Share** (⬆️), tap **Add to Home Screen**, type the name on the Add to Home screen, and then tap **Add**. You can then go straight to the page by tapping its icon on the Home screen.

Create Bookmarks

While browsing the web on your iPhone, you will likely find web pages you will want to access again. To access such a web page easily, create a bookmark for it. If you have set your iPhone to sync bookmarks with your iCloud account, the bookmark becomes available on your computer or online account as well when you sync.

If you create many bookmarks, it is usually helpful to store them in multiple folders. You can create folders easily on the iPhone and choose which folder to store each bookmark in.

Create Bookmarks

Create a Bookmark on the iPhone

1 Press the Home button.

The Home screen appears.

2 Tap **Safari**.

Safari opens and displays the last web page you were viewing.

3 Navigate to the web page you want to bookmark.

4 Tap **Share** (□).

The Share screen appears.

5 Tap **Add Bookmark**.

The Add Bookmark screen appears.

6 Edit the suggested name, or type a new name.

7 Tap **Location**.

The Choose a Folder screen appears.

8 Tap the folder in which to store the bookmark.

The Add Bookmark screen appears.

9 Tap **Save**.

Create a New Folder for Bookmarks

1 In Safari, tap **Bookmarks** (□).

The Bookmarks screen appears.

2 Tap **Edit**.

The editing controls appear.

3 Tap **New Folder**.

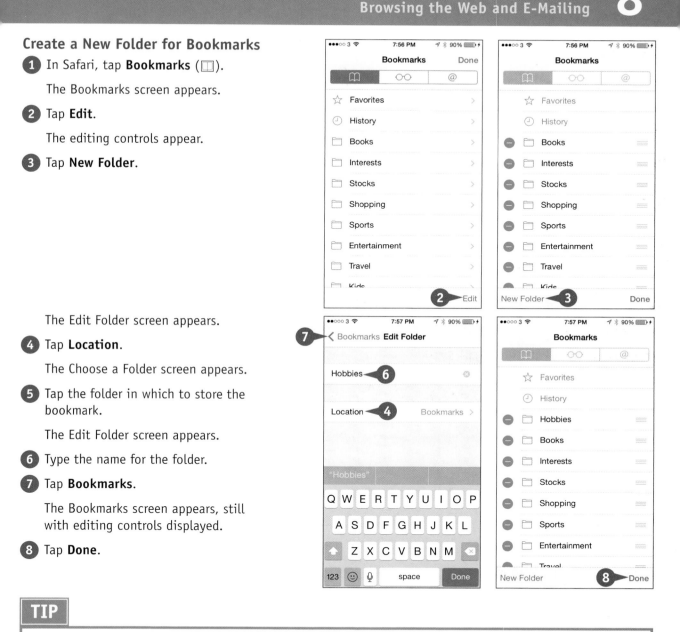

The Edit Folder screen appears.

4 Tap **Location**.

The Choose a Folder screen appears.

5 Tap the folder in which to store the bookmark.

The Edit Folder screen appears.

6 Type the name for the folder.

7 Tap **Bookmarks**.

The Bookmarks screen appears, still with editing controls displayed.

8 Tap **Done**.

TIP

Can I change a bookmark I have created?

Yes. Tap **Bookmarks** (□) to display the Bookmarks screen, and then navigate to the bookmark you want to change. Tap **Edit** to switch to editing mode. You can then tap a bookmark to open it on the Edit Bookmark screen, where you can change its name, address, or location. In editing mode, you can also delete a bookmark by tapping ⊖ and then tapping **Delete**, or rearrange your bookmarks by tapping ═ and dragging up or down the list.

Keep a Reading List of Web Pages

Bookmarks are a handy way of marking pages you want to be able to visit repeatedly, but you may also want to be able to save some web pages for later reading without creating bookmarks for them. You can do this easily by using Safari's Reading List feature.

You can quickly add the current web page to Reading List by using the Share screen. Once you have added pages, you access Reading List through the Bookmarks feature. When viewing Reading List, you can display either all the pages it contains or only those you have not read.

Keep a Reading List of Web Pages

Add a Web Page to Reading List

1 Press the Home button.

The Home screen appears.

2 Tap **Safari**.

Safari opens and displays the last web page you were viewing.

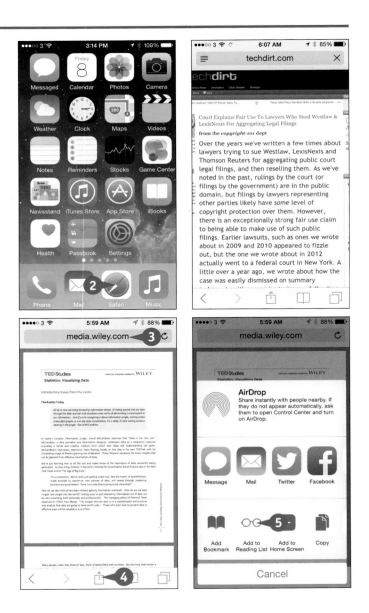

3 Navigate to the web page you want to add to Reading List.

4 Tap **Share** ().

The Share screen appears.

5 Tap **Add to Reading List**.

Safari adds the web page to Reading List.

Open Reading List and Display a Page

1 In Safari, tap **Bookmarks** (▢).

The Bookmarks screen appears.

2 Tap **Reading List** (▭).

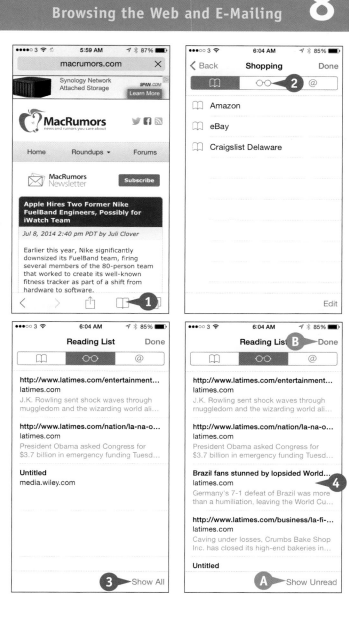

The Reading List screen appears.

3 Tap **Show All**.

Reading List displays all the pages it contains, including those you have read.

Ⓐ You can tap **Show Unread** to display only unread pages.

4 Tap the page you want to open.

Ⓑ If you decide not to open a page from Reading List, tap **Done** to hide the Reading List screen.

TIP

How do I remove an item from Reading List?

To remove an item from Reading List, tap **Bookmarks** (▢) and then **Reading List**. In the list of pages, tap the page you want to remove and swipe left, and then tap the **Delete** button that appears.

Share Web Pages with Others

When browsing the web, you will likely come across pages you want to share with other people. Safari makes it easy to share web page addresses via e-mail, instant messaging, Twitter, Facebook, and other apps.

When others share web pages with you via Twitter and similar apps, Safari adds them to the Shared Links list. You can open this list, browse the pages, and quickly display any pages you want to view.

Share Web Pages with Others

Share a Web Page with Others

1 Press the Home button.

The Home screen appears.

2 Tap **Safari**.

Safari opens and displays the last web page you were viewing.

3 Navigate to the web page you want to share.

4 Tap **Share** (⬆).

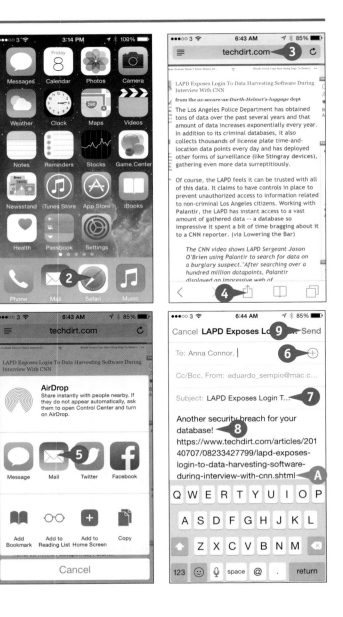

The Share sheet appears.

5 Tap **Mail**.

Your iPhone starts a new message in the Mail app.

Ⓐ The URL appears in the body of the message.

6 Tap ⊕ and type an address for the message.

7 Edit the suggested subject line as needed.

8 Type any explanatory text needed.

9 Tap **Send**.

Open a Page Someone Has Shared with You

1 In Safari, tap **Bookmarks** (📖).

The Bookmarks screen appears.

2 Tap **Shared Links** (@).

The Shared Links list appears.

3 If necessary, tap and drag up to scroll down to locate the link you want.

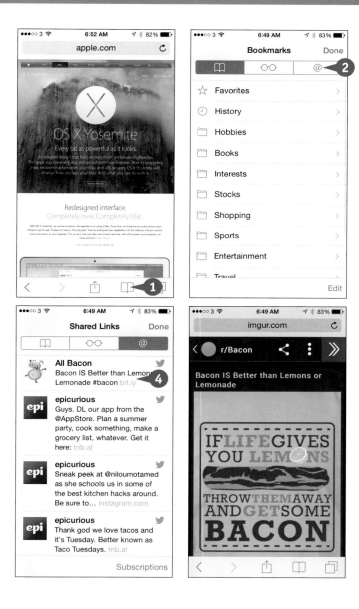

4 Tap the link.

Safari displays the linked page.

TIP

What other ways can I use to share a web page?

You can also share a web page address by including it in an instant message, by tweeting it to Twitter, or by posting it to Facebook. Another option is to use AirDrop to share the address with a local device. See Chapter 6 for instructions on using AirDrop.

Navigate Among Open Web Pages Using Tabs

I f you browse the web a lot, you will probably need to open many web pages in Safari at the same time. Safari presents your open pages as a list of scrollable tabs, making it easy to navigate from one page to another.

You can change the order of the tabs to suit your needs, and you can quickly close a tab by either tapping its **Close** button or simply swiping it off the list.

Navigate Among Open Web Pages Using Tabs

Open Safari and Display the List of Tabs

1 Press the Home button.

The Home screen appears.

2 Tap **Safari**.

Safari opens or becomes active.

3 Tap **Pages** ( ).

The list of pages appears.

Close Pages You Do Not Need to Keep Open

1 Tap on the tab for a page you want to close.

The page closes, and the tab disappears from the list.

2 Alternatively, you can tap a tab and swipe it left off the screen.

The page closes, and the tab disappears from the list.

Note: You can turn the iPhone 6 to landscape orientation and then tap to close the current tab.

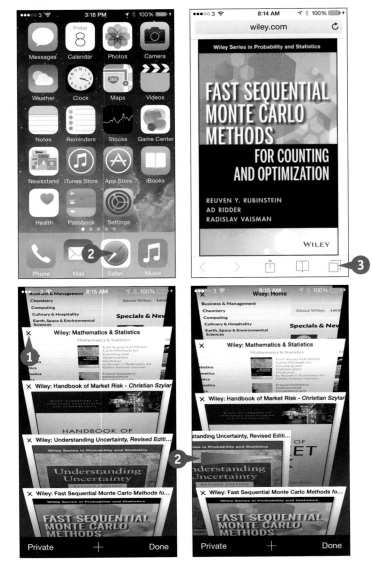

Change the Order of the Pages

1 Tap and hold the tab for a page you want to move.

The tab moves to the foreground.

2 Drag the tab to where you want it to appear in the list, and then release it.

Find a Page and Display It

1 Scroll up and down to browse through the tabs.

 Your current iCloud tabs from your other devices logged into iCloud appear at the bottom of the screen. You can tap a page to open it.

2 Tap the tab for the page you want to display.

The page opens.

Note: Turn the iPhone 6 to landscape orientation to display the tab bar at the top of the screen. You can then tap the tab you want to view.

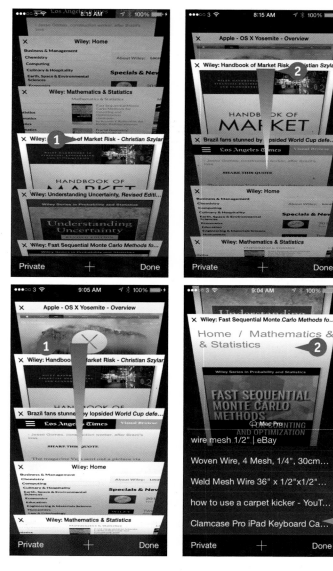

TIP

How do I return from the list of tabs to the page I was viewing before?
To return to the page you were viewing before, either tap the page's tab in the list of tabs, or tap **Done** in the lower-right corner of the screen.

Configure Your Default Search Engine

To find information with Safari, you often need to search using a search engine. Safari's default search engine is Google, but you can change to another search engine. Your choices depend on your location and carrier, but typically include Google, Yahoo!, and Bing. These search engines compete directly with one another and return similar results for many searches. But if you experiment with the search engines your iPhone offers, you will gradually discover which one suits you best. And if you find you prefer a search engine other than those available, you can search by using its website.

Configure Your Default Search Engine

Set the Default Search Engine for Safari

1 Press the Home button.

The Home screen appears.

2 Tap **Settings**.

The Settings screen appears.

3 Tap **Safari**.

The Safari screen appears.

4 Tap **Search Engine**.

The Search Engine screen appears.

5 Tap the search engine you want.

6 Tap **Safari**.

7 Set the **Search Engine Suggestions** switch to On (⬚) if you want to receive search suggestions.

8 Set the **Spotlight Suggestions** switch to On (⬚) if you want to see Spotlight suggestions.

9 Set the **Preload Top Hit** switch to On (⬚) if you want Safari to preload the first search result page so it will load quickly.

Search with a Search Engine Other than Google, Yahoo!, or Bing

1 Press the Home button.

The Home screen appears.

2 Tap **Safari**.

Safari opens.

3 Tap the Address box.

4 Enter the address of the search engine's website.

5 Tap the appropriate search result.

The search engine appears.

6 Tap in the Search box.

7 Type your search terms.

8 Tap **Search**.

The search results appear.

9 Tap a result to display its page.

Which is the best search engine?

This depends on what you are searching for and what is important to you. For most purposes, Google is the most comprehensive search engine, but you may be able to discover a more specialized search engine that focuses on your area of interest. If you value your privacy, use a search engine that emphasizes privacy, and verify its claims as far as possible.

What is Quick Website Search?

Quick Website Search enables you to search within a website by including the website name in your search. For example, type **apple ipad** to search for iPad information on the Apple website.

Fill In Forms Quickly Using AutoFill

If you fill in forms using your iPhone, you can save time and typos by enabling the AutoFill feature. AutoFill can automatically fill in standard form fields, such as name and address fields, using the information from a contact card you specify.

AutoFill can also automatically store other data you enter in fields, and can store usernames and passwords to enter them for you automatically. You can also add one or more credit cards to AutoFill so that you can easily pay for items online.

Fill In Forms Quickly Using AutoFill

1 Press the Home button.

The Home screen appears.

2 Tap **Settings**.

The Settings screen appears.

3 Scroll down, and then tap **Safari**.

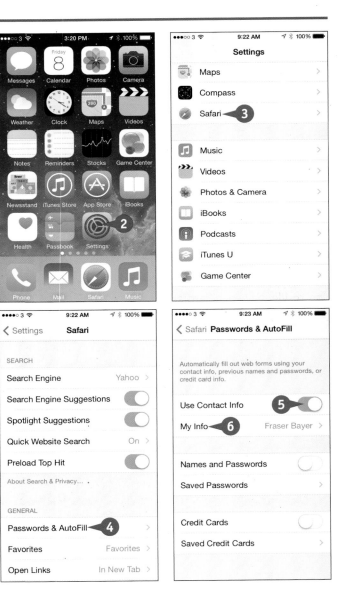

The Safari screen appears.

4 Tap **Passwords & AutoFill**.

The Passwords & AutoFill screen appears.

5 Set the **Use Contact Info** switch to On (⬜) if you want to use AutoFill with contact info.

6 Tap **My Info** to display the Contacts screen.

7 Tap the contact record that contains the information you want to use.

8 Set the **Names and Passwords** switch to On (■).

9 Tap **Saved Passwords**. On the Saved Passwords screen, tap **Edit**, select any sites you want to remove, and tap **Delete**. Tap **AutoFill** to return.

10 Set the **Credit Cards** switch to On (■).

11 Tap **Saved Credit Cards**.

12 Tap **Add Credit Card**.

A You can tap **Use Camera** and use the camera to recognize your card's details. This feature is clever but requires a steady hand or a tripod.

13 Enter your credit card details.

Note: Type a description that enables you to identify each card easily.

14 Tap **Done**.

15 Tap **AutoFill**.

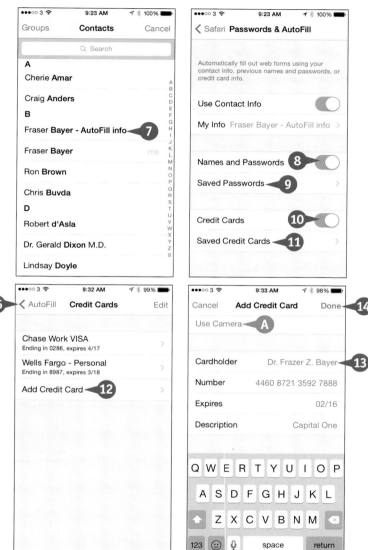

TIP

Is it safe to store my passwords and credit card information in AutoFill?
There is no hard-and-fast answer, but storing this sensitive information is reasonably safe because your iPhone encrypts it securely. The main threat to this data is from someone picking up your iPhone, so be sure to protect the device with your fingerprint, a passcode, or — better — a password. See Chapter 2 for instructions on setting up Touch ID, a passcode, or a password.

Tighten Up Safari's Security

To protect yourself against websites that infect computers with malware or try to gain your sensitive personal or financial information, turn on Safari's Fraudulent Website Warning feature. You can also turn off the JavaScript programming language, which can be used to attack your iPhone. Additionally, you can block pop-up windows, which some websites use to display unwanted information; choose which cookies to accept; and turn on the Do Not Track feature to reduce the footprint you leave on the Internet.

Tighten Up Safari's Security

1 Press the Home button.

The Home screen appears.

2 Tap **Settings**.

The Settings screen appears.

3 Scroll down, and then tap **Safari**.

The Safari screen appears.

4 Set the **Block Pop-ups** switch to On (⬤) to block unwanted pop-up windows.

5 Set the **Do Not Track** switch to On (⬤) or Off (◻), as needed.

6 Tap **Block Cookies**.

The Block Cookies screen appears.

7 Tap **Always Block**, **Allow from Current Website Only**, **Allow from Websites I Visit**, or **Always Allow**, as needed. See the tip for advice.

8 Tap **Safari**.

The Safari screen appears.

9 Set the **Fraudulent Website Warning** switch to On ().

10 Tap **Clear History and Website Data**.

A dialog opens.

11 Tap **Clear History and Data**.

12 Tap **Advanced**.

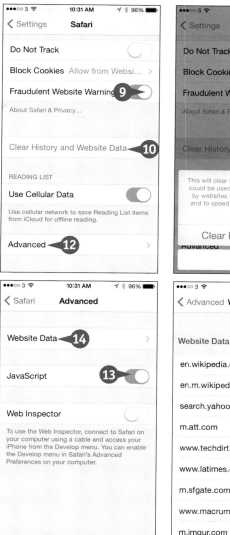

The Advanced screen appears.

13 Set the **JavaScript** switch to On (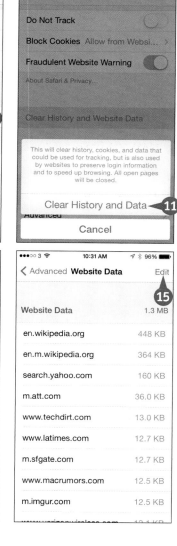) or Off (☐), as needed.

Note: Turning off JavaScript may remove some or most functionality of harmless sites.

14 Tap **Website Data**.

The Website Data screen appears.

15 Tap **Edit**.

⊖ appears to the left of each website.

16 To delete a website's data, tap ⊖, and then tap **Delete**.

What are cookies, and what threat do they pose?
A *cookie* is a small text file that a website places on a computer to identify that computer in the future. This is helpful for many sites, such as shopping sites in which you add items to a shopping cart, but when used by malevolent sites, cookies can pose a threat to your privacy. You can set Safari to never accept cookies, but this prevents many legitimate websites from working properly. So accepting cookies only from sites you visit is normally the best compromise.

Read E-Mail

After you have set up Mail by synchronizing accounts from your computer, as described in Chapter 1, or by setting up accounts manually on the iPhone, as described in Chapter 4, you are ready to send and receive e-mail messages using your iPhone.

This section shows you how to read your incoming e-mail messages. You learn to reply to messages and write messages from scratch later in this chapter.

Read E-Mail

 Press the Home button.

The Home screen appears.

 Tap **Mail**.

The Mailboxes screen appears.

Note: If Mail does not show the Mailboxes screen, tap ◁ until the Mailboxes screen appears.

③ Tap the inbox you want to see.

Ⓐ To see all your incoming messages together, tap **All Inboxes**. Depending on how you use e-mail, you may find seeing all your messages together helpful.

The inbox opens.

Ⓑ A blue dot to the left of a message indicates that you have not read the message yet.

Ⓒ A gray star to the left of a message indicates the message is from a VIP. See the second tip for information about VIPs.

④ Tap the message you want to open.

The message opens.

5 Turn the iPhone sideways if you want to view the message in landscape orientation.

In landscape orientation, you can see the message at a larger size, so it is easier to read.

6 Tap ⌃ or ⌄.

The previous or the next message appears.

7 If you want to delete the message, tap 🗑.

Note: If you want to reply to the message, see the next section, "Reply To or Forward an E-Mail Message." If you want to file the message in a folder, see the later section, "Organize Your Messages in Mailbox Folders."

Note: The badge on the Mail icon on the Home screen shows how many unread messages Mail has found so far.

< Inbox (1)   **6** ⌃ ⌄

Hi,

Please look at this marketing photo and let me know whether you want to use it for the upcoming campaign.

⚑   🗀   🗑   ↩   ✏

< Inbox   ⌃ ⌄

From: Eduardo Sempio >   Hide
To: Roman Kerze >

Industry spreadsheet
July 9, 2014 at 10:52 AM

Could you send me the latest industry spreadsheet?

⚑   🗀   🗑 **7**   ↩   ✏

TIPS

How do I view the contents of another mailbox?
From an open message, tap **Inbox** or **All Inboxes** to return to the inbox or the screen for all the inboxes. Tap **Mailboxes** to go back to the Mailboxes screen. You can then tap the mailbox you want to view.

What is the VIP inbox on the Mailboxes screen?
The VIP inbox is a tool for identifying important messages, no matter which e-mail account they come to. You mark particular contacts as being very important people to you, and Mail then adds messages from these VIPs to the VIP inbox. To add a VIP, tap the sender's name in an open message, then tap **Add to VIP** on the Sender screen.

Reply To or Forward an E-Mail Message

After receiving an e-mail message, you often need to reply to it. You can choose between replying only to the sender of the message and replying to the sender and all the other recipients in the To field and the Cc field, if there are any. Recipients in the message's Bcc field, whose names you cannot see, do not receive your reply.

Other times, you may need to forward a message you have received to one or more other people. The Mail app makes both replying and forwarding messages as easy as possible.

Reply To or Forward an E-Mail Message

Open the Message You Will Reply To or Forward

1 Press the Home button.

The Home screen appears.

2 Tap **Mail**.

The Mailboxes screen appears.

Note: When you launch Mail, the app checks for new messages. This is why the number of new messages you see on the Mailboxes screen may differ from the number on the Mail badge on the Home screen.

3 Tap the inbox you want to see.

The inbox opens.

4 Tap the message you want to open.

The message opens.

5 Tap **Action** (⬅).

The Action dialog opens.

Note: You can also reply to or forward a message by using Siri. For example, say "Reply to this message" or "Forward this message to Alice Smith," and then tell Siri what you want the message to say.

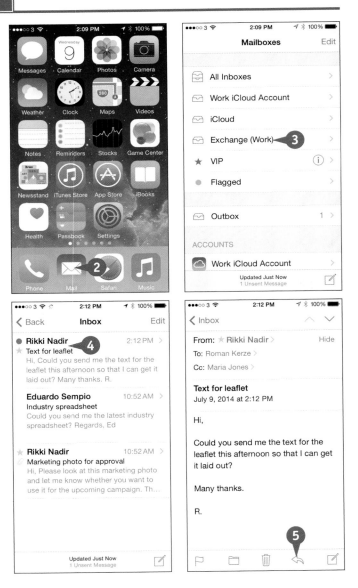

196

Reply To the Message

1 In the Action dialog, tap **Reply**.

A To reply to all recipients, tap **Reply All**. Reply to all recipients only when you are sure that they need to receive your reply. Often, it is better to reply only to the sender.

A screen containing the reply appears.

2 Type your reply to the message.

3 Tap **Send**.

Mail sends the message.

Forward the Message

1 In the Action dialog, tap **Forward**.

A screen containing the forwarded message appears.

2 Type the recipient's address.

B Alternatively, you can tap ⊕ and choose the recipient in your Contacts list.

3 Type a message if needed.

4 Tap **Send**.

Mail sends the message.

Can I reply to or forward only part of a message?
Yes. The quick way to do this is to select the part of the message you want to include before tapping **Action** (⟲). Mail then includes only your selection. Alternatively, you can start the reply or forwarded message, and then delete the parts you do not want to include.

How do I check for new messages?
In a mailbox, tap and drag your finger down the screen, pulling down the messages. When a progress circle appears at the top, lift your finger. Mail checks for new messages.

Organize Your Messages in Mailbox Folders

To keep your inbox or inboxes under control, you should organize your messages into mailbox folders.

You can quickly move a single message to a folder after reading it or after previewing it in the message list. Alternatively, you can select multiple messages in your inbox and move them all to a folder in a single action. You can also delete any message you no longer need.

Organize Your Messages in Mailbox Folders

Open Mail and Move a Single Message to a Folder

1 Press the Home button.

The Home screen appears.

2 Tap **Mail**.

The Mailboxes screen appears.

3 Tap the mailbox you want to open.

The mailbox opens.

Ⓐ 🔄 indicates you have replied to the message.

Ⓑ 🔄 indicates you have forwarded the message.

4 Tap the message you want to read.

The message opens.

5 Tap **Move** (📁).

The Move This Message to a New Mailbox screen appears.

6 Tap the mailbox to which you want to move the message.

Mail moves the message.

The next message in the mailbox appears, so that you can read it and file it if necessary.

Note: You can delete the open message by tapping 🗑.

Move Multiple Messages to a Folder

1 In the mailbox, tap **Edit**.

2 Tap the selection button (☐ changes to ✅) next to each message you want to move.

3 Tap **Move**.

4 Tap the destination mailbox.

Note: To move the messages to a mailbox in another account, tap **Accounts** on the Move This Message to a New Mailbox screen, tap the account, and then tap the mailbox.

Move a Message from a Mailbox

1 In the mailbox list, tap the message and swipe to the left.

Ⓒ Tap **Trash** to delete the message.

2 Tap **More**.

The More dialog opens.

3 Tap **Move Message**.

The Mailboxes screen appears.

4 Tap the mailbox to which you want to move the message.

TIP

What do the Flag command and the Mark as Unread command do?

Tap **Flag** (⚑) to set a flag on the message — for example, to indicate that you need to pay extra attention to it. The flag appears as an orange dot (🔴).

Tap **Mark as Unread** to mark the message as not having been read, even though you have opened it. Sometimes it is helpful to mark a message as unread as a reminder that you need to read it properly later. You can also mark a message as unread by tapping it in the message list, swiping right, and then tapping **Mark as Unread**.

Write and Send E-Mail Messages

Your iPhone is great for reading and replying to e-mail messages you receive, but you will likely also need to write new messages. When you do, you can use the data in the Contacts app to address your outgoing messages quickly and accurately. If the recipient's address is not one of your contacts, you can type the address manually.

You can attach one or more files to an e-mail message to send those files to the recipient. This works well for small files, but many mail servers reject files larger than several megabytes in size.

Write and Send E-Mail Messages

1 Press the Home button.

The Home screen appears.

2 Tap **Mail**.

The Mailboxes screen appears.

3 Tap **New Message** (✉).

The New Message screen appears.

4 Tap ⊕.

The Contacts list appears.

Note: If necessary, change the Contacts list displayed by tapping **Groups**, making your choice on the Groups screen, and then tapping **Done**.

Ⓐ If the person you are e-mailing is not a contact, type the address in the To area. You can also start typing here and then select a matching contact from the list that the Mail app displays.

5 Tap the contact you want to send the message to.

B The contact's name appears in the To area.

Note: You can add other contacts to the To area by repeating Steps 4 and 5.

6 If you need to add a Cc or Bcc recipient, tap **Cc/Bcc, From**.

The Cc, Bcc, and From fields expand.

7 Tap the Cc area or Bcc area, and then follow Steps 4 and 5 to add a recipient.

C To change the e-mail account you are sending the message from, tap **From**, and then tap the account to use.

8 Tap **Subject**, and then type the message's subject.

D You can tap 🔔 (🔔 changes to 🔔) to receive notifications when someone responds to the e-mail conversation.

9 Tap below the Subject line, and then type the body of the message.

10 Tap **Send**.

Mail sends the message.

View Files Attached to Incoming E-Mail Messages

E-mail is not just a great way to communicate; it is also a great way to transfer files quickly and easily. When you receive an e-mail message with a file attached to it, you can quickly view the file from the Mail app.

The Mail app automatically downloads small attachments. But if the attachment is a large file, the Mail app starts downloading it only when you open the message for reading. This behavior gives you the chance to delete the message and terminate the download if necessary.

View Files Attached to Incoming E-Mail Messages

1 Press the Home button.

The Home screen appears.

2 Tap **Mail**.

The Mailboxes screen appears.

3 Tap the inbox you want to open.

The inbox opens.

A A paperclip icon (⬚) indicates that a message has one or more files attached.

4 Tap the message you want to open.

The message opens.

B If the attached file is large, Mail begins to download it. A progress indicator appears.

A button for the attachment appears.

5 Tap the attachment's button.

The attached file opens in Mail's Viewer feature.

Note: The Viewer feature provides basic features for viewing widely used document types, such as PDF files, Microsoft Word documents, and Microsoft Excel workbooks. If the Viewer feature cannot open the file you try to open, your iPhone tries to suggest a suitable app.

6 Tap **Share** (⬆).

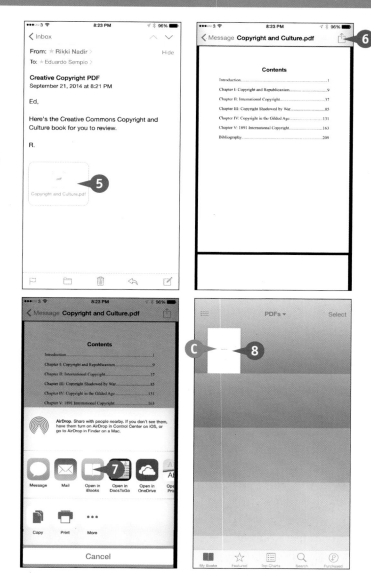

A screen for opening or using the attachment appears.

7 Tap the app in which you want to open the document. For example, tap **Open in iBooks**.

C The file opens in the app you chose.

8 Depending on the app, tap the file to open it.

Note: After you open an attached file in an app, your iPhone stores a copy of the file in that app's storage. You can then open the file again directly from that app.

TIP

How can I delete an attached file from an e-mail message?
You cannot directly delete an attached file from an e-mail message on the iPhone at this writing. You can delete only the message along with its attached file. If you use an e-mail app such as Apple Mail or web-based e-mail such as iCloud.com to manage the same e-mail account, you can remove the attached file using that app. When you update your mailbox on your iPhone, the iPhone deletes the attached file but leaves the message.

CHAPTER 9

Keeping Your Life Organized

You can use your iPhone to manage your contacts, keep your schedule, track commitments, and carry important documents. With the iPhone 6, you can also make payments easily using the Apple Pay service.

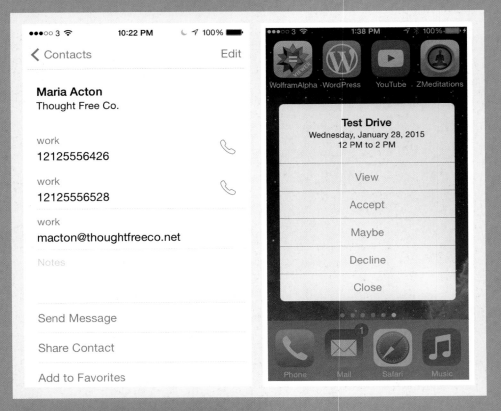

Your iPhone's Contacts app enables you to store contact data that you sync from your computer or online accounts or that you enter directly on your iPhone. You can access the contacts either via the Contacts app itself or through the Contacts tab in the Phone app.

To see which contacts you have synced to your iPhone, or to find a particular contact, you can browse through the contacts. You can either browse through your full list of contacts or display particular groups, such as your business contacts. You can also locate contacts by searching for them.

Browse or Search for Contacts

Browse Your Contacts

1. Press the Home button.

   The Home screen appears.

2. Tap **Extras**.

   The Extras folder opens.

3. Tap **Contacts**.

   The Contacts screen appears.

Note: You can also access your contacts by pressing the Home button, tapping **Phone**, and then tapping **Contacts**.

 To navigate the screen of contacts quickly, tap the letter on the right that you want to jump to. To navigate more slowly, scroll up or down.

4. Tap the contact whose information you want to view.

   The contact's screen appears.

Note: From the contact's screen, you can quickly phone the contact by tapping the phone number you want to use.

5. If necessary, tap and drag up to scroll down the screen to display more information.

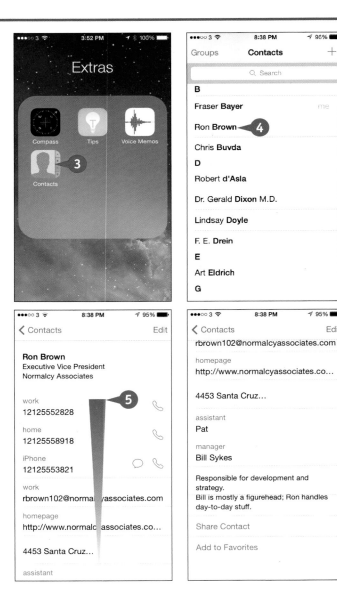

Choose Which Groups of Contacts to Display

1️⃣ From the Contacts screen, tap **Groups**.

The Groups screen appears.

2️⃣ Tap **Show All Contacts**.

Contacts displays a check mark next to each group.

Note: When you tap **Show All Contacts**, the Hide All Contacts button appears in place of the Show All Contacts button. You can tap **Hide All Contacts** to remove all the check marks.

3️⃣ Tap a group to apply a check mark to it or to remove the existing check mark.

4️⃣ Tap **Done**.

The Contacts screen appears, showing the contacts in the groups you selected.

Search for Contacts

1️⃣ From the Contacts screen, tap **Search**.

The Search screen appears.

2️⃣ Start typing the name you want to search for.

3️⃣ From the list of matches, tap the contact you want to view.

The contact's information appears.

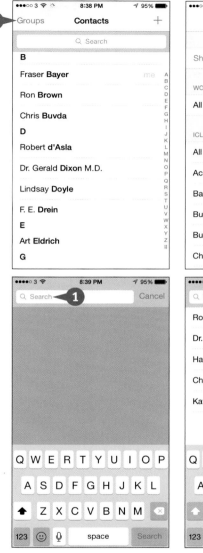

TIP

How do I make my iPhone sort my contacts by last names instead of first names?
Press the Home button. Tap **Settings** and then **Mail, Contacts, Calendars**. In the Contacts area, tap **Sort Order**. Tap **Last, First**.

Create a New Contact

Normally, you put contacts on your iPhone by syncing them from existing records on your computer or from an online service such as iCloud. But when necessary, you can create a new contact on your iPhone itself — for example, when you meet someone you want to remember.

You can then sync the contact record back to your computer or online service, adding the new contact to your existing contacts.

Create a New Contact

1 Press the Home button.

The Home screen appears.

2 Tap **Phone**.

The Phone app opens.

3 Tap **Contacts**.

The Contacts screen appears.

Note: You can also access the Contacts app by tapping the **Extras** folder on the Home screen, and then tapping the **Contacts** app.

4 Tap **Add** (⊞).

The New Contact screen appears.

5 Tap **First**.

The on-screen keyboard appears.

6 Type the first name.

7 Tap **Last**.

8 Type the last name.

9 Add other information as needed by tapping each field and then typing the information.

10 To add a photo of the contact, tap **add photo**.

The Photo dialog opens.

11 Tap **Take Photo**.

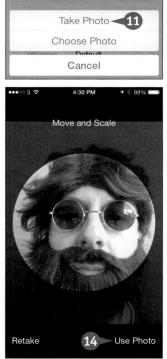

The Take Photo screen appears.

12 Compose the photo, and then tap **Take Photo** (⬤).

The Move and Scale screen appears.

13 Position the part of the photo you want to use in the middle.

Note: Pinch in with two fingers to zoom the photo out. Pinch out with two fingers to zoom the photo in.

14 Tap **Use Photo**.

The photo appears in the contact record.

15 Tap **Done**.

TIP

How do I assign my new contact an existing photo?

1 In the Photo dialog, tap **Choose Photo**.

2 On the Photos screen, tap the photo album.

3 Tap the photo.

4 On the Move and Scale screen, position the photo, and then tap **Choose**.

Share Contacts via E-Mail and Messages

Often in business or your personal life, you will need to share your contacts with other people. Your iPhone makes it easy to share a contact record via either e-mail or an instant message using the Multimedia Messaging Service, or MMS, as explained in this section. You can also share a contact record via AirDrop; see Chapter 6 for information on using AirDrop.

The iPhone shares the contact record as a virtual business card in the widely used vCard format. Most phones and personal-organizer software can easily import vCard files.

Share Contacts via E-Mail and Messages

Open the Contact You Want to Share

1 Press the Home button.

The Home screen appears.

2 Tap **Extras**.

The Extras folder opens.

3 Tap **Contacts**.

The Contacts screen appears.

Note: You can also access the Contacts app from within the Phone app. From the Home screen, tap **Phone**, and then tap the **Contacts** tab at the bottom.

4 Tap the contact you want to share.

The Info screen for the contact appears.

5 Tap **Share Contact**.

The Share Contact Using dialog opens.

Share a Contact via E-Mail

① In the Share Contact Using dialog, tap **Mail**.

Ⓐ A new message appears in the Mail app, with the contact record attached as a vCard file.

Ⓑ The contact's name appears in the Subject line.

② Address the message by typing the address or by tapping ⊕ and choosing a contact as the recipient.

③ Type a message.

④ Tap **Send**, and Mail sends the message with the contact record attached.

Share a Contact via Message

① In the Share Contact Using dialog, tap **Message**.

Ⓒ The New MMS screen appears, with the contact record attached to the message.

② Address the message by typing the name or number or by tapping ⊕ and choosing a contact as the recipient.

③ Type a message.

④ Tap **Send**, and the iPhone sends the message with the contact record attached.

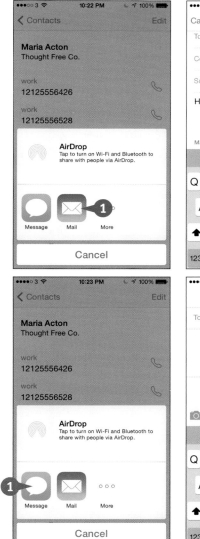

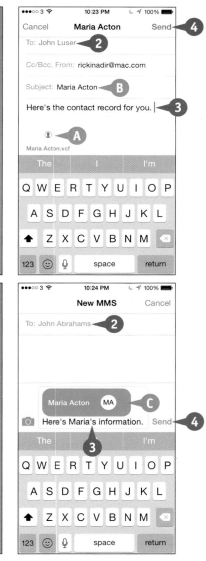

TIP

How do I add a vCard I receive in an e-mail message to my contacts?

In the Mail app, tap the button for the vCard file. A screen appears showing the vCard's contents. Scroll down to the bottom, and then tap **Create New Contact**. If the vCard contains extra information about an existing contact, tap **Add to Existing Contact**, and then tap the contact.

Browse Existing Events in Your Calendars

Your iPhone's Calendar app gives you a great way of managing your schedule and making sure you never miss an appointment.

After setting up your calendars to sync using iTunes, iCloud, or another calendar service, as described in Chapter 1, you can take your calendars with you everywhere and consult them whenever you need to. You can view either all your calendars or only ones you choose.

Browse Existing Events in Your Calendars

Browse Existing Events in Your Calendars

1 Press the Home button.

2 Tap **Calendar**.

A The black circle indicates the day shown. When the current date is selected, the circle is red.

B Your events appear on a scrollable timeline.

C An event's background color indicates the calendar it belongs to.

D You can tap **Today** to display the current day.

3 Tap the day you want to see.

The events for the day appear.

4 Tap the month.

The calendar for the month appears.

E You can tap the year to display the calendar for the full year, in which you can navigate quickly to other months.

5 Scroll up or down as needed, and then tap the date you want.

The date's appointments appear.

6 Tap **List** (☰ changes to ▤).

The appointments appear as a list, enabling you to see more.

7 Tap an event to see its details.

The Event Details screen appears.

8 To edit the event, tap **Edit**.

The Edit screen appears, and you can make changes to the event. When you finish, tap **Done**.

Choose Which Calendars to Display

1 Tap **Calendars**.

2 Tap to place or remove a check mark next to a calendar you want to display or hide.

Ⓕ Tap **Show All Calendars** to place a check mark next to each calendar. Tap **Hide All Calendars** to remove all check marks.

Ⓖ The Birthdays calendar automatically displays birthdays of contacts whose contact data includes the birthday.

Ⓗ You can set the **Show Declined Events** switch to On (🔘) to include invitations you have declined.

3 Tap **Done**.

The calendars you chose appear.

TIP

How can I quickly find an event?
In the Calendar app, tap **Search** (🔍). Calendar displays a list of your events. Type your search term. When Calendar displays a list of matches, tap the event you want to view.

Create New Events in Your Calendars

Normally, you will probably create most new events in your calendars on your computer, and then sync them to your iPhone. But when you need to create a new event using the iPhone, you can easily do so.

You can create either a straightforward, one-shot appointment or an appointment that repeats on a schedule. You can also choose the calendar in which to store the appointment.

Create New Events in Your Calendars

1 Press the Home button.

The Home screen appears.

2 Tap **Calendar**.

The Calendar screen appears.

3 Tap the day on which you want to create the new event.

Note: You can also tap the current month and use the month-by-month calendar to navigate to the date. Alternatively, leave the current date selected, and then change the date when creating the event.

4 Tap **New** (⊞).

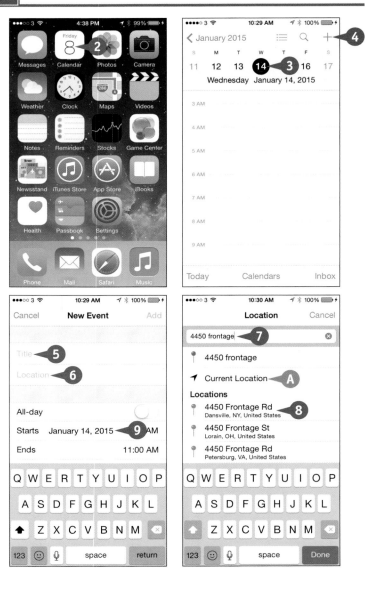

The New Event screen appears.

5 Tap **Title** and type the title of the event.

6 Tap **Location**.

Note: If the Allow "Calendar" to Access Your Location While You Use the App? dialog box opens when you tap **Location**, tap **Allow** to use locations.

A You can tap **Current Location** to use the current location.

7 Start typing the location.

8 Tap the appropriate match.

9 Tap **Starts**.

The time and date controls appear.

10 Tap the date and time controls to set the start time.

11 Tap **Ends**.

12 Tap the date and time wheels to set the end time.

B If this is an all-day appointment, set the **All-day** switch to On ().

C If you need to change the time zone, tap **Time Zone**, type the city name, and then tap the time zone.

13 Tap **Alert**.

The Event Alert screen appears.

14 Tap the timing for the alert.

The New Event screen appears.

15 Tap **Calendar**.

The Calendar screen appears.

16 Tap the calendar for the event.

The New Event screen appears.

17 Tap **Add**.

The event appears on your calendar.

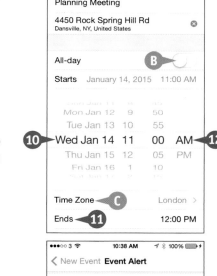

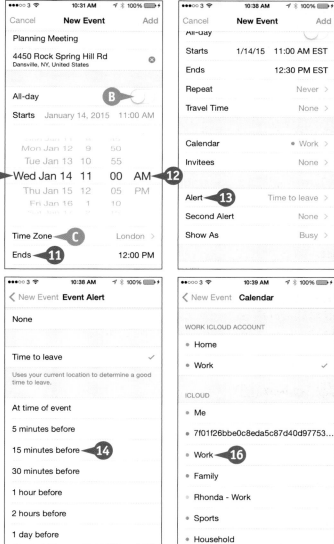

How do I set up an event that repeats every week?

On the New Event screen, tap **Repeat**. On the Repeat screen, tap **Every Week**, placing a check mark next to it, and then tap **Done**.

How do I set a time to the exact minute instead of to the nearest five minutes?

On the New Event screen, tap **Starts** to display the time and date controls. Double-tap the time readout — either the hours or the minutes — to switch the minutes between five-minute intervals and single minutes.

Work with Calendar Invitations

As well as events you create yourself, you may receive invitations to events that others create. When you receive an event invitation attached to an e-mail message, you can choose whether to accept the invitation or decline it. If you accept the invitation, you can add the event automatically to your calendar.

Work with Calendar Invitations

Deal with an Invitation from an Alert

1 When an invitation alert appears, tap **Options**.

The Options dialog opens.

2 Tap **View**.

Ⓐ You can tap **Accept**, **Maybe**, or **Decline** to deal with the invitation without viewing the details.

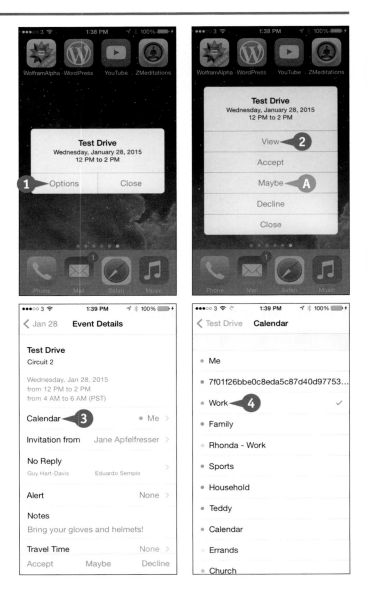

The Event Details screen appears.

3 Tap **Calendar** if you decide to accept the invitation.

The Calendar screen appears.

4 Tap the calendar to which you want to assign the event.

Note: To control how the event's time appears in your calendar, tap **Show As** on the Event Details screen, and then tap **Busy** or **Free**, as appropriate, on the Show As screen.

The Event Details screen appears.

5 Tap **Alert**.

The Event Alert screen appears

6 Tap the button for the alert interval. For example, tap **1 hour before**.

The Event Details screen appears.

7 Tap **Accept**.

Your calendar appears, showing the event you just accepted.

Deal with an Invitation from the Inbox Screen

B In your calendar, the Inbox button shows an alert giving the number of invitations.

1 Tap **Inbox**.

The Inbox screen appears.

2 Tap **Accept**, **Decline**, or **Maybe**, as needed.

Note: To see the full detail of the invitation, tap its button on the Inbox screen. The Event Details screen then appears, and you can accept the invitation as described earlier in this section.

3 Tap **Done**.

TIP

Why does an event appear at a different time than that shown in the invitation I accepted?
When you open the invitation, you see the event's time in the time zone in which it was created. If your iPhone is currently using a different time zone, the appointment appears in your calendar using that time zone's time, so the time appears to have changed.

Track Your Commitments with Reminders

Your iPhone's Reminders app gives you an easy way to note your commitments and keep track of them. The Reminders app comes with a built-in list called Reminders, but you can create as many other lists as you need, giving each a distinctive color.

You can create a reminder with no due time or location or tie a reminder to a due time, arriving at or leaving a location, or both. Your iPhone can remind you of time- or location-based reminders at the appropriate time or place.

Track Your Commitments with Reminders

Open the Reminders App and Create Your Reminder Lists

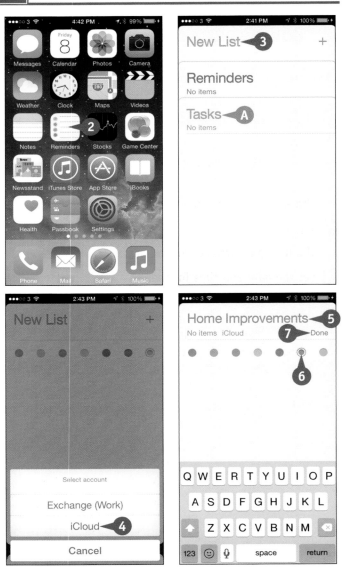

1. Press the Home button.

2. Tap **Reminders**.

   The Reminders app opens, displaying the Lists screen.

   A. The Tasks list appears on the Lists screen if you sync your iPhone with an Exchange account for which you have enabled Reminders.

3. Tap **New List**.

   The New List screen appears.

Note: If you have only one Notes account, Reminders does not prompt you to choose the account to use.

4. Tap the account in which you want to store the list.

5. Type the name for the list.

6. Tap the color to use for the list.

7. Tap **Done**.

   The list appears.

Create a New Reminder

1. To create a new reminder in this list, tap the first line.

B. To return to the Lists screen so you can switch to another list, tap the tabbed pages at the bottom of the screen.

The keyboard appears.

2. Type the text for the reminder.

3. Tap ⓘ.

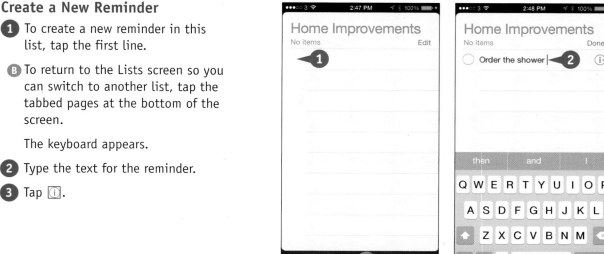

The Details screen appears.

4. To create a time-based reminder, set the **Remind me on a day** switch to On (◯).

The Alarm and Repeat controls appear.

5. Tap **Alarm**.

The date and time controls appear.

6. Set the date and time for the reminder.

7. If you need to repeat the reminder, tap **Repeat**, choose the repeat interval on the Repeat screen, and then tap **Details** to return to the Details screen.

TIP

How do I sync my iPhone's reminders with my Mac's reminders?

You can sync your iPhone's reminders with your Mac's reminders via your iCloud account.

On your iPhone, press the Home button to display the Home screen, and then tap **Settings** to display the Settings screen. Tap **iCloud** to display the iCloud screen, and then set the **Reminders** switch to On (◯).

On your Mac, click and **System Preferences** to open System Preferences. Click **iCloud** to display the iCloud pane, and then select the **Calendars** check box and the **Reminders** check box (☐ changes to ☑).

continued ▶

You can assign different priorities to your reminders to give yourself a quick visual reference of their urgency. You can also add notes to a reminder to keep relevant information at hand. When you have completed a reminder, you can mark it as completed. You can view your list of scheduled reminders for quick reference, and you can choose whether to include your completed reminders in the list. If you no longer need a reminder, you can delete it from the list.

Track Your Commitments with Reminders (continued)

8 To create a location-based reminder, set the **Remind me at a location** switch to On (🔘).

Note: If Reminders prompts you to allow it to use your current location, tap **Allow**.

9 Tap **Location**.

The Location screen appears.

10 Type the location in the search box.

ⓒ You can tap **Current Location** to use your current location.

11 Tap the location in the list of results.

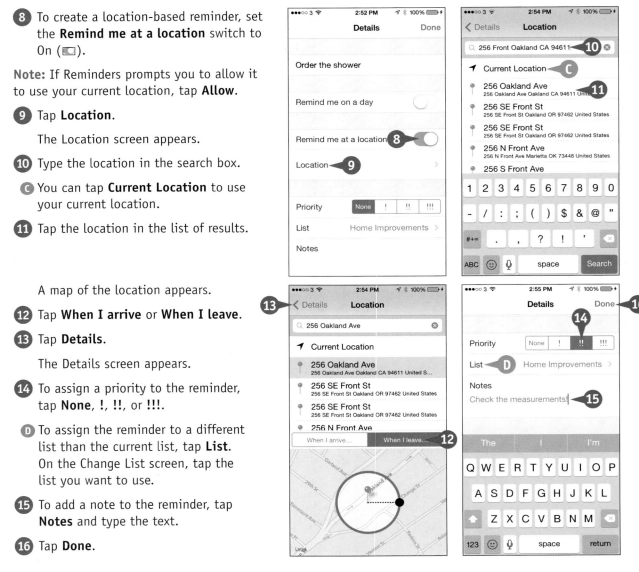

A map of the location appears.

12 Tap **When I arrive** or **When I leave**.

13 Tap **Details**.

The Details screen appears.

14 To assign a priority to the reminder, tap **None**, **!**, **!!**, or **!!!**.

ⓓ To assign the reminder to a different list than the current list, tap **List**. On the Change List screen, tap the list you want to use.

15 To add a note to the reminder, tap **Notes** and type the text.

16 Tap **Done**.

The new reminder appears on your list of reminders.

17 Tap the next line to start creating a new reminder.

E When you finish a task, tap ☐ (☐ changes to ◉) to mark the reminder as complete.

Note: To delete a reminder, tap **Edit** on the screen that contains it. Tap ⊖ to its left, and then tap **Delete**.

18 Tap the tabbed pages at the bottom of the screen to switch to another reminder list.

View a List of Your Scheduled Reminders

1 Tap the Lists screen and pull down a little way.

The Search bar appears.

2 Tap **Scheduled** (◉).

The Scheduled list appears.

3 Tap the reminder you want to see.

Note: You can turn the iPhone 6 to landscape orientation to view both your reminder lists and the current list's reminders at the same time.

TIP

How do I change the default list that Reminders puts my reminders in?
Press the Home button to display the Home screen, and then tap **Settings** to display the Settings screen. Tap **Reminders** to display the Reminders screen, tap **Default List** to display the Default List screen, and then tap the list you want to make the default. On the Reminders screen, you can also tap **Sync** and choose how many reminders to sync — **Reminders 2 Weeks Back**, **Reminders 1 Month Back**, **Reminders 3 Months Back**, **Reminders 6 Months Back**, or **All Reminders**.

Keep Essential Documents at Hand with Passbook

Passbook is an app for storing electronic versions of essential documents such as boarding passes, cinema tickets, and hotel reservations. To get your documents into Passbook, you use apps such as Mail and Safari. For example, when an airline sends you your travel details attached to an e-mail message, you can add the boarding pass to Passbook from Mail. You can also add documents using custom apps for shopping, booking hotels, and booking flights.

Keep Essential Documents at Hand with Passbook

Add a Document to Passbook

① In Mail, tap the message with the document attached.

The message opens.

② Tap the document's button.

The document appears.

③ Tap **Add**.

Mail adds the document to Passbook.

The message appears again.

Note: In Safari, open the web page containing the document, and then tap **Add** to add it to Passbook.

Open Passbook and Find the Documents You Need

① Press the Home button.

The Home screen appears.

② Tap **Passbook**.

Passbook opens.

The documents you have added appear.

Note: Until you add one or more documents to Passbook, the app displays an information screen highlighting its uses.

③ Tap the document you want to view.

The document appears above the other documents. You can then hold its barcode in front of a scanner to use the document.

④ To see another document, tap the current top document and drag down.

⑤ At the bottom of the screen, release the document.

Passbook reshuffles the documents so you can see them all.

Choose Settings for a Document or Delete It

① Tap ⓘ.

The document rotates so you can see its back.

② Set the **Automatic Updates** switch to On (⬜) if you want to receive updates to this document.

③ Set the **Show On Lock Screen** switch to On (⬜) if you want notifications about the document to appear on the lock screen.

Ⓑ If you have no further need for the document, tap **Delete** to delete it.

④ When you finish reviewing the document, tap **Done**.

The document rotates to display its front.

TIP

What other actions can I take with documents in Passbook?
You can share a document with other people via e-mail, instant messaging, or AirDrop. To access these features, tap **Share** (🔼), and then tap **AirDrop**, **Mail**, or **Message** on the sharing sheet that appears.

Make Payments with Your iPhone

If your iPhone is an iPhone 6 or an iPhone 6 Plus, you can use Apple's payment service to make payments directly from your iPhone. The iPhone 5s and iPhone 5c do not have this capability.

Apple's payment service is called Apple Pay. At this writing, you can use it at a wide variety of locations in North America. Apple will subsequently add other locations.

Understand How Apple Pay Works

The Apple Pay service links with the three major payment networks — Visa, MasterCard, and American Express — and enables you to use debit cards and credit cards issued on these networks by a wide variety of banks.

Apple Pay uses the Near Field Communications, or NFC, chip built into the iPhone 6 or iPhone 6 Plus to make contactless payments with card readers. On the iPhone, a chip called the Secure Element stores your payment information in an encrypted format for security.

Set Up Your Means of Payment

Before you can make a payment with Apple Pay, you must set up your means of payment. To do so, you add the details of your debit card or credit card to your account on the iTunes Store. The easiest way to do this is to use iTunes on a Windows PC or on a Mac.

If you have already set up the debit card or payment card you want to use, you are ready to use Apple Pay on your iPhone. Otherwise, open iTunes, click **Store** on the menu bar, and then click **View Account** to display the Account Information screen on the iTunes Store. Click **Edit** on the Payment Information line to display the Edit Payment Information screen. You can then enter the card details and click **Continue** or **Done**, depending on which button appears.

Make a Payment at a Payment Terminal

Apple Pay enables you to make payments easily at payment terminals located in retailers, cafes and restaurants, and places such as stations or airports.

To make a payment, you simply bring your iPhone up to the payment terminal, verify the amount displayed on-screen, and place one of your fingers that you have registered with Touch ID on the Home button to approve the transaction and authenticate your identity.

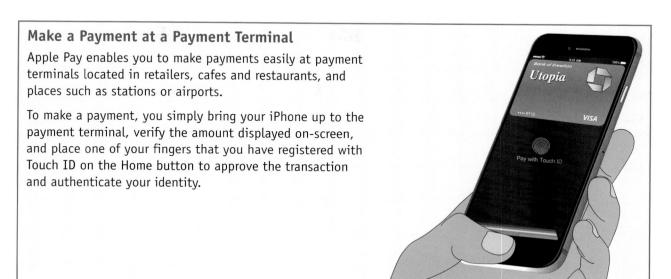

Make a Payment Online

You can also use Apple Pay to make payments online within apps on your iPhone.

When an app displays a button with Apple Pay logo on a payment screen, you can tap that button to use Apple Pay. On the subsequent screen, you place one of your fingers that you have registered with Touch ID on the Home button to confirm the purchase and authenticate your identity.

Using the Health App

The Health app integrates with third-party hardware and software to enable you to keep tabs on many different aspects of your health, ranging from your weight and blood pressure to your nutrition, activity levels, and body mass index. Press the Home button to display the Home screen, and then tap **Health** to launch the Health app.

Track Your Health with Dashboard

The Dashboard screen provides quick access to the health information you want to track closely. Tap **Dashboard** to display the Dashboard screen. You can then tap **Day**, **Week**, **Month**, or **Year** to view the data available for that unit of time. For example, you might view your blood pressure for the last week and then switch to viewing your weight for the past year.

Scroll up and down as needed to view information. Tap an item to go straight to the screen for managing its data and adding data points.

Work with Your Health Data

Tap **Health Data** to display the Health Data screen, which gives you access to the full range of health data you, your apps, and your device have entered in the Health app.

The main screen contains buttons for All, Diagnostics, Fitness, Lab Results, Me, Medication, Nutrition, Sleep, and Vital Signs. Tap the category you want to view, or tap **Search** at the top of the screen and then type your search terms.

After displaying the category screen, such as the Nutrition screen, you can tap the item with which you want to work. For example, from the Nutrition screen, you can tap **Protein** to display the Protein screen, which provides controls for entering and analyzing your protein intake.

Add Data Points

The Health app can automatically accept data points from sources you approve, as explained next, but you can also add data points manually. For example, if you weigh yourself on a manual scale or have your blood pressure taken, you can add your latest readings to the Health app so that you can track your weight and blood pressure over time.

Tap **Vital Signs** on the Health Data screen to display the Vital Signs screen. You can then tap the appropriate button to reach its screen. For example, tap **Blood Pressure** to display the Blood Pressure screen. You can then tap **Add Data Point** to display the Add Data screen. Enter the date, time, and systolic and diastolic pressures, and then tap the **Add** button.

On a screen such as the Blood Pressure screen, you can set the **Show on Dashboard** switch to On ( ) to add the item's graph to the Dashboard screen for quick reference.

Add Sources

Tap **Sources** to display the Sources screen. Here you can review the list of apps that have requested permission to update the data in the Health app; you can remove any apps that you no longer want to permit to update the data. You can also review the list of hardware devices that have gotten permission to update the data — for example, your iWatch — and revoke permissions as needed.

Add Your Medical ID

Tap **Medical ID** to display the Medical ID screen. You can then tap **Edit** to open the data for editing so that you can enter details of your medical conditions, medications, emergency contact, and blood type. Set the **Show Medical ID** switch to On ( ) if you want to display your medical ID on the lock screen, enabling others to access your essential information to help if you become unwell.

CHAPTER 10

Playing Music and Videos

As well as being a phone and a powerful handheld computer, your iPhone is also a full-scale music and video player. To play music, you use the Music app; to play videos, you use the Videos app. In this chapter, you learn to use the Music app to play music and radio and to create playlists. You also learn how to play videos and enjoy podcasts and iTunes U lectures.

Play Music Using the Music App

After loading music on your iPhone, as described in the section "Choose Which Items to Sync from Your Computer" in Chapter 1, you can play it back using the Music app. You can play music in several ways. You can play music by song or by album, as described in this section. You can play songs in exactly the order you want by creating a custom playlist, as described in the later section, "Create a Music Playlist." You can also play by artist, genre, or composer.

Play Music Using the Music App

1 Press the Home button.

2 Tap **Music**.

3 Tap the button by which to sort. This example uses **Songs**.

A To see the music listed by another category, such as Genres, tap **More**, and then tap the category by which you want to sort.

B Tap a letter on the right side to jump to the first item starting with that letter.

4 Tap the song you want to play.

The song's details appear, and the song plays.

5 Tap and drag the playhead to change the position in the song.

6 Tap and drag the volume control.

7 Tap the album artwork.

If the song contains the text of its lyrics, the Song Lyrics panel appears.

8 Tap the Song Lyrics panel to display the album artwork again.

9 Tap **Shuffle** if you want to shuffle the order of songs. Shuffle All replaces Shuffle. Tap **Shuffle All** to turn off shuffling.

10 Tap **Repeat**.

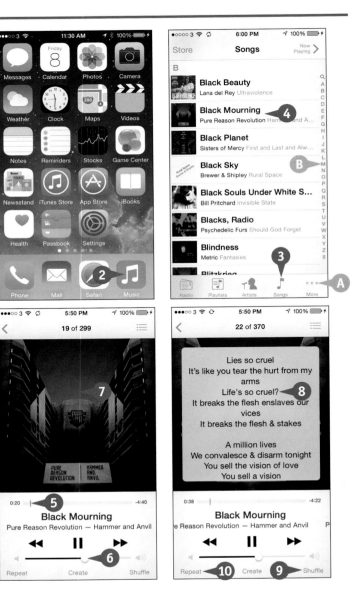

The Repeat dialog appears.

⑪ Tap **Repeat Song** to repeat just this song. Tap **Repeat All** to repeat all songs in the current list. Tap **Repeat Off** to turn off repeating.

⑫ Tap **Song List** (▤).

The list of songs in the current album appears.

⑬ Tap the song you want to play, or tap **Done** to continue playing the current song.

⑭ To navigate to another album visually, turn your iPhone to landscape orientation.

A screen of album covers appears.

⑮ Tap the album you want to play.

The list of songs on the album appears.

⑯ Tap the song you want to play.

The song starts playing.

Note: Only some songs include the text of their lyrics. You may need to add the text to other songs using iTunes or another app on your computer.

TIP

Is there a way to control the Music app's playback when I have switched to another app?
Yes. You can quickly control the Music app from Control Center. Swipe up from the bottom of the screen to display Control Center. You can then use the playhead to move through the song, control playback using the playback buttons, and tap and drag the volume slider to adjust the volume. When you finish using Control Center, drag down from the top to close it.

Play Videos Using the Videos App

To play videos — such as movies, TV shows, or music videos — you use the iPhone's Videos app. You can play a video either on the iPhone's screen, which is handy when you are traveling, or on a TV to which you connect the iPhone, or on a TV connected to an Apple TV box. Using a TV is great when you need to share a movie or other video with family, friends, or colleagues.

Play Videos Using the Videos App

1 Press the Home button.

The Home screen appears.

Note: You can also play videos included on web pages. To do so, press the Home button, tap **Safari**, navigate to the page, and then tap the video.

2 Tap **Videos**.

The Videos screen appears.

3 Tap the video you want to play.

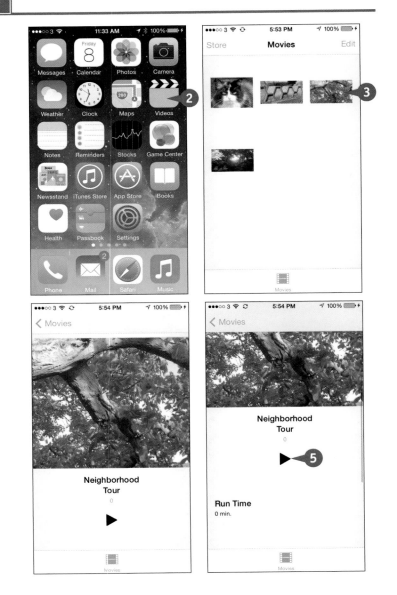

The information screen for the video appears, showing the video's preview frame and name.

4 Scroll down to see further details about the video.

Note: If you are about to play a landscape video, turn your iPhone sideways to view the video in landscape orientation.

5 Tap **Play** (▶).

The playback controls appear at first, but then disappear within a few seconds if you do not use them.

The video starts playing.

6 When you need to control playback, tap the screen.

The playback controls appear, and you can pause the video, move it forward, or take other actions.

7 Tap **Done** when you want to stop playing the video.

How do I play videos on my television from my iPhone?
If you have an Apple TV or AirPlay-compatible device, use AirPlay, as explained in the next section, "Play Music and Videos Using AirPlay." Otherwise, use the Apple Lightning Digital AV Adapter and an HDMI cable to connect your iPhone to a TV. The content of your iPhone's screen then appears on the TV's screen.

Play Music and Videos Using AirPlay

Using the AirPlay feature, you can play music from your iPhone on remote speakers connected to an AirPlay-compatible device such as an AirPort Express or Apple TV. Similarly, you can play video from your iPhone on a TV or monitor connected to an Apple TV. Even better, you can use the iOS feature called AirPlay Mirroring to display an iPhone app on a TV or monitor. For example, you can display a web page in Safari on your TV screen.

Play Music and Videos Using AirPlay

Play Music or Videos on External Speakers or an Apple TV

1 Press the Home button.

The Home screen appears.

2 Tap **Music**.

Note: This example shows the Music app, but the process is the same in the Videos app.

The Music app opens.

3 Tap the song you want to play.

The song's screen appears, and the song starts playing.

4 Tap and swipe up from the bottom of the screen.

Control Center opens.

5 Tap **AirPlay**.

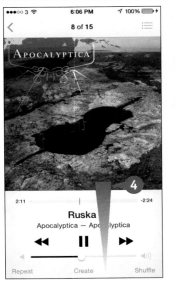

The AirPlay dialog opens.

6 Tap the speakers or Apple TV you want to use.

7 Tap **Done**.

The AirPlay dialog closes.

The AirPlay button shows the device you selected.

The music starts playing through the AirPlay device.

8 Tap in the Music app above Control Center.

Control Center closes, and the Music app appears full screen.

Display an iPhone App on Your TV's Screen

1 Open the app you want to use.

2 Tap and swipe up from the bottom of the screen to open Control Center.

3 Tap **AirPlay** (▣).

4 Tap the AirPlay device to use.

5 Set the **Mirroring** switch to On (▭).

Note: The Mirroring switch appears in the AirPlay dialog only when you have selected a device that supports AirPlay Mirroring, such as an Apple TV.

6 Tap **Done**.

The TV or monitor mirrors the iPhone's screen.

7 Tap in the app to close Control Center.

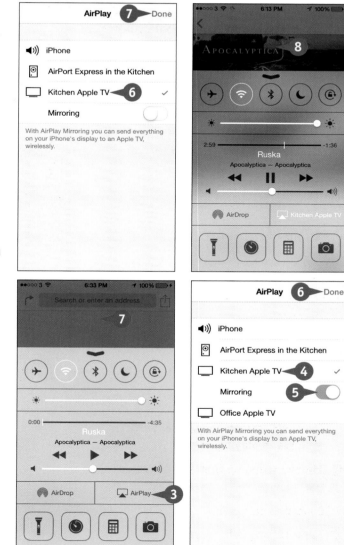

TIPS

Why does the AirPlay button not appear in Control Center?

The AirPlay button appears only when your iPhone is connected to a wireless network to which AirPlay devices are attached. If you use multiple wireless networks, make sure your iPhone is connected to the right network.

Can AirPlay play music through multiple sets of speakers at the same time?

AirPlay on the Mac or PC can play music through two or more sets of speakers at the same time, enabling you to play music throughout your home. But at this writing, AirPlay on the iPhone can play only to a single device at a time.

Create a Music Playlist

Instead of playing individual songs or playing a CD's songs from start to finish, you can create a playlist that contains only the songs you want in your preferred order. Playlists are a great way to enjoy music on your iPhone.

You can either create a standard playlist by putting the songs in order yourself, or use the Genius Playlist feature to have the Music app create the playlist for you.

Create a Music Playlist

① Press the Home button.

The Home screen appears.

② Tap **Music**.

The Music screen appears.

③ Tap **Playlists**.

The Playlists screen appears.

Ⓐ The Genius symbol (⊛) indicates a Genius playlist.

④ Tap **New Playlist**.

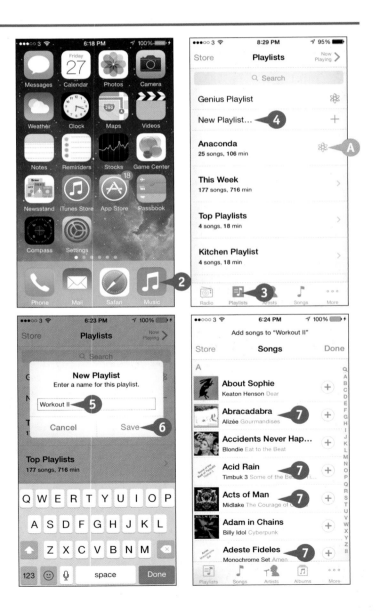

The New Playlist dialog opens.

⑤ Type the name for the playlist.

⑥ Tap **Save**.

The Songs screen appears.

⑦ Tap ⊞ for each song you want to add, or simply tap the song's button.

B The text on the song button fades to gray to show you have added the song to the playlist.

C To browse by artists for songs to add, tap **Artists**. To browse by playlists, tap **Playlists**. To browse by albums, tap **Albums**.

8 Tap **Done**.

The playlist screen appears.

9 Tap **Edit**.

The screen for editing the playlist appears.

10 Tap ▭ and drag a song up or down to move it.

D To remove a song, tap ⊖.

11 Tap **Done** at the top of the playlist editing screen.

12 Tap a song to start the playlist playing.

E Tap **Shuffle** (⋈) if you want to play the playlist's songs in random order.

How do I create a Genius playlist on my iPhone?

Press the Home button. Tap **Music**, tap **Playlists**, and then tap **Genius Playlist**. Tap the song to base the playlist on. The Music app creates the playlist and starts playing it.

Customize the Music App's Interface

The Music app comes set up so that you can easily browse by playlists, artists, songs, or albums. If you want to browse by other categories, such as by composers or by genres, you can customize the Music app's interface to put these items at the tip of your finger.

Customize the Music App's Interface

1 Press the Home button.

The Home screen appears.

2 Tap **Music**.

The Music screen appears.

3 Tap **More**.

The More screen appears.

4 Tap **Edit**.

The Configure screen appears.

5 Tap a button and drag it to replace a button on the button bar. For example, tap **Genres** and drag it on top of **Albums**.

The button you dropped replaces the button you dropped it on.

6 Change other buttons as needed.

Note: You can change the position of the buttons on the button bar by tapping a button and dragging it left or right to where you want it.

7 Tap **Done**.

A You can then use your customized version of the Music screen.

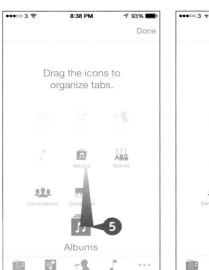

Listen to iTunes Radio

our iPhone's Music app includes iTunes Radio, a feature for listening to streaming radio across the Internet and setting up personalized stations that play the types of music you prefer. While listening to a song, you can choose to hear more songs like it, ask not to hear this song again, or create a custom station based on the artist or the song. When you find a song you must have, you can buy it from the iTunes Store. At this writing, iTunes Radio is available only in some countries because of the complexities of licensing music.

Listen to iTunes Radio

Open the Music App and Launch iTunes Radio

1 Press the Home button.

The Home screen appears.

2 Tap **Music**.

The Music app opens.

3 Tap **Radio**.

The Radio screen appears.

4 Tap a station you want to hear.

The station's screen appears.

The station starts playing.

Ⓐ Tap ❚❚ to pause playback.

Ⓑ Tap ▶▶ if you want to skip to the next song.

5 To control whether you hear music like the current song, tap ★.

The control dialog opens.

6 Tap the appropriate button:

Ⓒ Tap **Play More Like This** to indicate you like this type of music.

Ⓓ Tap **Never Play This Song** to register your dislike.

Ⓔ Tap **Add to iTunes Wish List** to add the song to your Wish List in iTunes.

The dialog closes.

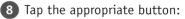 If you tapped **Play More Like This**, the star icon turns red (★ changes to ★).

If you tapped **Never Play This Song**, Radio starts playing the next song.

7 Tap ⓘ.

The information screen appears.

8 Tap the appropriate button:

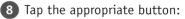 Tap the price button to display this song in the iTunes Store.

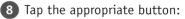 Tap **New Station from Artist** if you want to create a new station based on the artist.

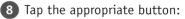 Tap **New Station from Song** to create a new station based on the song.

Add a Station to Your List

1 On the Radio home screen, tap **Edit** to the left of My Stations.

The My Stations screen appears.

2 Tap **New Station**.

The New Station screen appears.

3 Tap the type of music you want. For example, tap **Classic Alternative**.

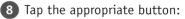 Alternatively, tap the search box and type an artist name, song name, or genre on which to base the station.

4 On the screen that appears, tap the station you want to add.

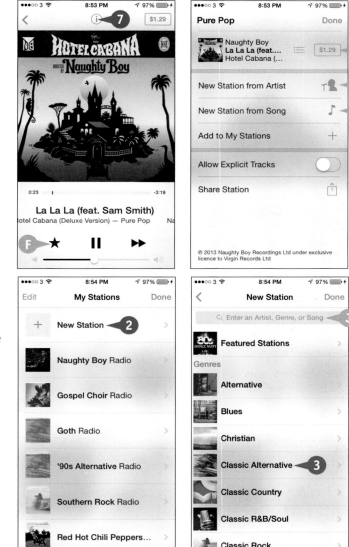

TIP

How do I remove a station I no longer want to listen to?

In the Music app, tap the **Radio** button, and then tap **Edit** to the left of My Stations. On the Edit Stations screen, tap the station you want to remove. At the bottom of the station's screen, tap **Delete Station**, then tap **Delete** in the confirmation dialog.

Choose Music Settings

To make the Music app work the way you prefer, you can enable shake-shuffling, turn on "normalization," and apply an equalization and volume control.

If you subscribe to iTunes Match, Apple's service for storing your music online so that you can play it back on all your devices, you can set up iTunes Match on your iPhone and stream your songs across the Internet instead of storing them on your iPhone. Turning on iTunes Match replaces any songs currently stored on your iPhone.

Choose Music Settings

1 Press the Home button.

The Home screen appears.

2 Tap **Settings**.

The Settings app opens.

3 Tap **Music**.

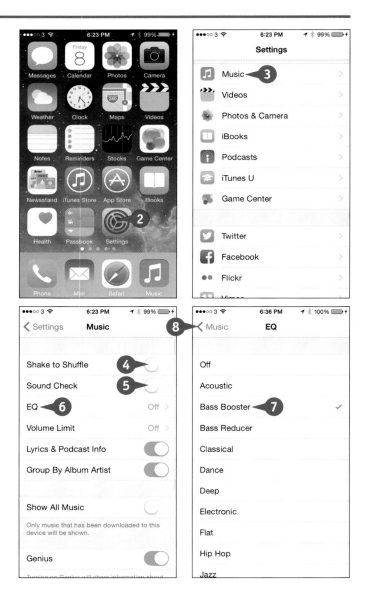

The Music screen appears.

4 Set the **Shake to Shuffle** switch to On () to be able to shuffle the current list by shaking your iPhone.

5 Set the **Sound Check** switch to On () to "normalize" the volume. See the Tip for details.

6 Tap **EQ**.

The EQ screen appears.

7 Tap the equalization you want to apply.

8 Tap **Music**.

242

The Music screen appears.

9 Tap **Volume Limit**.

The Volume Limit screen appears.

10 Drag the **Max Volume** slider to set the maximum volume.

Ⓐ In European markets, you can set the **EU Volume Limit** switch to On (☐) to implement the EU's volume limit.

11 Tap **Music**.

12 Set the **Lyrics & Podcast Info** switch to On (☐) to display song lyrics and podcast information.

13 Set the **Group By Album Artist** switch to On (☐) to group songs by the Album Artist tag rather than the Artist tag.

14 Set the **Show All Music** switch to On (☐) to show songs in iCloud as well as songs on your iPhone.

15 Set the **Genius** switch to On (☐) to use the Genius feature.

Ⓑ You can set the **iTunes Match** switch to On (☐) and then tap **Enable** to use iTunes Match.

TIP

Should I use the Sound Check feature?

This is up to you. Set the **Sound Check** switch to On (☐) if you want to "normalize" the volume, preventing songs recorded at a higher volume level from playing more loudly than songs recorded at a lower volume level. By reducing the variations in playback volume, Sound Check can help you avoid getting your ears blasted by a loud song that follows a quiet song for which you have turned up the volume. But Sound Check reduces the dynamic range of the music and gives audiophiles conniptions.

Watch Podcasts and iTunes U Lectures

Besides listening to music and watching videos, you can use your iPhone to watch or listen to *podcasts*, which are video or audio programs released via the Internet.

You can find podcasts covering many different topics by using Apple's Podcasts app. Similarly, you can use the iTunes U app to access podcasts containing free educational content. iTunes U also acts as a portal to other types of content, including paid material.

Watch Podcasts and iTunes U Lectures

① Press the Home button.

The Home screen appears.

② Tap **Podcasts**.

Note: If the Podcasts app does not appear on the Home screen, go to the App Store and install it. See Chapter 7 for instructions on installing apps.

The Podcasts app opens.

Note: At first, when you have added no podcasts, you see an informational message.

③ Tap **Featured** or **Top Charts**. This example uses **Featured**.

The Podcasts app displays the Featured screen in the iTunes Store.

④ Tap **Categories**.

The Categories screen appears.

⑤ Tap the category you want to browse.

The screen for the category appears.

6 Tap **All**, **Audio**, or **Video**, depending on the podcast type you want.

Ⓐ You can also search for podcasts by tapping **Search** and then typing search terms in the search box.

7 Tap the podcast you want to view.

8 Tap **Subscribe** if you want to subscribe to the podcast.

9 Tap ⬇ to download an episode of the podcast.

10 Tap **My Podcasts** to display your podcasts.

11 Tap the podcast whose episodes you want to see.

12 Tap the episode you want to play.

The episode starts playing.

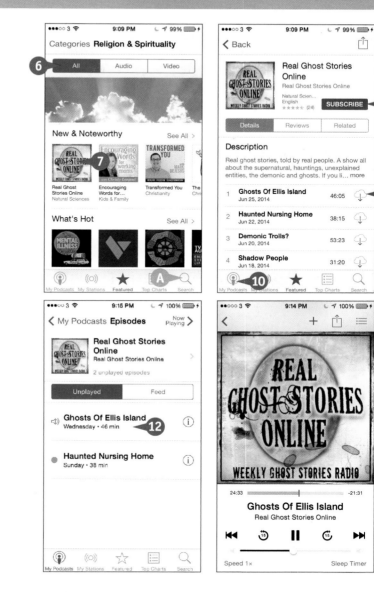

How do I use iTunes U?

iTunes U works in a similar way to the Podcasts app. Press the Home button, and then tap **iTunes U** to launch the app. Tap **Featured**, **Charts**, **Browse**, or **Search** to display the associated screen, and then use it to find a lecture that interests you. After that, tap **Library** to display the Library screen, and then tap the item you want to play.

CHAPTER 11

Working with Photos and Books

In this chapter, you learn to use the Photos app to view and share photos. You also learn to use iBooks to read e-books and PDF files.

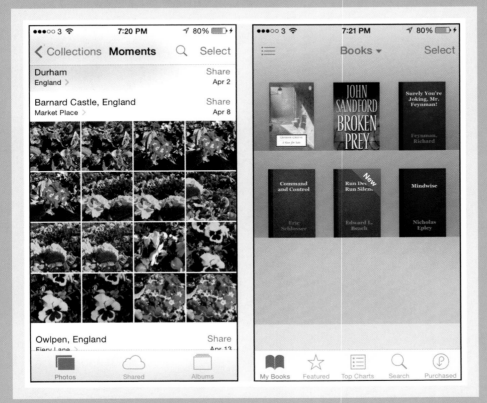

Browse Photos Using Years, Collections, and Moments

Y ou can use the Photos app to browse the photos you have taken with your iPhone's camera, photos you have synced using iTunes or via iCloud's Shared Streams feature, and images you receive in e-mail messages or download from web pages.

You can browse your photos by date and locations using the smart groupings that Photos creates. Each Year grouping contains Collections, which contain Moments, which contain your photos. Alternatively, you can browse by albums, as explained in the next section, "Browse Photos Using Streams."

Browse Photos Using Years, Collections, and Moments

① Press the Home button.

The Home screen appears.

② Tap **Photos**.

The Photos app opens.

③ Tap **Photos**.

The Photos screen appears, showing the Years list.

④ Tap the year you want to open.

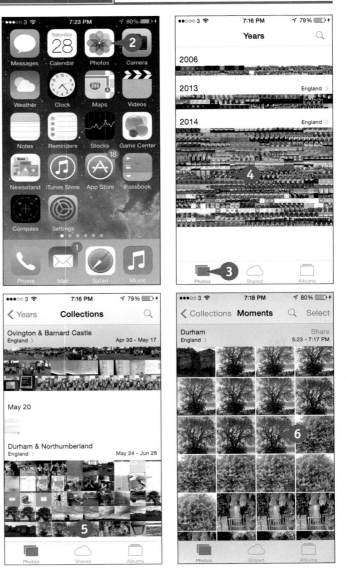

The Collections screen for the year appears.

⑤ Tap the collection you want to open.

Note: Scroll up or down as needed to see other collections.

The Moments screen for the collection appears.

⑥ Tap the photo you want to view.

The photo opens.

 You can tap **Edit** to edit the photo, as explained in Chapter 13.

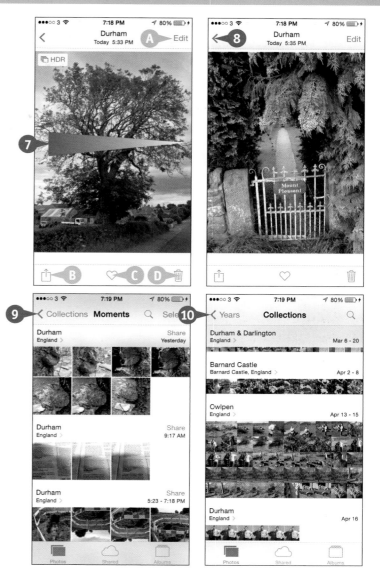

 You can tap **Share** (⬆️) to share the photo, as explained later in this chapter.

Ⓒ You can tap **Favorite** (♡ changes to ❤️) to make the photo a favorite.

Ⓓ You can tap **Trash** (🗑️) to delete the photo.

Note: The Trash icon does not appear for photos you cannot delete, such as photos in a shared photo stream.

7 Tap and swipe left or right to display other photos in the moment.

Another photo appears.

8 Tap 〈.

The Moments screen appears.

Note: You can scroll up or down to display other moments.

9 Tap **Collections**.

The Collections screen appears.

Note: You can scroll up or down to display other collections.

10 Tap **Years**.

The Years screen appears, and you can navigate to another year.

TIP

How can I move a photo to a different year?

To move a photo to a different year, you need to change the date set in the photo's metadata. You cannot do this with the Photos app, but you can change the date with a third-party app such as Pixelgarde, which is free from the App Store at this writing. Alternatively, if you sync the photos from your computer, you can change the date in the photo on your computer. For example, in iPhoto on OS X, click **Photos** and **Adjust Date and Time**.

Browse Photos Using Streams

Your iPhone's Photos app includes a feature called Shared Streams that enables you to share photos easily with others via iCloud and enjoy the photos they are sharing. In this section, you learn how to add other people's shared streams to the Photos app on your iPhone by accepting invitations. You also learn how to browse through the photos they are sharing.

Later in this chapter, you learn to share your own photos via Shared Streams.

Browse Photos Using Streams

Accept an Invitation to a Shared Stream

1. When you receive an invitation to a photo stream, open the e-mail message in Mail.

2. Tap **Subscribe to this Photo Stream**.

   The Photos app becomes active, and the Shared Streams screen appears.

   The new stream appears on the Shared Streams screen.

Note: The Activity item at the top of the Shared Streams screen shows new activity on your shared streams. When you add a shared stream, the Activity thumbnail shows the new stream's thumbnail.

3. Tap the new stream.

   The new stream's screen appears.

4. Tap a photo.

   The photo opens.

   Ⓐ You can tap **Add a comment** to add a comment on the photo.

   Ⓑ You can tap **Share** (□) to share the photo with others.

   Ⓒ You can swipe left or right to display other photos.

5. Tap ◁.

   The Shared Streams screen appears.

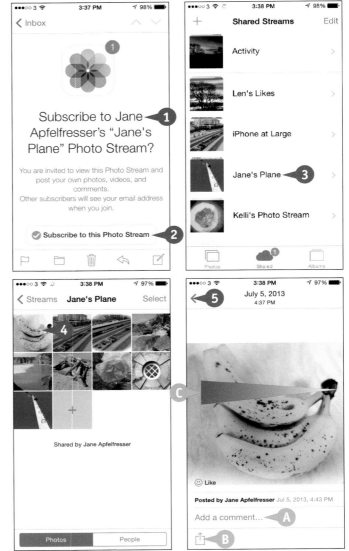

Browse the Latest Activity on Shared Streams

1 In the Photos app, tap **Shared**.

The Shared Streams screen appears.

2 Tap **Activity**.

The Activity screen appears.

3 Tap a photo.

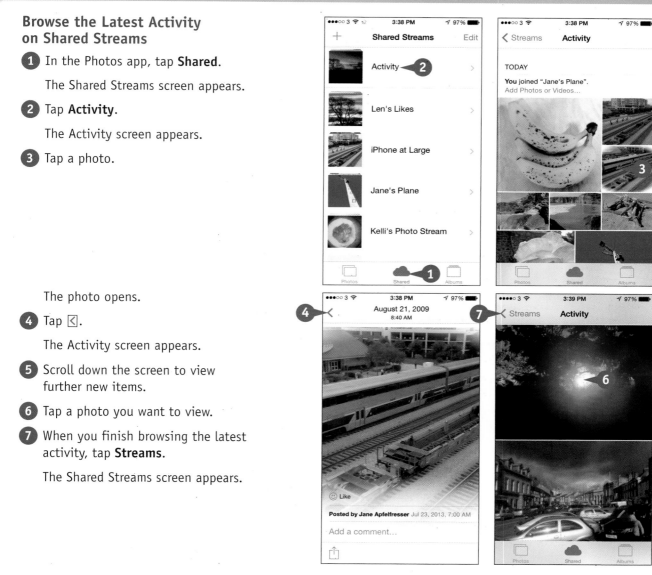

The photo opens.

4 Tap ◁.

The Activity screen appears.

5 Scroll down the screen to view further new items.

6 Tap a photo you want to view.

7 When you finish browsing the latest activity, tap **Streams**.

The Shared Streams screen appears.

How do I remove a shared stream?

In the Photos app, tap **Shared** to display the Shared Streams screen. Tap **Edit** to turn on Editing mode, and then tap ⊖ to the left of the stream you want to remove. Tap the **Delete** button that then appears. Tap **Done** to turn off Editing mode.

Browse Photos Using Albums

A long with browsing by collections and browsing shared photo streams, you can browse your photos by albums. Your iPhone's Camera app automatically maintains several albums, storing each conventional photo you take in an album called Camera Roll, each burst photo in an album called Bursts, and each video in an album called Videos. You can also create other albums manually from your photos or sync existing albums from your computer. If you sync your iPhone with iPhoto on the Mac, you can sync an album called Faces that contains known faces that iPhoto has recognized in your photos.

Browse Photos Using Albums

Open the Photos App and Browse an Album

1 Press the Home button.

The Home screen appears.

2 Tap **Photos**.

The Photos app opens.

3 Tap **Albums**.

The Albums screen appears.

4 Tap the album you want to browse. This example uses an album named Transfer.

The album appears.

Note: The Recently Added album is the album in which the Camera app places the photos you take; photos you save from web pages, e-mail messages, instant messages, and social media apps; and photos you edit from other people's streams.

5 Tap the photo you want to view.

The photo opens.

Note: Swipe left to display the next photo or right to display the previous photo.

6 Tap ◁.

The album appears.

7 Tap **Albums**.

The Albums screen appears.

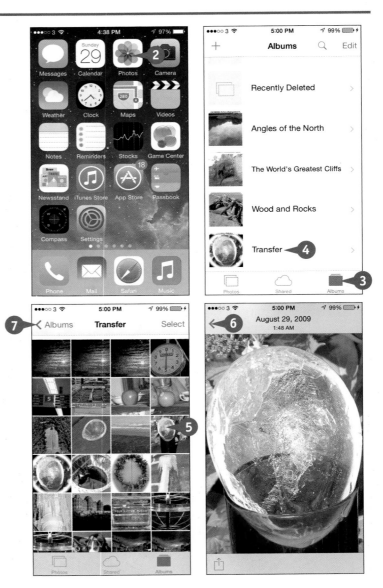

Create an Album

1 In the Photos app, tap **Albums**.

The Albums screen appears.

2 Tap **New** (⊞).

The New Album dialog opens.

3 Type the name to give the album.

4 Tap **Save**.

The Add Photos screen appears.

5 Tap the source of the photos. For example, tap **Photos**, tap the year, tap the collection, and then tap the moment.

6 Tap each photo to add to the collection, placing ⊘ on each.

7 Tap **Done**.

Ⓐ The album appears on the Albums screen.

TIPS

How can I move through a long list of photos more quickly?
You can move through the photos more quickly by using momentum scrolling. Tap and flick up with your finger to set the photos scrolling. As the momentum drops, you can tap and flick up again to scroll further. Tap and drag your finger in the opposite direction to stop the scrolling.

How can I recover photos I deleted by mistake?
Tap **Albums**, and then tap **Recently Deleted**. In the Recently Deleted album, tap **Select**, tap the photos, and then tap **Recover**.

Share Photos Using My Photo Stream

I f you have an iCloud account, you can use the My Photo Stream feature to share your photos among your iOS devices and your computer.

After you turn on My Photo Stream on your iPhone, other iOS devices, and your Macs or PCs, Photo Stream automatically syncs your 1,000 most recent photos among the devices and your computers.

Share Photos Using My Photo Stream

Turn On My Photo Stream on Your iPhone

1 Press the Home button.

The Home screen appears.

2 Tap **Settings**.

The Settings screen appears.

3 Tap **iCloud**.

The iCloud screen appears.

4 Tap **Photos**.

The Photos screen appears.

Ⓐ You can set the **iCloud Photo Library** switch to On (⬜) to store all your library in iCloud.

5 Set the **My Photo Stream** switch to On (⬜).

Ⓑ You can set the **Upload Burst Photos** switch to On (⬜) to upload bursts of photos to iCloud.

6 If you want to share photo streams with others, set the **Photo Sharing** switch to On (⬜). See the next section, "Share Photo Streams with Other People," for more.

7 Tap ◁.

The iCloud screen appears.

Use Photo Stream on Your Mac

1 Click and **System Preferences**.

The System Preferences window opens.

2 Click **iCloud**.

The iCloud pane appears.

3 Click **Photos** (☐ changes to ☑).

4 Click **Options**.

The iCloud Photo Options dialog opens.

5 Click **My Photo Stream** (☐ changes to ☑).

6 If you want to share photo streams with others, click **Photo Sharing** (☐ changes to ☑).

7 Click **Done**.

8 Click **System Preferences** and **Quit System Preferences**.

9 Click **iPhoto** (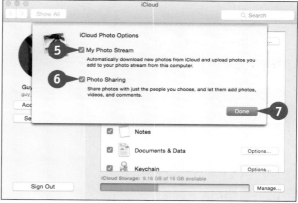) on the Dock.

10 In iPhoto, click **iCloud**.

The iCloud screen appears, showing your streams and your family and friends' streams.

How do I use Photo Stream in Windows?

In Windows 8, display the Start screen and click **iCloud Photos** in the Apps section of the Apps list. In earlier versions of Windows, click **Start** to open the Start menu, and then locate and click the **iCloud Photos** item on it.

In the iCloud Photos window, click **Open iCloud Control Panel**. Click **Photos** (☐ changes to ☑). Click **Options** to display the Photos Options dialog box. Click **My Photo Stream** (☐ changes to ☑) and **Photo Sharing** (☐ changes to ☑). Click **Change** and select the folder. Click **OK** and then click **Apply**.

Share Photo Streams with Other People

After turning on the Photo Sharing feature on the iCloud screen in the Settings app, you can create shared photo streams, invite people to subscribe to them, and add photos. See the previous section, "Share Photos Using My Photo Stream," to turn on the Photo Sharing feature.

You can also control whether subscribers can post photos and videos to your shared photo stream, decide whether to make the stream publicly available on the iCloud.com website, and choose whether to receive notifications when subscribers comment on your photos or post their own.

Share Photo Streams with Other People

1 Press the Home button.

The Home screen appears.

2 Tap **Photos**.

The Photos app opens.

3 Tap **Shared**.

The Shared Streams screen appears.

4 Tap **New Shared Stream** (⊞).

The New Stream dialog opens.

5 Type the name for the stream.

6 Tap **Next**.

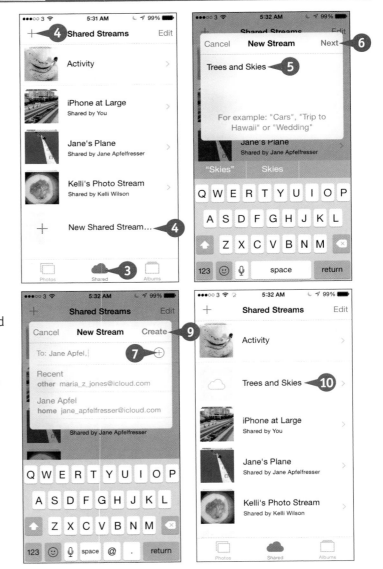

Another New Stream dialog opens.

7 Tap ⊕ to display the Contacts screen, and then tap the contact to add.

8 Repeat Step 7 to add other contacts as needed. You can also type contact names.

9 Tap **Create**.

The Shared Streams screen appears.

10 Tap the new stream.

The stream's screen appears.

11 Tap ⊞.

The Moments screen appears, with the selection controls displayed.

12 Tap each photo you want to add.

13 Tap **Done**.

The iCloud dialog opens.

14 Type the text you want to post with the photos.

15 Tap **Post**.

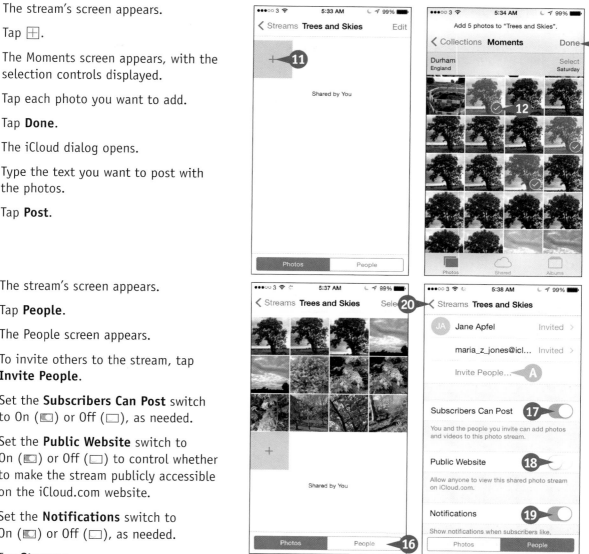

The stream's screen appears.

16 Tap **People**.

The People screen appears.

Ⓐ To invite others to the stream, tap **Invite People**.

17 Set the **Subscribers Can Post** switch to On (▣) or Off (▢), as needed.

18 Set the **Public Website** switch to On (▣) or Off (▢) to control whether to make the stream publicly accessible on the iCloud.com website.

19 Set the **Notifications** switch to On (▣) or Off (▢), as needed.

20 Tap **Streams**.

The Streams screen appears.

TIP

If I make a photo stream public, how do people find the website?
When you set the **Public Website** switch on the People screen for a photo stream to On (▣), a Share Link button appears. Tap **Share Link** to display the Share sheet, and then tap the means of sharing you want to use — for example, Message, Mail, Twitter, or Facebook.

Share Photos via E-Mail and Instant Messaging

rom your iPhone's Photos app, you can quickly share a photo either by sending it as an attachment to an e-mail message or by inserting it in an instant message.

When you send a photo via e-mail, your iPhone prompts you to choose whether to send the photo at its actual size or at a smaller size.

Share Photos via E-Mail and Instant Messaging

Select the Photo and Display the Share Screen

1 Press the Home button.

The Home screen appears.

2 Tap **Photos**.

The Photos app opens.

3 Navigate to the photo you want to share. For example, tap **Years**, tap the appropriate collection, and then tap the moment that contains the photo.

4 Tap the photo to open it.

5 Tap **Share** ().

The Share screen appears.

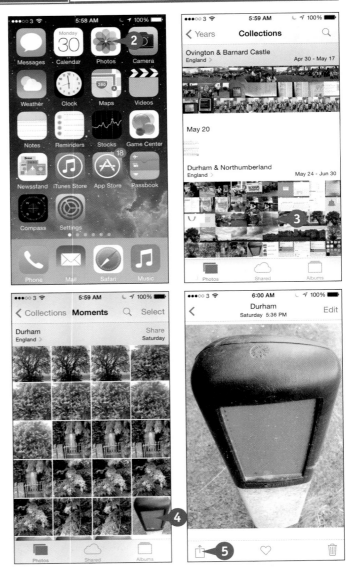

Share the Photo via Instant Messaging

Ⓐ If you want to send another photo at the same time, tap it (☐ changes to ✅).

① On the Share screen, tap **Message**.

② Tap in the To field and address the message.

③ Tap in the body area, and then type any text needed.

④ Tap **Send**.

The Messages app sends the message.

Share the Photo via E-Mail

① On the Share screen, tap **Mail**.

② Tap in the To field and address the e-mail message.

③ Tap in the Subject line and type the subject for the e-mail message.

④ Tap in the body area, and then type any text needed.

⑤ Tap **Send**.

⑥ If the Photos Size dialog opens, tap the button for the size of photo you want to send.

Mail sends the message.

What is the best size for sending photos via e-mail?
This depends on what the recipient will do with the photo. If the recipient needs to edit or print the photo, choose **Actual Size**. If the recipient will merely view the photo on-screen, choose **Large** or **Medium**. The **Small** size works for contact card images, but its picture quality is too low for most other uses.

Play Slide Shows of Photos

Your iPhone can not only display your photos but also play them as a slide show. The slide show feature is limited to using existing groups of photos — you cannot create a slide show group on the iPhone — but you can shuffle the photos into a different order. You can also choose to repeat the slide show or run the photos in random order. Then, when you start the slide show, you can choose which transition to use and add music. To make the most of your slide shows, you can choose the slide timing in the Photos screen in Settings.

Play Slide Shows of Photos

1 Press the Home button.

The Home screen appears.

Note: To play your photos on a bigger screen, either use AirPlay to play a TV connected to an Apple TV or use the Apple Lightning Digital AV Adapter and an HDMI cable to connect your iPhone to a TV or monitor with an HDMI input.

2 Tap **Photos**.

The Photos screen appears.

3 Navigate to the photo with which you want to start the slide show. For example, tap **Photos**, tap the appropriate year, tap the appropriate collection, and then tap the moment that contains the photo.

The moment or other photo collection opens.

4 Tap the photo you want to use at the beginning of the slide show.

The photo opens.

5 Tap **Share** (📤).

260

The Share screen appears.

6 Tap **Slideshow**.

The Slideshow Options screen appears.

7 If you have a choice of output devices, such as an Apple TV instead of your iPhone, tap the one you want to use.

8 Tap **Transitions**.

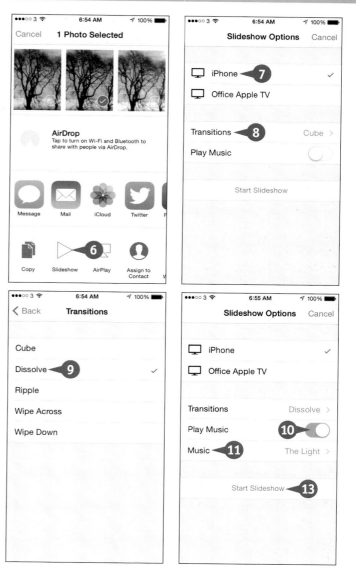

The Transitions screen appears.

9 Tap the transition you want.

The Slideshow Options screen appears.

10 If you want to play music during the slide show, set the **Play Music** switch to On (⬜).

The Music button appears.

11 Tap **Music**.

The Music screen appears.

12 Tap the song, album, or playlist you want to play.

The Slideshow Options screen appears.

13 Tap **Start Slideshow**.

The slide show starts.

How do I choose other settings for a slide show?

You can set timing, repeat, and shuffling in the Settings app. Press the Home button to display the Home screen, and then tap **Settings**. On the Settings screen, tap **Photos & Camera**. In the Slideshow area, tap **Play Each Slide For**, and then tap the length of time — for example, **10 Seconds**. Also on the Photos & Camera screen, set the **Repeat** switch and the **Shuffle** switch to On (⬜) or Off (☐), as needed.

Read Digital Books with iBooks

The iBooks app enables you to read e-books or PDF files that you load on the iPhone from your computer. You can also read e-books you download from online stores, download from web pages, or save from e-mail messages.

If you have already loaded some e-books, you can read them as described in this section. If iBooks contains no books, tap the **Store** button and browse the iBooks Store. Alternatively, see the next section, "Add PDF Files to iBooks and Read Them," for instructions on adding PDF files to iBooks.

Read Digital Books with iBooks

1 Press the Home button.

The Home screen appears.

2 Tap **iBooks**.

iBooks opens, and the Books screen appears.

Ⓐ If the Books button does not appear in the upper middle area of the iBooks screen, tap the button that appears there. On the Collections screen that appears, tap **Books** to display the Books screen.

3 If you want to view the books as a list, tap **List** () at the top of the screen.

Ⓑ You can search to locate the book you want.

The list of books appears.

4 Tap the book you want to open.

The book opens.

Note: When you open a book, iBooks displays your current page. When you open a book for the first time, iBooks displays the book's cover, first page, or default page.

Ⓒ To change the font, tap **Font Settings** (⒜) and work in the Font Settings dialog.

5 Tap anywhere on the screen to hide the reading controls.

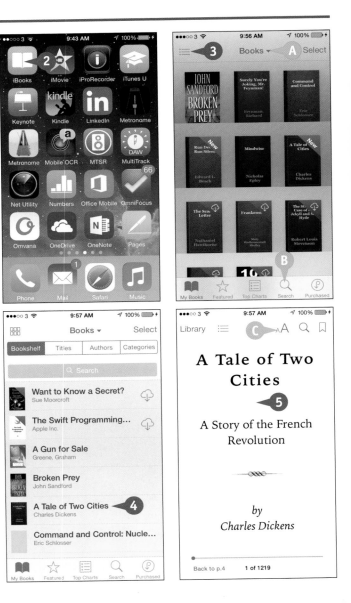

The reading controls disappear.

Note: To display the reading controls again, tap anywhere on the screen.

6 Tap the right side of the page to display the next page.

Note: To display the previous page, tap the left side of the page. Alternatively, tap the left side of the page and drag to the right.

7 To look at the next page without fully revealing it, tap the right side and drag to the left. You can then either drag further to turn the page or release the page and let it fall closed.

8 To jump to another part of the book, tap **Table of Contents** (▤).

Note: Alternatively, you can drag the slider at the bottom of the screen.

9 When the table of contents appears, tap the part of the book you want to display.

10 To search in the book, tap **Search** (🔍).

11 On the Search screen, type the search term.

12 Tap the match you want to display.

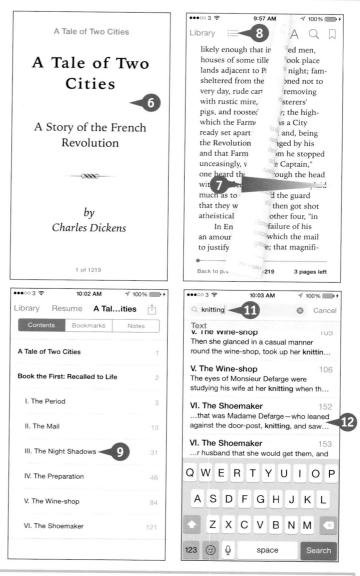

TIPS

How do I get my books from iBooks on my Mac onto my iPhone?

You need to set iBooks on your iPhone to sync your collections. Press the Home button, tap **Settings**, and then tap **iBooks**. Set the **Sync Collections** switch to On (⬜). To sync your bookmarks and notes, set the **Sync Bookmarks and Notes** switch to On (⬜) as well.

Where can I find free e-books to read in iBooks?

On the iBooks Store, look at the Free Books listing on the Top Charts screen or the Top Authors screen, or tap **Featured** and then tap **Free Books** in the Browse area. Other sources of free e-books include ManyBooks.net (www.manybooks.net), Project Gutenberg (www.gutenberg.org), and the Baen Free Library (www.baen.com/library).

Add PDF Files to iBooks and Read Them

These days, many books, reports, and other documents are available as Portable Document Format files, or PDF files. You can add your PDF files to iBooks on the Mac or load PDF files on your iPhone and read them using iBooks. This is a great way to take your required reading with you so that you can catch up on it anywhere.

Add PDF Files to iBooks and Read Them

Add PDFs to iBooks on Your Mac

1 On your Mac, click **iBooks** (▣) on the Dock.

Note: If iBooks (▣) does not appear on the Dock, click **Launchpad** (◉) on the Dock, and then click **iBooks** (▣) on the Launchpad screen.

The iBooks window opens.

2 Click **File**.

The File menu opens.

3 Click **Add to Library**.

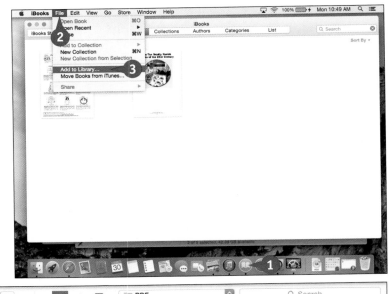

The Add To Library dialog opens.

4 Click the PDF file or select the PDF files you want to add.

5 Click **Add**.

iBooks adds the PDF file or files to your PDFs collection.

iBooks syncs the PDF files to your collection in iCloud.

Now, provided you have set the **Sync Collections** switch to On (▭) on the iBooks screen in the Settings app, iBooks on your iPhone syncs the PDFs from iCloud.

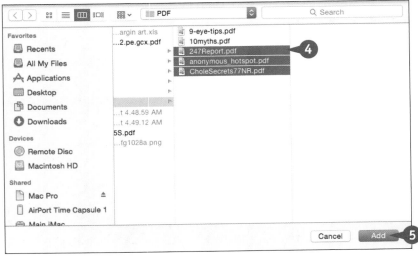

Read a PDF File Using iBooks

 Press the Home button.

The Home screen appears.

 Tap **iBooks**.

The Books screen appears.

 Tap **Books**.

The Collections screen appears.

 Tap **PDFs**.

The PDFs screen appears.

 Tap the PDF file you want to open.

The PDF file appears. You can then read the PDF file by scrolling up and down and zooming in and out as needed.

Note: If you open a PDF file while browsing the web in Safari, you can open the file in iBooks. To do so, tap the screen, and then tap **Open in iBooks** on the command bar that pops up.

TIP

How do I change the font size on the PDF file?
You cannot change the font size on the PDF file. This is because PDF is a graphical format — essentially a picture — instead of a text format. To make the PDF file more readable on the iPhone, rotate the iPhone to a landscape orientation, so that the screen is wider than it is tall. Then pinch outward to zoom the text to a larger size.

CHAPTER 12

Using the Built-In Apps

Your iPhone comes with apps that enable you to make the most of its features right out of the box. You can get your bearings with Compass, find your way and explore with Maps, track prices with Stocks, keep the time with Clock, or check the forecast with Weather.

Get Your Bearings with Compass

When you need to get your bearings, use the Compass app that comes installed on your iPhone. With Compass, you can establish your relationship to the points of the compass, learn your precise GPS location, and measure an angle between two points.

Compass includes a Level feature that you can use to level an object or surface precisely or to measure its current slant.

Get Your Bearings with Compass

Open Compass and Get Your Bearings

1 Press the Home button.

2 Tap **Compass**.

Note: If Compass does not appear on the Home screen, look in the Extras folder.

Note: If Compass displays a message prompting you to complete the circle to calibrate it, turn your iPhone this way and that until the circle is filled in. The compass then appears.

3 Point your iPhone in the direction whose bearing you want to take.

Ⓐ The readout shows the bearing.

Ⓑ You can tap the GPS location to switch to the Maps app and display the map for that location.

Measure an Angle

1 On the Compass screen, tap anywhere on the compass to fix the current bearing.

Ⓒ The bearing appears at the top of the compass.

2 Turn the iPhone toward the target point.

Ⓓ The red arc measures the difference between the two bearings.

Use the Level Feature

1 From the Compass screen, tap and drag left or swipe left.

E You can also tap the gray dot to switch to the Level screen.

The Level screen appears.

F The figure shows the angle of the object or surface.

2 Tilt your iPhone toward a level position to move the circles on top of each other.

3 If the black-and-white color scheme is hard to see, tap anywhere on the screen.

The background color changes to red.

Note: You can tap again to switch the background color back from red to black.

G When you align the circles, the screen goes green.

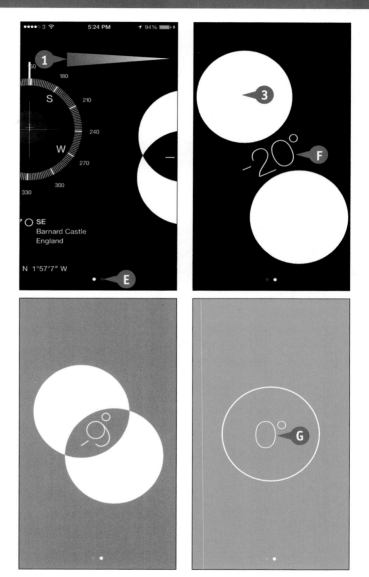

TIP

Does the Compass app use True North or Magnetic North?
The Compass app can show either True North or Magnetic North. To switch, press the Home button, and then tap **Settings**. In the Settings app, tap **Compass**, and then set the **Use True North** switch to On (⬜) or Off (⬜), as needed.

Find Your Location with Maps

Your iPhone's Maps app can pinpoint your location by using the Global Positioning System, known as GPS, or wireless networks. You can view your location on a road map, a satellite picture, or a hybrid that shows street and place names on the satellite picture. You can easily switch among map types to find the most useful one for your current needs. To help you get your bearings, the Tracking feature in the Maps app can show you which direction you are facing.

Find Your Location with Maps

1 Press the Home button.

The Home screen appears.

2 Tap **Maps**.

The Maps screen appears.

A A blue dot shows your current location. The expanding circle around the blue dot shows that Maps is determining your location.

Note: It may take a minute for Maps to work out your location accurately. While Maps determines the location, the blue dot moves, even though the iPhone remains stationary.

3 Tap and pinch in with two fingers.

Note: You can tap and pinch out with two fingers to zoom in.

The map zooms out, showing a larger area.

4 Tap .

The Maps dialog opens.

5 Tap **Satellite**.

The Satellite view appears.

6 Tap ⓘ.

The Maps dialog opens.

7 Tap **Hybrid**.

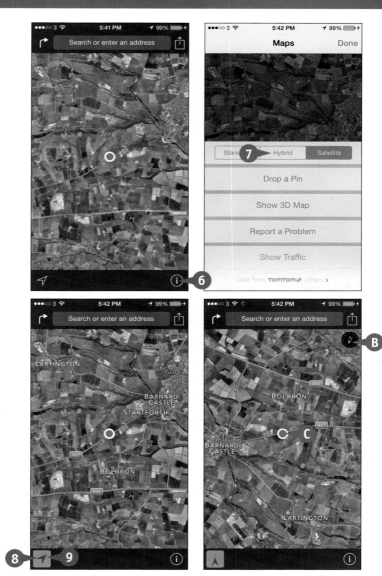

The satellite map appears with street and place names overlaid on it.

8 Tap **Location** (⟋ changes to ◂), turning on the Location service.

9 Tap **Location** (◂ changes to ▲).

Ⓑ The Compass icon appears (◉). The red arrow indicates north.

Ⓒ The map turns to show the direction the iPhone is facing, so that you can orient yourself.

TIP

How can I tell the scale of the map?

Place two fingers on the screen as if about to pinch outward or inward. Maps displays a scale in the upper-left part of the screen.

Find Directions with Maps

Your iPhone's Maps app can give you directions to where you want to go. Maps can also show you current traffic congestion in some locales to help you identify the most viable route for a journey.

Maps displays driving directions by default, but you can make it display public transit directions and walking directions.

Find Directions with Maps

1 Press the Home button.

The Home screen appears.

2 Tap **Maps**.

The Maps screen appears.

3 Tap ↱.

The Directions screen appears.

4 Tap **Start**.

The Current Location text changes to a blue button.

5 Tap ⊗ to delete the Current Location button.

Note: If you want the directions to start from your current location, leave Current Location in the Start field. Skip to Step **7**.

6 Type the start location for the directions.

Note: If the starting location or ending location is an address in the Contacts app, start typing the name, and then tap the match in the list.

7 Type the end location.

A Tap **Switch Places** (⇅) if you need to switch the start location and end location.

8 Tap **Route**.

B A screen showing the driving directions appears. The green pin marks the start, and the red pin marks the end.

C If multiple routes are available, tap a time button to view a different route. The time button changes to blue to indicate it is active.

9 Tap **Start**.

The first screen of directions appears.

10 Tap and scroll as needed to follow the directions.

11 If you want to see the full list of directions, tap **Overview**.

The overview screen appears.

12 Tap **List Steps**.

The Directions screen appears, showing a complete list of the directions.

D You can tap a direction to display it on the map.

13 Tap **Done** to return to the map.

14 Tap **Resume** to resume step-by-step navigation.

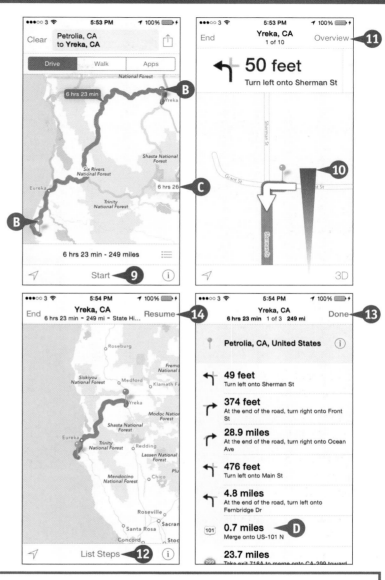

TIP

How do I get directions for walking or public transit?

Tap **Walk** to display the distance and time for a walking route. Be aware that walking directions may be inaccurate. Before walking the route, check that it does not send you across pedestrian-free bridges or through rail tunnels.

For public transit, you need to use a third-party app. Tap **Apps** to see a list of related apps. If an app is already installed on your iPhone, tap **Route** on the app's button to open that app and make Maps pass the start location and end location to the app. If an app is not installed, tap its button to go to the app's page on the App Store, where you can download the app.

Explore with 3D Flyover

Maps is not only great for finding out where you are and for getting directions to places, but it can also show you 3D flyovers of the places on the map. Flyovers can be a great way to explore a place virtually so that you can find your way around later in real life.

After switching on the 3D feature, you can zoom in and out, pan around, and move backward and forward.

Explore with 3D Flyover

1 Press the Home button.

The Home screen appears.

2 Tap **Maps**.

The Maps screen appears.

3 Display the area of interest in the middle of the screen. For example, tap and drag the map, or search for the location you want.

4 Tap ⓘ.

The Maps dialog opens.

5 Tap **Show 3D Map**.

The Maps dialog closes.

The screen switches to 3D view.

6 Pinch out with two fingers to zoom in.

Note: You can pinch in with two fingers to zoom out.

Note: Tap and drag to scroll the map as needed.

7 Place two fingers on the screen and twist clockwise or counterclockwise to rotate the view.

The rotated view appears.

A The Compass arrow () appears. You can tap it to restore the direction to north.

Note: Pan and zoom as needed to explore the area.

8 Tap and drag down with two fingers.

The viewing angle steepens until you reach a straight-down position.

9 Tap and drag up with two fingers.

The viewing angle becomes shallower.

10 Tap 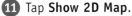.

The Maps dialog opens.

11 Tap **Show 2D Map**.

The standard view reappears.

TIP

What does 3D do with the Standard map?
When you tap **Show 3D Map** to switch on Flyover with the Standard map displayed, Maps tilts the map at an angle, as you might do with a paper map. In cities, building shapes appear when you zoom in on the map, enabling to see the layout without using the full detail of the satellite photos.

Using Maps' Favorites and Contacts

W hen you need to be able to return to a location easily in the Maps app, you can create a favorite for the location.

Similarly, you can add a location to your contacts, so that you can access it either from the Contacts app or from the Maps app. You can either create a new contact or add the location to an existing contact. You can also return quickly to locations you have visited recently but for which you have not created a favorite or contact.

Using Maps' Favorites and Contacts

1 Press the Home button.

The Home screen appears.

2 Tap **Maps**.

The Maps screen appears.

3 Find the place for which you want to create a favorite. For example, tap and drag the map, or search for the location you want.

4 Tap and hold the place you want to bookmark.

The Maps app drops a pin on the place.

Note: To get rid of a pin you have dropped, tap the pin to display its pop-up label, and then tap the label. On the Dropped Pin screen that appears, tap **Remove Pin**.

5 Tap ▷.

The Dropped Pin screen appears.

6 Tap ⬆.

The Share sheet opens.

7 Tap **Add to Favorites**.

The Add to Favorites screen appears.

8 Type the name for the favorite. Alternatively, you can accept the default name, if there is one.

9 Tap **Save**.

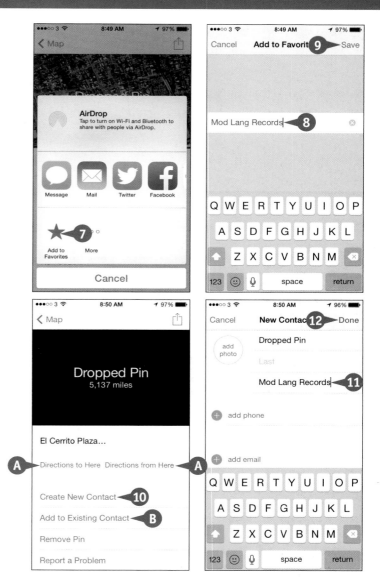

The Location screen appears again.

A You can quickly get directions to or from this location by tapping **Directions to Here** or **Directions from Here**.

10 Tap **Create New Contact**.

B You can tap **Add to Existing Contact** and then tap the contact to which you want to add the location instead.

11 Type the details for the contact.

12 Tap **Done**.

 TIP

How do I go to a location for which I have created a favorite or a contact?

1 In the Maps app, tap the Search box to display the Search screen.

2 Tap **Favorites** to display the Favorites screen.

3 To go to a favorite, tap the favorite in the list. To go to a contact, tap **Contacts** at the bottom of the screen, and then tap the contact. You can also go back to a recent location by tapping **Recents** and then tapping the location.

Track Stock Prices with the Stocks App

I f you own or follow stocks, you can use the iPhone's Stocks app to track stock prices so that you can take immediate action as needed.

The Stocks app displays a default selection of stock information at first, including the Dow Jones Industrial Average, the NASDAQ Composite, the Standard & Poor's 500, and Apple, Google, and Yahoo! stocks. You can customize the Stocks app to display only those stocks that interest you.

Track Stock Prices with the Stocks App

Open the Stocks App

1 Press the Home button.

The Home screen appears.

2 Tap **Stocks**.

The Stocks screen appears, showing a default selection of stocks.

Choose the Stocks You Want to Track

1 Tap **Info** (▤).

The Stocks configuration screen appears.

2 Tap **Add** (⊞).

The Search screen appears.

3 Type the company's name or stock ID.

4 Either tap **Search** or simply wait for the Stocks app to search.

A list of matching company names and stock symbols appears.

5 Tap the item you want to add.

The stock listing appears.

6 To remove a stock listing, tap , and then tap **Delete**.

The stock listing disappears.

7 To change the order, tap ≡ and drag up or down.

8 Tap **percentage**, **price**, or **market cap** to control which statistic the Stocks app displays first.

9 Tap **Done**.

View Information for a Stock

1 On the Stocks screen, tap the stock for which you want to see information at the bottom of the screen.

2 Tap the first dot to see the summary information, the second dot to see the stock chart, or the third dot to see stock-related headlines.

Note: You can also scroll the lower part of the screen to switch among the summary information, the stock chart, and the headlines.

3 Tap to switch among percentage changes, price changes, and market capitalization.

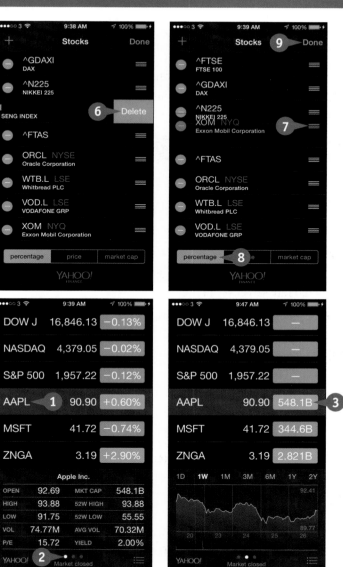

Using the Clock App

T he Clock app on your iPhone provides four helpful time-keeping features. The World Clock feature enables you to keep track of the time easily in different cities. The Alarm feature lets you set as many alarms as you need, each with a different schedule and your choice of sound. The Stopwatch feature allows you to time events to the hundredth of a second. And the Timer feature enables you to count down a set amount of time and play a sound when the timer ends.

Open the Clock App

To open the Clock app, press the Home button and then tap **Clock** on the Home screen. The app displays the screen for the feature you last used. You can switch among the four features by tapping **World Clock**, **Alarm**, **Stopwatch**, or **Timer** at the bottom of the screen.

The World Clock shows a dark face for a clock where the local time is between 6:00PM and 5:59AM and a white face for a clock where the local time is between 6:00AM and 5:59PM.

Set Up the World Clock with Multiple Locations

Tap **World Clock** at the bottom of the screen to display the World Clock screen.

To add cities, tap  and then either type the start of the city name or simply browse the list. Tap the city you want to add, and it appears at the bottom of the list on the World Clock screen.

You can edit the list of cities by tapping **Edit** on the World Clock screen. To remove a city, tap ⊖, and then tap **Delete**. To change the order, tap ☰ and drag up or down. Tap **Done** when you finish editing. You can turn the iPhone 6 to landscape orientation to display a world map that shows all your world clocks at once.

Set Alarms

Tap **Alarm** at the bottom of the screen to display the Alarm screen, which shows the current alarms with switches for enabling and disabling them.

Tap ⊞ to start creating a new alarm. On the Add Alarm screen, spin the dials to set the time. To create a repeating alarm, tap **Repeat** and then tap the days on the Repeat screen. Tap **Back** to return to the Add Alarm screen, and then tap **Label**, type a descriptive name for the alarm, and tap **Done**. Tap **Sound** and choose the sound to play, and set the **Snooze** switch to On (⬛) or Off (☐), as needed. Tap **Save** to save the alarm.

Time Events with the Stopwatch

Tap **Stopwatch** at the bottom of the screen to display the Stopwatch screen. You can then tap **Start** to start the stopwatch running.

If you need to mark lap times, tap **Lap** at the appropriate points. The elapsed lap times appear at the bottom of the screen. The current lap time appears above the right side of the main time readout.

Tap **Stop** to stop the stopwatch. You can then tap **Start** to restart the stopwatch or tap **Reset** to reset it ready for its next use.

Use the Timer

Tap **Timer** at the bottom of the screen to display the Timer screen. Spin the Hours dial and the Minutes dial to set the amount of time you want to count down. Tap **When Timer Ends** to display the When Timer Ends screen, tap the sound you want to play or the **Stop Playing** action, and then tap **Set**. You can then tap **Start** to start the timer.

If you need to interrupt the timer, tap **Cancel** or **Pause**. Otherwise, when the timer sound plays, tap the prompt to stop it. The Stop Playing action enables you to play music for a period of time and have it stop automatically — for example, to lull you to sleep.

Look Up Weather Forecasts

Along with much other useful information, your iPhone can put the weather forecasts in the palm of your hand. By using the Weather app, you can quickly learn the current conditions and forecast for as many cities as you need. The Weather app comes set to show the weather in Cupertino, the city where Apple's headquarters are located, but you can choose whatever cities you want. You can also make Weather show the weather for your current location. You can then move quickly from location to location as needed.

Look Up Weather Forecasts

1 Press the Home button.

The Home screen appears.

2 Tap **Weather**.

The Weather app opens and displays the weather for either your current location or for Cupertino.

Note: To get local weather, you must allow Weather to use Location Services. On the Home screen, tap **Settings**, tap **Privacy**, and then tap **Location Services**. On the Location Services screen, tap **Weather** and then tap **Always**.

3 Tap the hourly weather timeline and drag left to display later hours.

4 Tap .

The list of weather locations appears.

5 Tap ⊕.

The Search screen appears.

6 Start typing the city or location.

7 Tap **Search**.

8 Tap the appropriate result in the list.

The city appears on the list of weather locations.

Note: You can now add other cities as needed.

9 Tap and hold a location until it moves, and then drag it to where you want it in the list.

10 Tap the location you want to display.

Note: To delete a city, swipe it to the left, and then tap **Delete**.

The location's weather appears.

11 Swipe left or right.

A You can also tap a dot to the left or right of the current dot to display a different screen.

The next screen in that direction appears.

Note: To view the current weather quickly, open the notification panel. You can tap the weather summary to jump to the weather app.

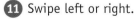

TIPS

How do I change from Centigrade to Fahrenheit?
Tap **Info** (🖼) to display the Weather screen, and then tap **°F** or **°C**, as needed.

What does the button called The Weather Channel in the Weather app do?
Tap the button called **The Weather Channel** to display the Weather.com page for the current city in Safari.

CHAPTER 13

Taking Photos and Videos

With your iPhone's Camera app, you can take high-quality still photos, apply filters to give photos different looks, and edit photos to improve them. You can also capture video and trim your clips down to length. You can easily share both the photos and the videos you take.

Take Photos with the Camera App

Your iPhone includes a high-resolution camera in the back for taking both still photos and videos, plus a lower-resolution camera in the front for taking photos and videos of yourself and for making video calls. To take photos using the camera, you use the Camera app. This app includes a digital zoom feature for zooming in and out; a flash that you can set to On, Off, or Auto; and a High Dynamic Range (HDR) feature that combines several photos into a single photo with adjusted color balance and intensity.

Take Photos with the Camera App

Open the Camera App

1 Press the Home button.

The Home screen appears.

Note: From the lock screen, you can open the Camera app by tapping the **Camera** icon in the lower-right corner and dragging up.

2 Tap **Camera**.

The Camera app opens and displays whatever is in front of the lens.

Compose the Photo and Zoom If Necessary

1 Aim the iPhone so that your subject appears in the middle of the photo area. To focus on an item not in the center of the frame, tap that item to move the focus rectangle to it.

Note: If you need to take tightly composed photos, get a tripod mount for the iPhone. You can find various models on eBay and photography sites.

2 If you need to zoom in or out, place two fingers together on the screen and pinch outward.

The zoom slider appears.

3 Tap ▬ to zoom in or ✚ to zoom out. Tap as many times as needed.

 You can also zoom by tapping and dragging the zoom slider ().

Choose Whether and How to Use the Flash

1 Tap the **Flash** button.

The Flash settings appear.

2 Tap **On** to use the flash, **Auto** to use the flash if there is not enough light without it, or **Off** to turn the flash off.

3 Tap the **HDR** button.

The HDR settings appear.

4 Tap **Auto**, **On**, or **Off**, as needed.

B The HDR readout appears.

Take the Photo and View It

1 Tap **Take Photo** (⬜).

Note: You can tap and hold **Take Photo** (⬜) to take a burst of photos.

The Camera app takes the photo and displays a thumbnail.

2 Tap the thumbnail.

The photo appears.

C From the photo screen, you can navigate as discussed in Chapter 11. For example, swipe your finger to the left to display the next photo, or swipe to the right to display the previous photo. Tap 🗑 to delete the photo.

3 Tap **Done** when you want to go back to the Camera app.

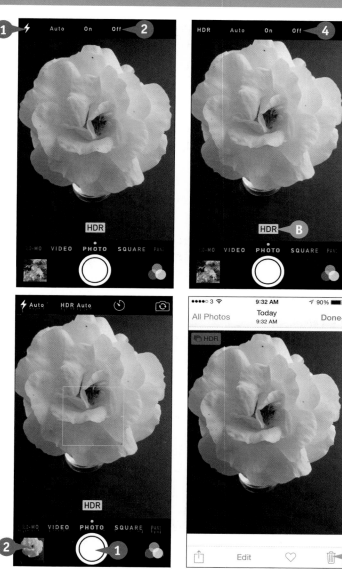

TIP

How do I switch to the front-facing camera?

Tap **Switch Cameras** (📷) to switch from the rear-facing camera to the front-facing camera. The image that the front-facing camera is seeing appears on-screen, and you can take pictures as described in this section. HDR is available for the front-facing camera, but flash is not. Tap **Switch Cameras** (📷) again when you want to switch back to the rear-facing camera.

Take Square and Panorama Photos

The Camera app includes a self-timer feature that enables you to set the app to take a photo 3 seconds or 10 seconds after you tap the Take Photo button. By using the self-timer, you can include yourself in group shots or simply minimize camera shake when taking photos of still subjects.

The Camera app also includes a feature for capturing square photos, a panorama mode for capturing landscapes, and a time-lapse feature for taking time-lapse movies.

Take Square and Panorama Photos

Open the Camera App and Take a Timed Photo

1 Press the Home button.

The Home screen appears.

2 Tap **Camera**.

The Camera app opens.

3 Tap **Timer** (🕐).

The Timer settings appear.

4 Tap **3s** or **10s** to set the delay.

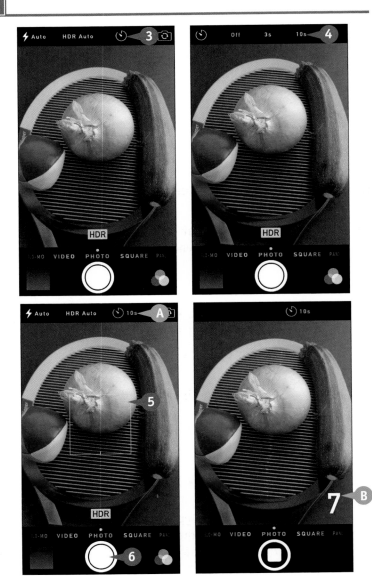

Ⓐ The delay appears next to the Timer icon.

5 Compose the photo.

6 Tap **Take Photo** (⬜).

Ⓑ The Camera app displays an on-screen countdown.

When the countdown ends, the app takes the photo.

Note: The timer remains set until you change it.

Take a Square Photo

1 Tap **Square**.

Note: Square photos are useful for adding to contact records and similar needs.

Camera reduces the frame to a square.

2 Tap **Take Photo** (○).

Camera takes a photo.

Take a Panorama Photo

1 Slide the **Type** slider to the left and tap **Pano**.

2 Holding the iPhone in portrait orientation, aim at the left end of the panorama.

3 Tap **Take Photo** (○).

4 Turn the iPhone to the right, keeping the white arrow on the horizontal line.

ⓒ The Camera app may prompt you to slow down.

5 Tap **Stop** (○) to stop shooting.

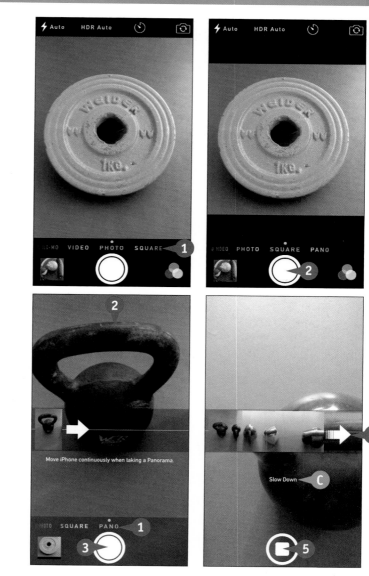

TIP

How do I take time-lapse movies?
In the Camera app, move the **Type** slider to the right and tap **Time-Lapse**. Set the iPhone up on a tripod or other steady holder, aim it at the subject, and then tap ○. When you have captured enough, tap ○ to stop shooting. You can then tap the thumbnail to view the time-lapse movie.

Apply Filters to Your Photos

You can use the Filter feature in the Camera app to change the look of a photo by applying a filter such as Mono, Tonal, Chrome, Transfer, or Instant.

You can apply a filter either before taking the photo or after taking it. If you apply the filter before taking the photo, you can remove the filter afterward; the filter is an effect applied to the photo, not an integral part of the photo.

Apply Filters to Your Photos

1 Press the Home button.

   The Home screen appears.

2 Tap **Camera**.

   The Camera app opens.

3 Tap **Filters** (⬤).

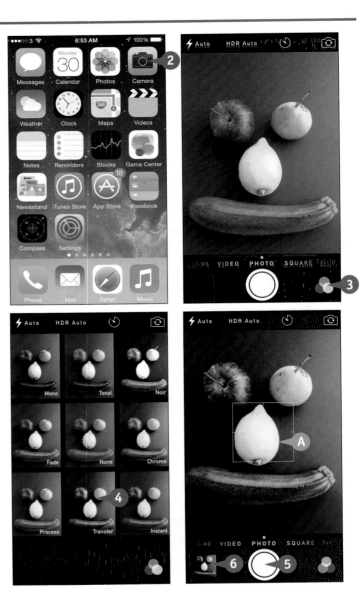

   The Filters screen appears.

4 Tap the filter you want to apply.

Ⓐ Camera applies the filter to the screen.

5 Tap **Take Photo** (⬤).

6 Tap the photo's thumbnail.

The photo appears.

7 Tap **Edit**.

The Edit Photo screen appears, showing the editing tools.

8 Tap **Filters** ().

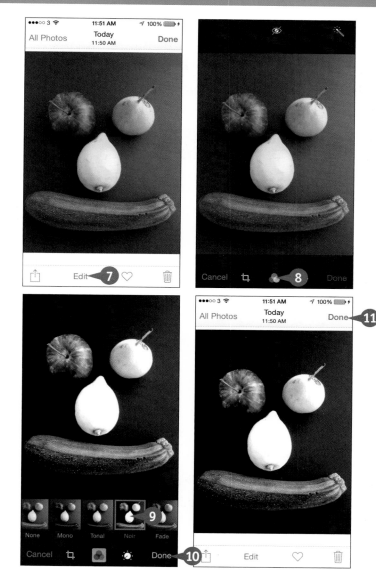

The Choose Filter screen appears.

9 Tap the filter you want to apply. Scroll left or right to display other filters.

Note: Tap **None** if you want to remove filtering.

The Edit Photo screen appears, showing the photo with the filter applied.

10 Tap **Done**.

iOS saves the change to the photo.

11 Tap **Done** to return to the Camera app.

TIP

Is it better to apply a filter before taking a photo or after taking it?
This is up to you. Sometimes it is helpful to have the filter effect in place when composing a photo so that you can arrange the composition and lighting to complement the filtering. Other times, especially when you do not have time to experiment with filters, it is more practical to take the photos and then try applying filters afterward.

Edit Your Photos

To improve your photos, you can use the powerful but easy-to-use editing tools your iPhone includes. These tools include rotating a photo to a different orientation, straightening it by rotating it a little, and cropping off the parts you do not need.

You can access the editing tools either through the Recently Added album in the Photos app or through the Photos app. To start editing a photo, you open the photo by tapping it, and then tap **Edit**.

Edit Your Photos

Open a Photo for Editing

1 Press the Home button.

The Home screen appears.

2 Tap **Photos**.

The Photos app opens.

3 Navigate to the photo you want to edit.

4 Tap **Edit**.

The Editing controls appear.

Crop, Rotate, and Straighten a Photo

1 Tap **Crop** (▣).

The tools for cropping, straightening, and rotating appear.

A You can tap **Rotate** (▣) to rotate the photo 90 degrees counterclockwise.

2 Tap and hold the degree dial.

B The grid appears.

3 Drag the degree dial left or right to straighten the photo.

C You can tap **Reset** to reset the photo.

4 Tap and hold an edge or corner of the crop box.

D The nine-square grid appears. This is to help you compose the cropped photo.

5 Drag the edge or corner of the crop box to select only the area you want to keep.

Enhance the Colors in a Photo

1 Tap **Auto-Enhance** (■ changes to ■).

iOS enhances the colors.

Note: Tap **Auto-Enhance** again (■ changes to ■) if you want to remove the color change.

TIP

What does the three-squares button on the cropping screen do?
The button with three squares (▭) is the Aspect button. Tap ▭ when you need to crop to a specific aspect ratio, such as a square or the 16:9 widescreen aspect ratio. In the Aspect dialog that opens, tap the constraint you want to use. iOS adjusts the current cropping to match the aspect ratio. You may then need to move the portion of the photo shown to get the composition you want. If you adjust the cropping, tap ▭ again and reapply the aspect ratio.

continued ▶

The Red-Eye Reduction feature enables you to restore feral eyes to normality. The Enhance feature enables you to adjust a photo's color balance and lighting quickly using default algorithms that analyze the photo and try to improve it. The Enhance feature often works well, but for greater control, you can use the Light settings and the Color settings to tweak the exposure, highlights, shadows, brightness, black point, contrast, vibrancy, and other settings manually.

Edit Your Photos (continued)

Remove Red Eye from a Photo

Note: You may need to zoom in on the photo in order to touch the red-eye patches accurately.

 Tap **Red-Eye Reduction** (![icon]).

iOS prompts you to tap each eye.

2 Tap each red eye.

iOS removes the red eye.

Adjust the Colors in a Photo

1 Tap **Adjust** (![icon]).

The Adjust controls appear.

2 Tap **Light**.

The Light settings appear.

3 Tap the setting you want to adjust. This example uses **Brightness**.

④ Drag the scale to adjust the setting.

⑤ Tap **List** (▤).

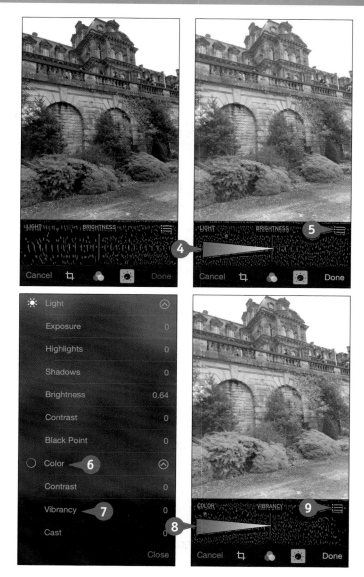

The list of Light settings appear.

⑥ Tap **Color**.

The list of Color settings appears.

⑦ Tap the setting you want to adjust. This example uses **Vibrancy**.

⑧ Drag the scale to adjust the setting.

⑨ Tap ▤.

The list of settings appears, and you can adjust further settings as needed.

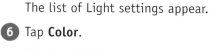

TIPS

How do I save the changes I have made to a photo?

When you finish making changes to a photo, tap **Done** to save the changes.

How do I get rid of changes I have made to a photo?

Tap **Cancel**, and then tap **Discard Changes** in the confirmation dialog that opens.

Capture Video

As well as capturing still photos, your iPhone's camera can capture high-quality, full-motion video in either portrait orientation or landscape orientation. To capture video, you use the Camera app. You launch the Camera app as usual, and then switch it to Video mode for regular-speed shooting or to Slo-Mo mode to shoot slow-motion footage. After taking the video, you can view it on the iPhone's screen.

Capture Video

1 Press the Home button.

The Home screen appears.

2 Tap **Camera**.

The Camera screen appears, showing the image the lens is seeing.

3 Tap **Video**.

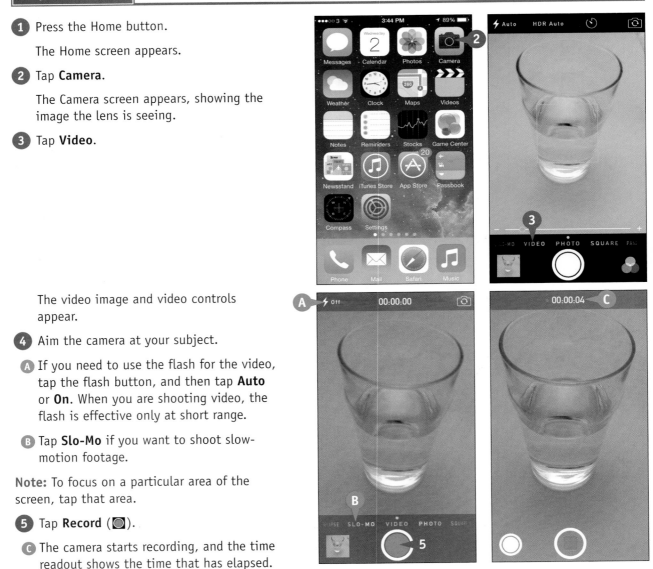

The video image and video controls appear.

4 Aim the camera at your subject.

A If you need to use the flash for the video, tap the flash button, and then tap **Auto** or **On**. When you are shooting video, the flash is effective only at short range.

B Tap **Slo-Mo** if you want to shoot slow-motion footage.

Note: To focus on a particular area of the screen, tap that area.

5 Tap **Record** (⬛).

C The camera starts recording, and the time readout shows the time that has elapsed.

6 To zoom in, place two fingers on the screen and pinch outward. You can then tap ▬ to zoom in, tap ➕ to zoom out, or drag the zoom slider (◉).

Ⓓ To take a still photo while shooting video, tap **Take Photo** (○).

7 To finish recording, tap **Stop** (◉).

The Camera app stops recording and displays a thumbnail of the video's first frame.

8 Tap the thumbnail.

The video appears.

9 Tap **Play** (▶).

The video starts playing.

10 Tap anywhere on the screen to display the video controls. These disappear automatically after a few seconds of not being used.

Note: If you want to trim the video, follow the procedure described in the next section, "Edit Video with the Trim Feature," before tapping **Done**.

11 When you finish viewing the video, tap **Done**.

The Camera app appears again.

TIP

What does the bar of miniature pictures at the top of the video playback screen do?
The navigation bar gives you a quick way of moving forward and backward through the movie. Tap the vertical playhead bar, and then drag to the right or to the left until the movie reaches the part you want. You can use the navigation bar either when the movie is playing or when it is paused.

Edit Video with the Trim Feature

When you capture video, you normally shoot more footage than you want to keep. You then edit the video down to keep only the footage you need.

The Camera app includes a straightforward Trim feature that you can use to trim the beginning and end of a video clip to where you want them. For greater precision in editing, or to make a movie out of multiple clips, you can use the iMovie app, which is available from the App Store.

Edit Video with the Trim Feature

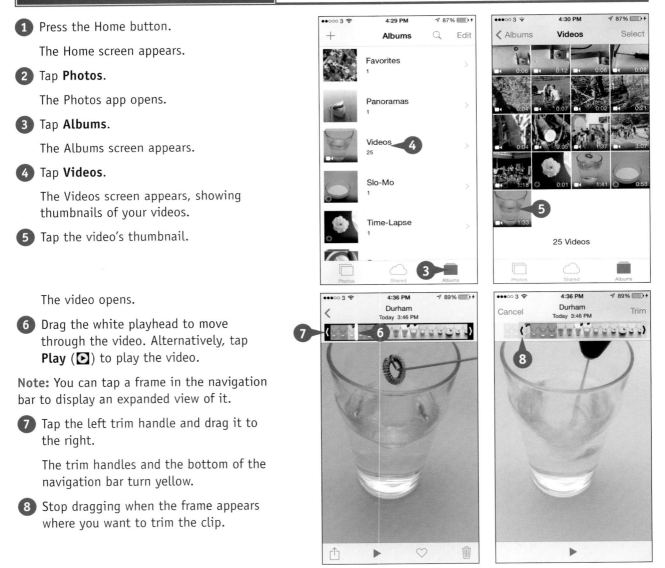

1 Press the Home button.

The Home screen appears.

2 Tap **Photos**.

The Photos app opens.

3 Tap **Albums**.

The Albums screen appears.

4 Tap **Videos**.

The Videos screen appears, showing thumbnails of your videos.

5 Tap the video's thumbnail.

The video opens.

6 Drag the white playhead to move through the video. Alternatively, tap **Play** (▶) to play the video.

Note: You can tap a frame in the navigation bar to display an expanded view of it.

7 Tap the left trim handle and drag it to the right.

The trim handles and the bottom of the navigation bar turn yellow.

8 Stop dragging when the frame appears where you want to trim the clip.

9 Tap the right handle and drag it to the left until the frame to which you want to trim the end appears.

10 Tap **Trim**.

The Trim dialog appears.

11 Tap **Trim Original** if you want to trim the original clip. Tap **Save as New Clip** to create a new clip from the trimmed content, leaving the original clip unchanged.

A The Trimming Video progress indicator appears while the Camera app trims the video.

Note: Tap **Play** (▶) if you want to play back the trimmed video.

12 Tap ◁.

The Videos screen appears.

TIP

Is there an easier way of trimming my videos?

If you need to trim your videos on your iPhone, try turning the iPhone to landscape orientation. This makes the navigation bar longer and the trimming handles easier to use.

You can also trim your videos, edit them, and create movies from them by using Apple's iMovie app, which is available from the App Store. If you have a Mac, you can trim your videos more precisely, and make many other changes by importing the clips into iMovie on the Mac, and then working with them there.

Share Your Photos and Videos

A fter taking photos and videos with your iPhone's camera, or after loading photos and videos on the iPhone using iTunes, you can share them with other people.

Chapter 11 explains how to share photos via e-mail and instant messaging, and Chapter 6 explains how to share items via the AirDrop feature. This section explains how to tweet photos to your Twitter account, assign photos to contacts, use photos as wallpaper, or print photos.

Share Your Photos and Videos

Select the Photo or Video to Share

1 Press the Home button.

2 On the Home screen, tap **Photos**.

3 On the Photos screen, tap the item that contains the photo or video you want to share. For example, tap an album.

4 Tap the photo or video you want to share.

5 Tap **Share** (⬆) to open the Share screen.

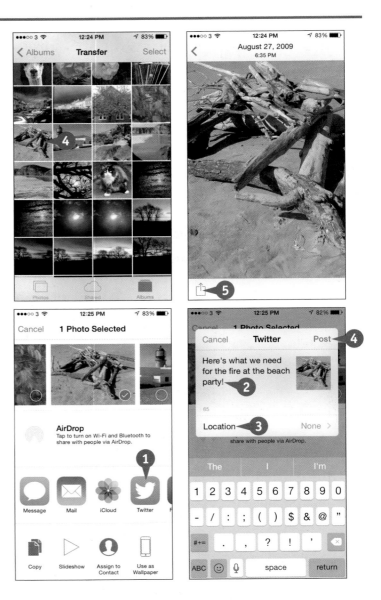

Share a Photo on Twitter

1 On the Share screen, tap **Twitter**.

2 Type the text of the tweet.

3 Tap **Location** if you want to add your location to the tweet.

4 Tap **Post**.

Assign a Photo to a Contact

1. On the Share screen, tap **Assign to Contact**.

   The list of contacts appears.

2. Tap the contact to which you want to assign the photo.

   The Move and Scale screen appears.

3. If necessary, move the photo so that the face appears centrally.

4. If necessary, pinch in to shrink the photo or pinch out to enlarge it.

5. Tap **Choose**.

Set a Photo as Wallpaper

1. On the Share screen, tap **Use as Wallpaper**.

   The Move and Scale screen appears.

2. Move the photo to display the part you want.

3. If necessary, pinch in to shrink the photo or pinch out to enlarge it.

4. Tap **Set**.

   The Set Wallpaper dialog appears.

5. Tap **Set Lock Screen**, **Set Home Screen**, or **Set Both**, as needed.

TIP

How do I print a photo?

Display the photo you want to print, and then tap **Share** (📤) to display the Share screen. Tap **Print** to display the Printer Options screen. If the Printer readout does not show the correct printer, tap **Select Printer**, and then tap the printer. Tap **Print** to print the photo.

CHAPTER 14

Troubleshooting Your iPhone

You can connect your iPhone to VPNs and Exchange Server, troubleshoot problems, and locate it when it goes missing.

Install Configuration Profiles on Your iPhone

You can configure your iPhone directly by choosing settings in the Settings app, but you can also configure the iPhone by installing one or more configuration profiles provided by an administrator. The most common way of providing a configuration profile is via e-mail.

Usually, you need to install configuration profiles only when an administrator manages your iPhone instead of you managing it. For example, a configuration profile can contain the settings needed for your iPhone to connect to a corporate network or a campus network.

Install Configuration Profiles on Your iPhone

1 Press the Home button.

The Home screen appears.

2 Tap **Mail**.

The Mailboxes screen appears.

3 Tap the mailbox that contains the message with the configuration profile.

Ⓐ You can tap **All Inboxes** to display all your inboxes.

The Inbox opens.

4 Tap the message that contains the configuration profile.

The message opens.

5 Tap the button for the configuration profile.

6 On the Install Profile screen, look for the Verified readout.

Note: Never install a configuration profile that does not have the Verified readout. The configuration profile may not be from the source claimed and may damage your iPhone, compromise your data, or both.

7 Review the configuration profile.

8 Tap **More Details** for more information.

Note: You can tap an item on the Details screen to see further details.

9 Tap **Back** (◁).

10 On the Install Profile screen, tap **Install**.

Your iPhone installs the configuration profile.

11 If the configuration profile prompts you to enter information, such as a VPN username, type the information and tap **Next**.

The Profile Installed screen appears.

12 Tap **Done**.

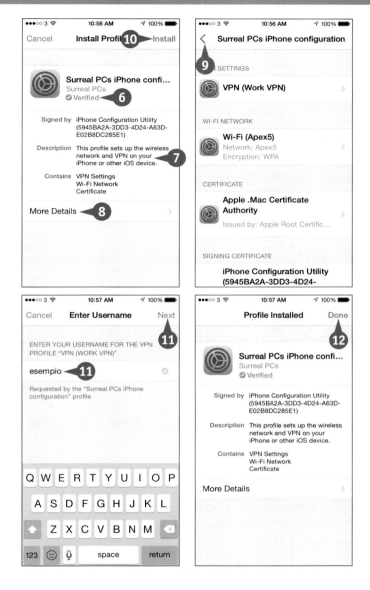

TIP

Is there a way of installing a configuration profile other than using e-mail?
Yes. An administrator can place a configuration profile on a web page. You download the configuration profile using Safari, and then install it using installation screens similar to those shown in this section. By sending a text message to your iPhone, an administrator can easily direct you to a web page that contains a configuration profile specific to your iPhone rather than a general profile for iPhones.

Connect to a Network via VPN

If you use your iPhone for work, you may need to connect it to your work network. By using the settings, username, and password that the network's administrator provides, you can connect via virtual private networking, or VPN, across the Internet. You can also use VPN to connect to your home network if you set up a VPN server on it.

VPN uses encryption to create a secure connection across the Internet. By using VPN, you can connect securely from anywhere you have an Internet connection.

Connect to a Network via VPN

Set Up the VPN Connection on the iPhone

1 Press the Home button.

The Home screen appears.

2 Tap **Settings**.

The Settings screen appears.

Note: After you have set up a VPN configuration, the VPN switch appears in the top area of the Settings screen. You can connect to the virtual private network by tapping the switch and moving it to On (□ changes to ▣).

3 Tap **General**.

The General screen appears.

4 At the bottom of the screen, tap **VPN**.

The VPN screen appears.

5 Tap **Add VPN Configuration**.

Note: If your iPhone already has a VPN configuration you want to use, tap it, and then go to Step **1** of the next set of steps, "Connect to the Virtual Private Network."

The Add Configuration screen appears.

6 Tap the tab for the VPN type: **L2TP**, **PPTP**, or **IPSec**.

7 Fill in the details of the virtual private network.

Note: Set the **Send All Traffic** switch to On (🔘) if you want your iPhone to send all Internet traffic across the virtual private network after you connect.

8 Tap **Save**.

The VPN configuration appears on the VPN screen.

Connect to the Virtual Private Network

1 On the VPN screen, set the **VPN** switch to On (☐ changes to 🔘).

The iPhone connects to the virtual private network.

A The VPN indicator appears in the status bar.

2 Work across the network connection as if you were connected directly to the network.

3 To see how long your iPhone has been connected, or to learn its IP address, tap **Info** (ⓘ).

4 Tap **General** to return.

5 When you are ready to disconnect from the virtual private network, set the **VPN** switch to Off (🔘 changes to ☐).

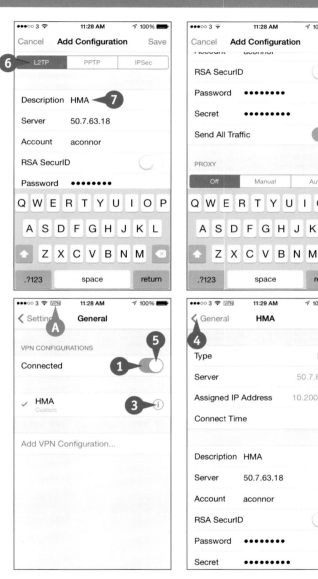

TIP

Is there an easier way to set up a VPN connection?
Yes. An administrator can provide the VPN details in a configuration profile, as discussed earlier in this chapter. When you install the configuration profile, your iPhone adds the VPN configuration automatically. You can then connect to the virtual private network.

Connect Your iPhone to Exchange Server

If your company or organization uses Microsoft Exchange Server, you can set up your iPhone to connect to Exchange for e-mail, contacts, calendaring, reminders, and notes.

Before setting up your Exchange account, ask an administrator for the connection details you need: your e-mail address, your password, the server name if required, and the domain name if required. You may be able to set up the account using only the e-mail address and password, but often you need the server name and domain as well.

Connect Your iPhone to Exchange Server

1 Press the Home button.

The Home screen appears.

2 Tap **Settings**.

The Settings screen appears.

Note: If you have not yet set up an e-mail account on the iPhone, you can also open the Add Account screen by tapping **Mail** on the iPhone's Home screen.

3 Tap **Mail, Contacts, Calendars**.

The Mail, Contacts, Calendars screen appears.

4 Tap **Add Account**.

The Add Account screen appears.

5 Tap **Exchange**.

6 Type your e-mail address.

7 Type your password.

8 Type a descriptive name for the account field.

9 Tap **Next**.

If Mail needs more information, another screen appears.

10 Type the server's address.

11 Type the domain if needed.

12 Type your username.

13 Tap **Next**.

14 Set the **Mail** switch to On (🔘) or Off (⬜).

15 Set the **Contacts** switch to On (🔘) or Off (⬜).

16 Set the **Calendars** switch to On (🔘) or Off (⬜).

17 Set the **Reminders** switch to On (🔘) or Off (⬜).

18 Set the **Notes** switch to On (🔘) or Off (⬜).

19 Tap **Save**.

A The new account appears on the Mail, Contacts, Calendars screen.

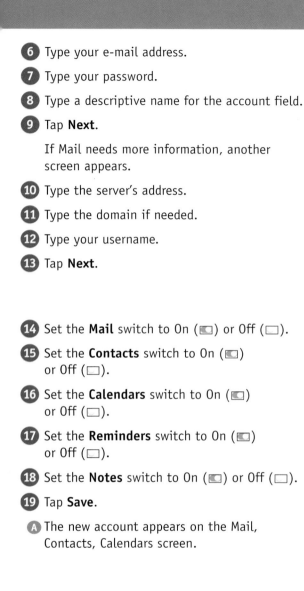

Is there an alternative way to set up an Exchange account?
Yes. An administrator can provide the Exchange details in a configuration profile, as discussed earlier in this chapter. If you have another e-mail account on your iPhone, the administrator can send you the profile. Otherwise, you may need to download the profile from a web page.

How do I know whether to enter a domain name when setting up my Exchange account?
You need to ask an administrator because some Exchange implementations require you to enter a domain, whereas others do not.

Update Your iPhone's Software

Apple periodically releases new versions of the iPhone's software to fix problems, improve performance, and add new features. To keep your iPhone running quickly and smoothly, and to add the latest features that Apple provides, you should update the iPhone's software when a new version becomes available.

iTunes and your iPhone notify you automatically when a new version of the iPhone's software is available. You can also check manually for new versions of the software.

Update Your iPhone's Software

1 Connect your iPhone to your computer via the USB cable.

The iPhone appears on the navigation bar in iTunes.

A dialog appears, telling you that a new software version is available.

2 Click **Update**.

iTunes downloads the new software, extracts it, and begins to install it.

The Summary screen shows the progress of the installation.

A If iTunes does not display the iPhone's management screens, click the iPhone button on the navigation bar to make the management screens appear.

When the installation is complete, iTunes displays a dialog telling you that the iPhone will restart in 15 seconds.

③ Click **OK**, or wait for the countdown to complete.

The iPhone restarts, and its button then appears on the navigation bar in iTunes.

④ If iTunes does not display the management screens for your iPhone, click **iPhone** (▢) on the navigation bar.

The iPhone's management screens appear.

⑤ Verify the version number in the Software Version readout in the iPhone area.

⑥ Disconnect your iPhone from the USB cable. You can now start using the iPhone as usual.

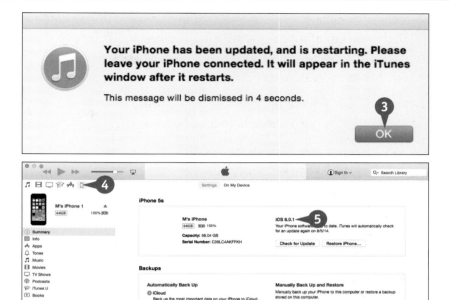

TIPS

How do I make iTunes check for a new version of my iPhone's software?

Connect your iPhone to your computer via the USB cable so that the iPhone appears on the navigation bar in iTunes. Click **iPhone** to display the Summary screen, and then click **Check for Update** in the upper area.

Can I update my iPhone's software without using a computer?

Yes. If your iPhone has enough free space, you can update it "over the air" by using a wireless network. Press the Home button, tap **Settings**, tap **General**, and then tap **Software Update** to check for new software. You can also update over the air using the cellular network if your data plan is generous.

Extend Your iPhone's Runtime on the Battery

To keep your iPhone running all day long, you need to charge the battery fully by plugging the iPhone into a USB socket, the iPhone Power Adapter, or another power source. You can extend your iPhone's runtime by reducing the demands on the battery. You can dim your iPhone's screen so that it consumes less power. You can set your iPhone to go to sleep quickly. You can turn off Wi-Fi and Bluetooth when you do not need them, and you can turn off the power-hungry GPS feature when you do not need to track your iPhone with the Find My iPhone feature.

Extend Your iPhone's Runtime on the Battery

Dim the iPhone's Screen

1 Press the Home button.

2 On the Home screen, tap **Settings**.

3 On the Settings screen, tap **Display & Brightness**.

4 On the Brightness & Wallpaper screen, tap the **Brightness** slider and drag it to the left to dim the screen.

A Set the **Auto-Brightness** switch to On (🔘) if you want the iPhone to adjust the brightness automatically.

5 Tap **Settings**.

Turn Off Wi-Fi and Bluetooth

1 On the Settings screen, tap **Wi-Fi**.

2 On the Wi-Fi screen, set the **Wi-Fi** switch to Off (🔲).

3 Tap **Settings**.

4 On the Settings screen, tap **Bluetooth**.

The Bluetooth screen appears.

5 Set the **Bluetooth** switch to Off (☐).

6 Tap **Settings**.

The Settings screen appears.

Note: Updating your iPhone's software may turn Bluetooth on automatically, so you may need to turn it off again.

Turn Off the GPS Feature

1 On the Settings screen, tap **Privacy**.

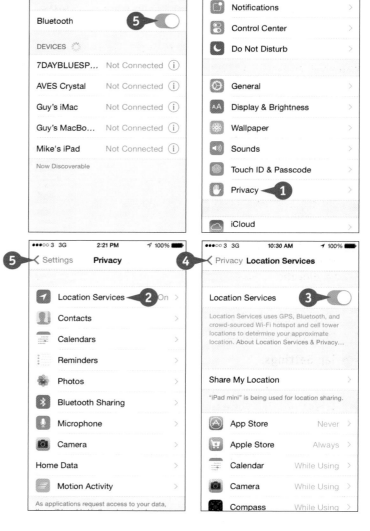

The Privacy screen appears.

2 Tap **Location Services**.

The Location Services screen appears.

3 Set the **Location Services** switch to Off (☐).

Note: If your iPhone warns you that turning off Location Services will turn off Find My iPhone, tap **Turn Off**.

4 Tap **Privacy**.

The Privacy screen appears.

5 Tap **Settings**.

The Settings screen appears.

TIPS

Is there a quicker way of controlling power consumption?
You can control Wi-Fi, Bluetooth, and screen brightness from Control Center. Swipe up from the bottom of the screen to open Control Center, and then tap **Wi-Fi** or **Bluetooth** or drag the Brightness slider.

What else can I do to save power?
You can set a short time for Auto-Lock. Press the Home button, tap **Settings**, tap **General**, and then tap **Auto-Lock**. Tap a short interval — for example, **1 Minute**.

Back Up and Restore Using Your Computer

When you sync your iPhone with your computer, iTunes automatically backs up the iPhone's data and settings. If your iPhone suffers a software or hardware failure, you can restore the data and settings to your iPhone. You can also sync your data and settings to a new iPhone, an iPad, or an iPod touch. iTunes backs up the iPhone's unique data, such as the settings and notes you have created on the iPhone, but does not back up music files, video files, or photos that you have synced to the iPhone from your computer.

Back Up and Restore Using Your Computer

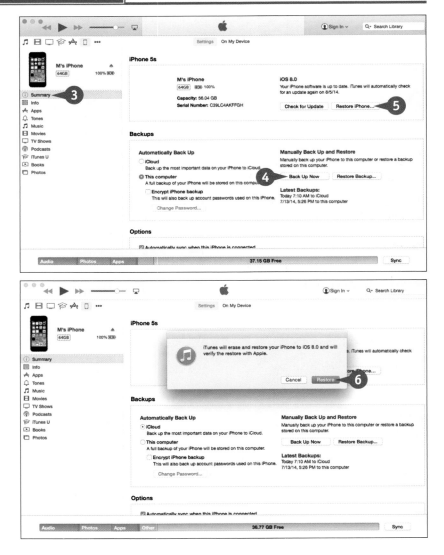

1. Connect your iPhone to your computer via the USB cable or via Wi-Fi.

   The iPhone appears on the navigation bar in iTunes.

2. Click the iPhone button on the navigation bar.

   The iPhone's management screens appear.

3. Click **Summary** if the Summary screen is not yet shown.

4. Click **Back Up Now**.

   iTunes backs up your iPhone.

5. Click **Restore iPhone**.

Note: Instead of restoring the iPhone's software, you can restore only the iPhone's data by clicking **Restore Backup**.

   iTunes confirms that you want to restore the iPhone to its factory settings.

6. Click **Restore**.

iTunes confirms the restore operation again.

7 Click **Restore**.

iTunes backs up the iPhone's data, restores the software on the iPhone, and returns the iPhone to its factory settings.

Note: Do not disconnect the iPhone during the restore process. Doing so can leave the iPhone in an unusable state.

iTunes displays the Welcome to Your New iPhone screen.

8 Click **Restore from this backup** (☐ changes to ◉).

9 Click ⬍ and choose your iPhone by name.

10 Click **Continue**.

iTunes restores the data and settings to your iPhone.

Your iPhone restarts, appears on the navigation bar in iTunes, and then syncs.

11 Disconnect the iPhone.

TIP

How can I protect confidential information in my iPhone's backups?
On the Summary screen in iTunes, click **Encrypt iPhone backup** (☐ changes to ☑). In the Set Password dialog, type the password, and then click **Set Password**. iTunes then encrypts your backups using strong encryption.

Back Up and Restore Using iCloud

Instead of backing up your iPhone to your computer, you can back it up to iCloud. If your iPhone suffers a software or hardware failure, you can restore its data and settings from backup.

At this writing, a standard free iCloud account gives you 5GB of data storage, but you can buy more space as needed. You can choose which items to back up to iCloud. The iTunes Store lets you download again all the apps, media files, and games you have bought, so you do not need to back up these files.

Back Up and Restore Using iCloud

1 Press the Home button.

The Home screen appears.

2 Tap **Settings**.

The Settings screen appears.

3 Tap **iCloud**.

The iCloud screen appears, showing the name of the iCloud account you have set up.

4 Choose the data you want to synchronize with iCloud by moving the **Mail**, **Contacts**, **Calendars**, **Reminders**, **Safari**, **Notes**, and **Passbook** switches to On (⬛) or Off (☐), as needed.

Note: The 5GB of storage in a standard free iCloud account is enough space to store your iPhone's settings and your most important data and files. If you need to store more data, buy more space.

5 If you need to buy more storage, tap **Storage**.

The Account screen appears, showing your storage amount in the Storage Plan area.

6 Tap the **Change Storage Plan** button.

7 Tap the storage plan you want, tap **Buy**, and follow the payment process.

8 On the Account screen, tap **Photos**.

9 On the Photos Stream screen, set the **My Photo Stream** switch and the **Photo Sharing** switch to On (◼) or Off (◻), as needed.

10 Tap **iCloud**.

11 On the Account screen, tap **iCloud Drive**.

12 Set the **iCloud Drive** switch to On (◼) or Off (◻), as needed.

13 In the apps list, set each app's switch to On (◼) or Off (◻), as needed.

14 Tap **iCloud**.

15 Set the **Find My iPhone** switch to On (◼) or Off (◻), as needed.

16 Tap **Storage & Backup**.

17 Set the **iCloud Backup** switch to On (◼).

18 If you want to back up your iPhone now, tap **Back Up Now**.

TIP

How do I restore my iPhone from its iCloud backup?
First, reset the iPhone to factory settings. Press the Home button, tap **Settings**, tap **General**, tap **Reset**, and tap **Erase All Content and Settings**. Tap **Erase iPhone** in the confirmation dialog. When the iPhone restarts and displays its setup screens, choose your language and country. On the Set Up iPhone screen, tap **Restore from iCloud Backup**, and then tap **Next**. On the Apple ID screen, enter your Apple ID, and then tap **Next**. On the Choose Backup screen, tap the backup you want to use — normally, the most recent backup — and then tap **Restore**.

Reset Your iPhone's Settings

If your iPhone starts malfunctioning, you may need to reset its settings. From the Reset screen in the Settings app, you can reset your network settings, reset the Home screen's icons, reset your keyboard dictionary, reset your location and privacy settings, or reset all settings to eliminate tricky configuration issues. If your iPhone has intractable problems, you may need to back it up, erase all content and settings, and then set it up from scratch. You can also erase your iPhone to get it ready to sell or give to someone else.

Reset Your iPhone's Settings

Display the Reset Screen

 Press the Home button.

The Home screen appears.

 Tap **Settings**.

The Settings screen appears.

Note: If your iPhone is not responding to the Home button or your taps, press and hold the Sleep/Wake button and the Home button for about 15 seconds to reset the iPhone.

③ Tap **General**.

The General screen appears.

④ Tap **Reset**.

The Reset screen appears.

You can then tap the appropriate button: **Reset All Settings**, **Erase All Content and Settings**, **Reset Network Settings**, **Reset Keyboard Dictionary**, **Reset Home Screen Layout**, or **Reset Location & Privacy**. ·

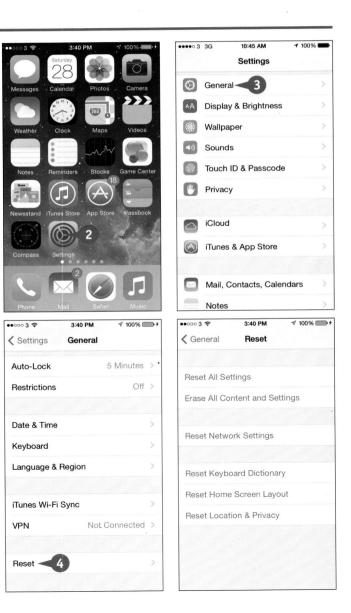

Reset Your Network Settings

1 On the Reset screen, tap **Reset Network Settings.**

A dialog opens, warning you that this action will delete all network settings and return them to their factory defaults.

2 Tap **Reset Network Settings**.

iOS resets your iPhone's network settings.

Restore Your iPhone to Factory Settings

1 On the Reset screen, tap **Erase All Content and Settings**.

A dialog opens to confirm that you want to delete all your media and data and reset all settings.

2 Tap **Erase iPhone**.

A second dialog opens to double-check that you want to perform this drastic action.

3 Tap **Erase iPhone**.

iOS wipes your media and data and restores your iPhone to factory settings.

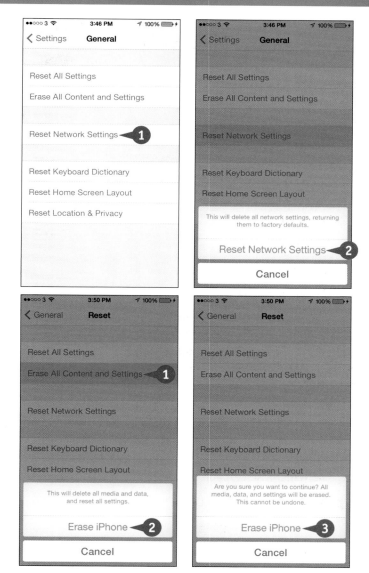

TIP

Does the Reset All Settings command delete my data and my music files?
No. When you reset all the iPhone's settings, the settings go back to their defaults, but your data remains in place. But you need to set the iPhone's settings again, either by restoring them using iTunes or by setting them manually, in order to get your iPhone working the way you prefer.

Troubleshoot Wi-Fi Connections

To get the most out of your iPhone without exceeding your data plan, use Wi-Fi networks whenever they are available instead of using your cellular connection.

Normally, the iPhone establishes and maintains Wi-Fi connections without problems. But you may sometimes need to request your iPhone's network address again, a process called renewing the lease on the IP address. You may also need to tell your iPhone to forget a network, and then rejoin the network manually, providing the password again.

Troubleshoot Wi-Fi Connections

Renew the Lease on Your iPhone's IP Address

1 Press the Home button.

The Home screen appears.

Note: You can sometimes resolve a Wi-Fi problem by turning Wi-Fi off and back on. Swipe up from the bottom of the screen to open Control Center, tap **Wi-Fi** (changes to), and then tap **Wi-Fi** again (changes to).

2 Tap **Settings**.

The Settings screen appears.

3 Tap **Wi-Fi**.

The Wi-Fi screen appears.

4 Tap to the right of the network for which you want to renew the lease.

The network's screen appears.

5 Tap **Renew Lease**.

The Renew Lease dialog opens.

6 Tap **Renew Lease**.

7 Tap **Wi-Fi Networks**.

The Wi-Fi screen appears.

Forget a Network and Then Rejoin It

1 On the Wi-Fi screen, tap ⓘ to the right of the network.

The network's screen appears.

2 Tap **Forget This Network**.

The Forget This Network dialog opens.

3 Tap **Forget**.

The iPhone removes the network's details.

4 Tap **Wi-Fi**.

The Wi-Fi screen appears.

5 Tap the network's name.

The password screen appears.

6 Type the password for the network.

7 Tap **Join**.

The iPhone joins the network.

TIP

What else can I do to reestablish my Wi-Fi network connections?
If you are unable to fix your Wi-Fi network connections by renewing the IP address lease or by forgetting and rejoining the network, as described in this section, try restarting your iPhone. If that does not work, reset your network settings, as described earlier in this chapter, and then set up each connection again manually.

Locate Your iPhone with Find My iPhone

If you have an iCloud account, you can use the Find My iPhone feature to locate your iPhone when you have lost it or it has been stolen. You can also display a message on the iPhone — for example, to tell the person who has found the iPhone how to contact you — or remotely wipe the data on the iPhone.

To use Find My iPhone, you must first set up your iCloud account on your iPhone, and then enable the Find My iPhone feature.

Locate Your iPhone with Find My iPhone

Turn On the Find My iPhone Feature

1 Set up your iCloud account on your iPhone as discussed in "Set Up Your iPhone as New Using iCloud" in Chapter 1.

2 Press the Home button.

The Home screen appears.

3 Tap **Settings**.

The Settings screen appears.

4 Tap **iCloud**.

The iCloud screen appears.

5 Tap **Find My iPhone**.

The Find My iPhone screen appears.

6 Set the **Find My iPhone** switch to On (⬜).

The Find My iPhone dialog appears.

7 Tap **Allow**.

8 Tap **iCloud**.

The iCloud screen appears.

Locate Your iPhone Using Find My iPhone

1 Open a web browser, such as Internet Explorer or Safari.

2 Click the Address box.

3 Type **www.icloud.com**, and press `Enter` in Windows or `Return` on a Mac.

The iCloud Sign In web page appears.

4 Type your username.

5 Type your password.

6 Click 🠖.

The iCloud site appears, displaying the page you last used.

7 Click **iCloud** (⬜).

The iCloud apps screen appears.

8 Click **Find My iPhone**.

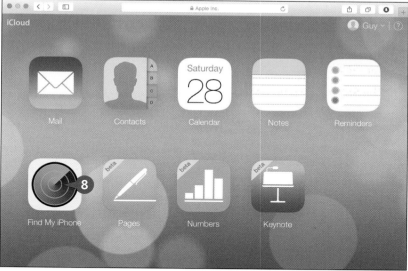

TIP

Is it worth displaying a message on my iPhone, or should I simply wipe it?
Almost always, it is definitely worth displaying a message on your iPhone. If you have lost your iPhone, and someone has found it, that person may be trying to return it to you. The chances are good that the finder is honest, even if he has not discovered that you have locked the iPhone with a passcode. That said, if you are certain someone has stolen your iPhone, you may prefer simply to wipe it, using the technique explained next.

continued ►

Find My iPhone is a powerful feature that you can use both when you have mislaid your iPhone and when someone has deliberately taken it from you.

If Find My iPhone reveals that someone has taken your iPhone, you can wipe its contents to prevent whoever has taken it from hacking into your data. Be clear that wiping your iPhone prevents you from locating the iPhone again — ever — except by chance. Wipe your iPhone only when you have lost it, you have no hope of recovering it, and you must destroy the data on it.

Locate Your iPhone with Find My iPhone (continued)

The iCloud Find My iPhone screen appears.

9 Click **All Devices**.

A The My Devices dialog appears.

10 Click your iPhone.

The Info dialog appears, showing the iPhone's location.

11 If you want to play a sound on the iPhone, click **Play Sound**. This feature is primarily helpful for locating your iPhone if you have mislaid it somewhere nearby.

B A message indicates that the iPhone has played the sound.

Lock the iPhone with a Passcode

1 Click **Lost Mode** in the Info dialog.

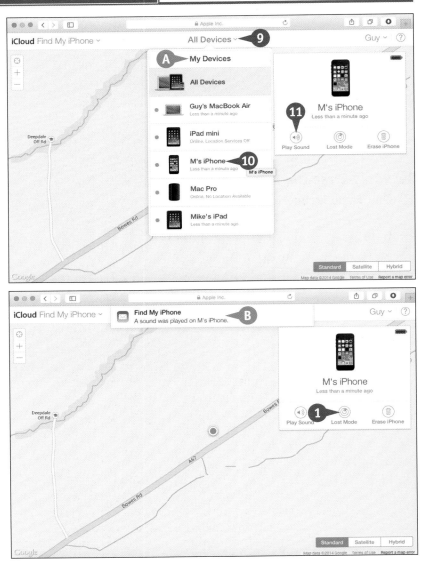

The Lost Mode dialog appears.

2 Click the numbers for a new passcode to apply to the iPhone.

The Lost Mode dialog displays its Re-enter Passcode screen.

3 Click the passcode numbers again.

4 Type a contact phone number.

5 Click **Next**.

6 Type a message to whoever finds your iPhone.

7 Click **Done**.

iCloud sends the lock request to the iPhone, and then displays a dialog telling you it sent the request.

Remotely Erase the iPhone

1 Click **Erase iPhone** in the Info dialog.

The Enter Your Apple ID Password dialog appears.

2 Click **Erase**.

The Erase iPhone dialog appears.

3 Type your password.

4 Click **Done**.

iCloud sends the erase request to the iPhone, which erases its data.

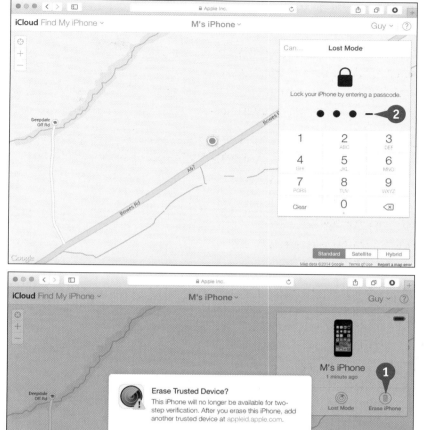

TIP

Can I remotely wipe the data on my iPhone if I do not have an iCloud account?
You can set a passcode for the iPhone as discussed in Chapter 2, and then set the **Erase Data** switch on the Touch ID & Passcode screen to On (⬜). This setting makes the iPhone automatically erase its data after ten successive failed attempts to enter the passcode. After five failed attempts, the iPhone enforces a delay before the next attempt; further failures increase the delay.

Index

Index

Index

Read Less-Learn More®

Visual

There's a Visual book for every learning level...

Microsoft®
Office 2013
Simplified

Step-by-step instructions for easy learning

Elaine Marmel

Simplified®

The place to start if you're new to computers. Full color.

- Computers
- Creating Web Pages
- Digital Photography
- Excel

- Internet
- Laptops
- Mac OS
- Office

- PCs
- Windows
- Word

Teach Yourself
VISUALLY
iPhone 5
The Fast and Easy Way to Learn

Guy Hart-Davis

Teach Yourself VISUALLY™

Get beginning to intermediate-level training in a variety of topics. Full color.

- Access
- Adobe Muse
- Computers
- Digital Photography
- Digital Video
- Dreamweaver
- Excel
- Flash
- HTML5
- iLife

- iPad
- iPhone
- iPod
- Macs
- Mac OS
- Office
- Outlook
- Photoshop
- Photoshop Elements
- Photoshop Lightroom

- PowerPoint
- Salesforce.com
- Search Engine Optimization
- Social Media
- Web Design
- Windows
- Wireless Networking
- Word
- WordPress

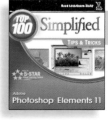

Adobe
Photoshop Elements 11

Top 100 Simplified® Tips & Tricks

Tips and techniques to take your skills beyond the basics. Full color.

- Digital Photography
- eBay
- Excel

- Google
- Office
- Photoshop

- Photoshop Elements
- PowerPoint
- Windows

...all designed for visual learners—just like you!

Master VISUALLY®

Your complete visual reference. Two-color interior.

- 3ds Max
- Creating Web Pages
- Dreamweaver and Flash
- Excel
- iPod and iTunes
- Mac OS
- Office
- Optimizing PC Performance
- Windows
- Windows Server

Visual Blueprint™

Where to go for professional-level programming instruction. Two-color interior.

- ActionScript
- Excel Data Analysis
- Excel Pivot Tables
- Excel Programming
- HTML5
- JavaScript
- Mambo
- Mobile App Development
- Perl and Apache
- PHP 5
- SEO
- Ubuntu Linux
- Vista Sidebar
- Visual Basic
- XML

Visual™ Quick Tips

Shortcuts, tricks, and techniques for getting more done in less time. Full color.

- Digital Photography
- Excel
- Internet
- iPhone
- iPod & iTunes
- Mac OS
- Office
- PowerPoint
- Windows

e **Available in print and e-book formats.**

For a complete listing of Visual books, go to wiley.com/go/visual

24.99   WITHDRAWN   2/27/15